AVERTING DOOMSDAY

Miller Center Studies on the Presidency

GUIAN A. MCKEE AND MARC J. SELVERSTONE, EDITORS

AVERTING DOOMSDAY

Arms Control during the Nixon Presidency

Patrick J. Garrity and
Erin R. Mahan

University of Virginia Press • *Charlottesville and London*
Published in association with the University of Virginia's Miller Center of Public Affairs

University of Virginia Press
© 2021 by the Rector and Visitors of the University of Virginia
Printed in the United States of America on acid-free paper

First published 2021

9 8 7 6 5 4 3 2 1

Library of Congress Cataloging-in-Publication Data

Names: Garrity, Patrick J., author. | Mahan, Erin R., author.
Title: Averting doomsday : arms control during the Nixon presidency / Patrick J.
    Garrity and Erin R. Mahan.
Other titles: Arms control during the Nixon presidency
Description: Charlottesville ; London : University of Virginia Press, 2021. | Series:
    Miller Center Studies on the Presidency | Includes bibliographical references
    and index.
Identifiers: LCCN 2021021074 (print) | LCCN 2021021075 (ebook) | ISBN
    9780813946696 (Hardcover : acid-free paper) | ISBN 9780813946719 (eBook)
Subjects: LCSH: Nixon, Richard M. (Richard Milhous), 1913–1994. | United States—
    Military policy—History—20th century. | Nuclear weapons—United States—
    History—20th century. | Arms control—History—20th century. | Strategic
    Arms Limitation Talks. | Strategic Arms Limitation Talks II. | United States—
    Foreign relations—1969–1974.
Classification: LCC E855 .G37 2021 (print) | LCC E855 (ebook) |
    DDC 327.1/745097309047—dc23
LC record available at https://lccn.loc.gov/2021021074
LC ebook record available at https://lccn.loc.gov/2021021075

Cover art: iStock/CSA-Printstock; National Museum of the U.S. Air Force; White
House Photo Office Collection/Nixon Administration; Nevada National Security Site,
Department of Energy

To Patrick, my coauthor and comrade in arms control—
you lived to finish our manuscript but not to see our book
in print. May your legacy live on on through your writings.

CONTENTS

PREFACE

Issues of weapons of mass destruction—whether chemical, biological, or nuclear—occupy a major place in the current national security agenda. Since 11 September 2001, high-ranking US officials have lamented that the prospect of weapons of mass destruction (WMD) falling into the hands of terrorists or hostile regimes is what keeps them up at night. Fears about WMD have not been limited to nuclear weapons. The recent COVID-19, colloquially known as the coronavirus, pandemic has inspired conspiracy theories that it was deliberately engineered and then accidentally released from a high-security Institute of Virology in Wuhan province, China. And the use of chemical weapons by the regime of Syrian president Bashar Hafez al-Assad during the Syrian civil war that began in 2013 resurrected the problem of how to address that insidious WMD.

There have been numerous national commissions devoted to WMD issues. Policy makers and the public need to know how we got to where we are today. Unfortunately, many of them point somewhat wistfully to the Cold War as a bygone era when measures such as arms control and nonproliferation, rightly practiced, sufficed. This myopic view distorts the historical reality. Providing antecedents to contemporary issues of weapons of mass destruction will provide practitioners in the national security realm a deeper understanding of WMD history and the underlying geopolitical circumstances surrounding these vexing problems that persist today.

The administration of Richard M. Nixon represented a critical juncture in US efforts to limit the number and to control the spread of nuclear, biological, and chemical weapons. Policy makers during that period dealt with a panoply of arms control and nonproliferation issues and reached a number of significant agreements, many of which served for decades and some of which continue to serve as cornerstones to international treaty regimes: the Strategic Arms Limitation Talks (SALT) agreement; the Antiballistic Missile (ABM) Treaty; the Nonproliferation Treaty; the Seabed Treaty; ratification of the Geneva Protocol of 1925 banning the use of chemical and biological weapons during war; the Biological Weapons Convention (BWC); and the creation of a nuclear-free zone in Latin America. In some instances, the administration drove certain agreements—namely SALT, the ABM Treaty, and to a lesser extent the BWC. In other cases, Nixon officials grappled with the implementation or aftermath of agreements largely reached before they came into office. While nuclear arms control issues remained central to the Nixon White House, other categories of WMD were also addressed seriously for the first time since World War II.

The totality of the Nixon record on combating WMD warrants examination, as contemporary strategies and tactics have their origins in the period 1969–72. For example, Nixon's director of the arms control and disarmament agency was perhaps the first high-ranking official to remark with some prescience that chemical and biological weapons "may soon offer a 'poor man's alternative' to nuclear weapons." The role that chemical weapons have played in the contemporary Syrian civil war or the concern over North Korea's acceleration of its biological weapons program (its nuclear program has long been a concern) shows how once peripheral arms control issues have gained increasing centrality. One Nixon-era WMD concern, namely the limitation (and then reduction) of US and Soviet nuclear arsenals, has diminished as an international focus, but current policy makers continue to grapple with how arms control fits in current US-Russian relations especially with the 2019 US withdrawal from the 1987 Intermediate-Range Nuclear Forces Treaty, which leaves only the 2010 New Strategic Arms Reduction Treaty, which entered into force in February 2011, in place to limit US and Russian nuclear weapons deployments.

Our study seeks to fill a large hole in the scholarly coverage of the critical Nixon period. At present there are two distinct bodies of work relevant to this study: the national security policies of the Nixon administration as a whole and the more specialized literature on WMD arms control and nonproliferation. The former typically treats SALT and other WMD control efforts as relatively isolated episodes within the broader context of the Nixon-Kissinger approach to the world. In fact, most studies of the Nixon administration barely touch on non-SALT/ABM arms control and nonproliferation topics. In scholarly literature and popular perception, the Nixon administration's arms control policies have become equated almost exclusively with those two agreements. This work builds on the best and most influential of these analyses to bridge the gap between the Nixon administration's worldview and approach to domestic politics and the way in which it treated specific aspects of the WMD problem.

Some of these studies deal with the Nixon administration's national security decision-making processes, often critically. Our book considers various processes that touched upon WMD issues—National Security Council decision-making, interagency reviews, and White House involvement—in each instance, evaluating the effect and effectiveness of given approaches. We are well aware that on most issues the Nixon White House dominated foreign policy issues, including those related to strategic nuclear weapons. The general literature on the history of arms control and nonproliferation is sparse and understudied for the years covering Nixon's presidency with the exception of SALT and the ABM Treaty. Works tend to cover agreements and treaties from the Nixon period as a list of milestones. Often arms control and nonproliferation treaties are cataloged with brief nonanalytic descriptions. For SALT, with a few recent exceptions, the few detailed studies and accounts are typically decades old and suffer from the vices as well as the virtues of personal accounts. Of the few recent monographs published on SALT, the focus is on the second agreement, the SALT II treaty. We do not offer a comprehensive account of the SALT I negotiations and its impact but rather highlight those detailed elements that help make sense of what the administration was trying to accomplish and what legacies it left for future arms control agreements. On the whole, we expect that we will make a particularly valuable contribution to understanding the non-SALT aspects of Nixon's WMD arms control and nonproliferation policies, where the literature is even more sparse and specialized.

In that vein, our methodology draws on the extensive collection of presidential recordings (hundreds of hours listened to or transcribed by both authors), documents, and books and articles on the Nixon administration's national security policies. We conducted extensive research into primary source materials across executive agencies and legislative bodies that involve arms control and WMD and that have not been used in detail in the secondary literature, including the Nixon White House recordings, oral histories, and a wide range of archival documentation generated by the assistant to the president for national security affairs, Henry Kissinger, and the National Security Council staff, the Arms Control and Disarmament Agency, the Department of Defense, the Central Intelligence Agency, and the Kissinger telephone transcripts. That information is integrated with findings from the secondary literature, both historical and theoretical, to develop conclusions about the Nixon administration's conceptual and practical approach to arms control and the WMD threat.

The Nixon administration inherited a number of layers of arms control and nonproliferation ideas and policies that had accumulated over time— some technical, others diplomatic, domestic political, and utopian. They typically resulted in formal agreements and domestic and international norms or proved to be a dead end. As chapter 1 outlines, the United States has placed varying degrees of emphasis at various times on certain aspects of the general goal to control WMD. These include

- supporting international agreements and norms that delegitimize WMD acquisition and use—particularly by outlawing the possession of specific categories of WMD;
- dissuading other powers from obtaining independent WMD capabilities, either by offering reassurance that the United States will extend deterrence against hostile WMD use or by using diplomatic, economic, and military pressures—and incentives—against hostile WMD proliferant candidates; both of these aspects of dissuasion have generally been thought to require the retention of an effective US WMD posture of some sort;
- developing US policies and a strategic posture—unilaterally or combined with selective arms control agreements—that reduce technical pressures for WMD acquisition or a WMD arms race and that create a general environment of strategic stability (e.g., by eliminating the military incentive to strike first with WMD in a crisis);
- reaching bilateral or multilateral agreements that limit WMD postures (e.g., their military characteristics, number of weapons, testing and geographical restrictions), in conjunction with more comprehensive diplomatic arrangements that aim to stabilize the overall geopolitical situation and thus constrain pressures for WMD proliferation;
- using covert action or military force to prevent a hostile nation from acquiring a specific WMD capability or to remove an existing capability; and
- reassuring the American public that the United States is behaving responsibly with respect to WMD and national security policy in general; depending on the circumstances, the public may desire evidence of American restraint, or a more assertive posture in a rising threat environment.

The Nixon administration, like those that came before and after it, inherited the residue of these WMD policy layers from its predecessors, including arms control agreements and commitments related to nonproliferation that invariably shaped and limited its own policy choices. As we discuss in chapter 2, the Nixon administration was no exception to this rule, even as the president was determined to chart his own path. He came into office inheriting this political and intellectual history, a set of partial agreements covering nuclear weapons and widespread public expectations that more could and should be done. And as we also discuss in chapter 2, Nixon and his national security advisor, Henry Kissinger, were experienced in the foreign policy realm and well aware of past efforts to control nuclear weapons. They embraced an approach generally referred to as "realism," putting concrete national interests above goals such as democratization, alleviating global poverty, and what they regarded as woolly-headed schemes for disarmament. They sought a practical understanding with the Soviet Union about rules of the road that would reduce superpower tensions, but they expected that their competition would continue. They were sensitive to the need to shore up domestic support for an internationalist foreign policy and strong defense posture, which had come under attack because of opposition to the Vietnam War. They concluded that the further pursuit of WMD controls should not be undertaken in isolation from this broad approach to national security policy but should be subordinate to that policy and take advantage of diplomatic leverage the United States had in other areas—what they termed "linkage."

Above all they needed to manage a fractious domestic national security bureaucratic process. How well they dealt with those elements would in large part determine whether arms control would succeed as an integral foundation for their general restructuring of the US national security posture for a new, stable geopolitical era. While Nixon and Kissinger strove to exclude elements of that bureaucracy from arms control discussions, they quickly discovered that they could not. Whether it was director of Arms Control and Disarmament Agency Gerard Smith pushing early for a SALT agreement and completion of the Seabed Treaty, which prohibited placement of WMD on the ocean floors, or Secretary of Defense Melvin Laird clamoring for biological weapons controls, or the Joint Chiefs pushing to maintain a chemical war program, the Nixon White House learned that each issue had a powerful "constituency" with its own agenda. One cannot write about the Nixon administration without accounting for the colorful personalities and internecine feuds that perpetually impacted decision-making. Once after an exasperating conversation with Laird about SALT, Nixon exclaimed to press secretary Robert Ziegler that "it would be goddamn easy to run this office if you didn't have to deal with people."[1]

Although SALT quickly became the dominant arms control concern in the Nixon administration (see chapters 4 and 6), it first had to deal with several other issues related to WMD, namely biological and chemical weapons control, that intruded somewhat unexpectedly and required immediate attention (chapter 3). The administration further had to address arms control concerns that carried over from the past. These included ratification of the 1968 Nonproliferation Treaty (NPT) and the establishment of a Latin American nuclear-weapons–free zone and proposals for a seabed treaty (chapter 5). And a perennial public relations problem surrounding nuclear testing reared its ugly head and could not be ignored by the White House (Chapter 7).

We have chosen to employ a topical rather than chronological approach to the presentation of our research. Although we deal with each of these issues discretely in separate chapters in large measure because the Nixon administration pursued a piecemeal approach, we endeavor within those to analyze the agreements holistically, showing how each impacted the others and affected the overall international arms control and nonproliferation regime. The totality of the Nixon arms control and nonproliferation agenda across the WMD spectrum contains implications for our understanding of contemporary arms control issues as well as those of the Nixon era. By offering a synthesis and bringing together all elements of the Nixon administration's efforts to combat germs, gases, and the bomb, this book additionally offers a context for understanding many policies of that presidency—whether its pursuit of détente with the Soviet Union, attempts to end the Vietnam War, the opening to China, or conundrums in the Middle East.

THIS BOOK project as a general concept developed over a decade ago when we were colleagues working on the Residential Recordings Project at the Miller Center of Public Affairs, University of Virginia. We coauthored a digital publication with the University of Virginia Press on SALT recordings; Mahan's work on the *Foreign Relations of the United States* (*FRUS*) series arms controls volumes at the Department of State and her chemical and biological weapons (CBW) research at the National Defense University's WMD Center and Garrity's career as an analyst at the Los Alamos National Laboratory with an expertise in strategic nuclear arms control created a natural intellectual partnership. Given Mahan's current position at the Department of Defense, certain topics especially regarding nonproliferation had to be framed generally, and the views expressed in the entire manuscript reflect those of the authors and not that of the US government. The public release clearance of this publication by the Department of Defense does not imply Department of Defense endorsement of the material.

As with any book, we have benefited from the assistance and goodwill of many people. This project would not have happened without the encouragement and support of Marc Selverstone and his presidential recordings team, notably Ken Hughes and Keri Matthews at the Miller Center of Public Affairs at the University of Virginia. We also appreciate the patience of Nadine Zimmerli and Richard Holloway at the University of Virginia Press as well as our copyeditor, George Roupe; we're indebted to the insights and recommendations offered by their anonymous peer reviewers. We also thank historian colleagues Jessica Shirvanian-Wolfe and Michael Fasulo for their assistance with formatting and photo selection. Librarians Marshall Geniske and Linda McGuire were invaluable for finding numerous articles and procuring interlibrary loan books. Mahan feels an intellectual debt to John Caves and Seth Carus, her former mentors at the National Defense University WMD Center, for sparking her interest in CBW; to Melvyn Leffler, her doctoral advisor and now colleague and friend from the University of Virginia; and Edward Keefer, former general editor of the *FRUS* series, who helped her refine her research skills in government documents. Among the many individuals who aided Garrity's understanding of these issues, he would especially like to note J. D. Crouch II, president and CEO of the United Services Organization; Keith Payne, National Institute for Public Policy; and Stephen Cambone, Texas A&M University.

AVERTING DOOMSDAY

1

Nixon's Arms Control Inheritance

> Arms control by the Seventies had had a complicated history.... By the
> time Nixon came into office, arms control doctrine was well established
> among opinion leaders.
>
> —Henry Kissinger, 1982

On 24 January 1946, the United Nations General Assembly issued its
first resolution as an international body. This resolution called for the
"elimination . . . of all other major weapons capable of mass destruction" in addition to atomic weapons. In August 1948, the UN Security
Council's Commission for Conventional Armaments adopted the short-
ened term "weapons of mass destruction," defined as "atomic explosive
weapons, radio active materials weapons, lethal chemical and biological
weapons, and any weapons developed in the future which have characteristics comparable in destructive effect to those of the atomic bomb or
other weapons mentioned above."[1]

Since the early twentieth century, the international community felt a
general revulsion toward weapons of mass destruction (WMD) because
they were widely thought to be beyond the civilized pale. In some
cases, national leaders concluded that the use of such weapons might
provide an adversary with a decisive strategic advantage or threaten
the existence of their societies. As a result of these sentiments and calculations, various nations sought periodically to limit or prohibit the
possession or use of different categories of WMD and to oppose the
proliferation of those weapons beyond those powers already possessing
a specific capability. At other times, certain nations, especially those
with or aspiring to great power status, sought to maintain the maximum freedom of political and military action consistent with their
concern with the new destructive effects of WMD, whether to retain
their own capabilities for the purposes of deterrence, diplomatic leverage, or even possible military advantage by exploiting a technological
breakthrough.[2]

Richard Nixon entered the presidency inheriting a legacy of half a century of US government efforts to control WMD. In some instances, the United States had taken the lead internationally, including exercising unilateral restraint designed to encourage arms control and nonproliferation norms and agreements. At other times, it had followed the nonproliferation lead of others and made corresponding adjustments in its own national security posture, often grudgingly. And in a few cases, it had remained aloof from or opposed to the nonproliferation initiatives of other key nations or the international community as a whole. Washington's policy calculations did not take place in a domestic political vacuum. Although WMD issues were not always high on the public agenda, they tended to spike during times when national opinion was emotionally engaged, such as during an international crisis.

Early Arms Control Efforts in Chemical and Biological Warfare

Diplomatic efforts to control the development, production, and use of what later became known as weapons of mass destruction began in earnest after World War I, after the widespread use of chemical weapons during that conflict was seen as portending a horrific future of warfare unless such agents were outlawed. Chemical and biological warfare had existed for thousands of years. Even before the mid-nineteenth century, when scientists identified diseases caused by microorganisms, CBW existed in forms such as poisoned arrows and the catapulting of diseased corpses into besieged cities. The twentieth century, however, witnessed the first mass wartime use of poison gases. Bans on gas warfare negotiated at the Hague conferences of 1899 and 1907 had not prevented the large-scale use of chemical warfare (mustard gas, chlorine, and phosgene) in World War I that had resulted in more than a million casualties.[3]

The 1920s saw two landmark efforts that shaped expectations of CBW arms control far into the future. The United States assumed an early activist role in outlawing poison gas in future warfare. The Senate first ratified a ban on "the use in war of asphyxiating, poisonous or other gases" in the Washington Treaty of 1922, but the agreement never went into effect because France withheld ratification over objections to restrictions on submarine warfare. The United States again took the lead and inserted the same language into the Geneva Protocol of 1925. Although the Senate Foreign Relations Committee approved the treaty, it died on the Senate floor after filibusters by its fierce opponents. The protocol was returned to the Foreign Relations Committee, where it languished until 1947, when it was sent to the State Department for revisions. In 1959, Congressman Robert Kastenmeier (D-WI) introduced a resolution reaffirming the language in the Geneva Protocol. The Departments of Defense and State Department opposed that resolution, and no action was taken in the Senate. Not until Nixon took office in 1969 was the issue revived.[4]

The Geneva Protocol did not discourage the great powers from maintaining active chemical weapons (CW) and (to a lesser extent) biological weapons (BW) programs in the interwar period and during World War II. At the outset of World War II, Great Britain and France declared that they intended to abide by the Geneva Protocol if Germany followed suit, which it agreed to do. While the various combatants contemplated using gas warfare, they ultimately concluded that the use of CW would not gain them any enduring military advantage if their adversary retaliated in kind. President Franklin D. Roosevelt found gas warfare morally abhorrent, and in 1937 he vetoed a bill that would have changed the US Army's Chemical Warfare Service to the "Chemical Corps" because he thought dignifying the service as a "corps" would be contrary to his intention of discouraging the use of chemical warfare between nations. In 1943, he went further and made a "no first use" pledge, which in essence made the United States an adherent to the Geneva Protocol and formed the basis of official US policy on gas and germ warfare in the immediate postwar years: "This country has not used them, and I hope that we never will be compelled to use them. I state categorically that we shall under no circumstances resort to the use of such weapons unless they are first used by our enemies."[5] Poison gas was not used on the battlefield during World War II with the flagrant exception of its use by the Japanese, who used it at various times in its war with China between 1937 and 1945, and Italian use of mustard gas in invading Ethiopia in 1936 (and Germany of course used poison gas on concentration camp victims). Japan also used new biological weapons on a large scale against China during the war.[6]

During this same period, the enhancement of US CBW programs greatly surpassed efforts to curtail them. To an even larger extent than the US nuclear arsenal, chemical and biological warfare programs were enshrouded in secrecy and rarely exposed to public view. The exact extent of these programs also largely escaped congressional scrutiny, and budgetary accounting was buried deep in defense authorization bills. By 1969, the Defense Department spent on average $300 million per year. In August 1946, Congress changed the Chemical Warfare Service to the Chemical Corps, making it an official branch within the army. While the army retained sole control of CW and BW and concentrated program efforts on delivery means as well, in the early 1960s the other services began maintaining an additional ten production and storage facilities. The chain of command for control of these programs was from the secretary of defense through the War Department (renamed the Department of the Army) to the chief chemical officer and on to the various facilities. The heart of the programs lay within six army installations devoted primarily and often exclusively to producing or testing CBW agents. The oldest was the sprawling Edgewood Arsenal, built in 1917 and located some fifteen miles northeast of Baltimore and focused on nerve gas research and testing. Since the interwar period chemical weapons rapidly moved beyond the more primitive, commonly used industrial gases such as chlorine and phosgene and included the lethal family of nerve agents such as soman, sarin, and VX. And after World War II modern CW agents expanded to include nonlethal ones such as tear gas. Basic biological warfare research was done at Fort Detrick, also located in Maryland, near Frederick, on a campus-like facility of thirteen hundred acres. There, the diseases tested in laboratories for their potentialities as biological warfare agents included the following: Venezuelan equine encephalomyelitis (damages the human nervous system); anthrax (bacterial disease found naturally in animals but that can be fatal within twenty-four hours if it attacks human lungs); brucellosis (bacterial disease found naturally in farm animals and sometimes fatal to humans); plague (highly infectious and usually fatal bacterial disease carried by rodents); Q fever (rarely fatal but prolonged rickettsial disease); and tularemia (causes high fever, chills, pains, and weakness in humans but not always fatal). Biological as well as chemical agents were field-tested at the Dugway Proving Grounds in Utah, an area larger than the state of Rhode Island. Poison gas production took place primarily at Rocky Mountain Arsenal, a deceptively attractive facility on the hillside ten miles north of Denver, Colorado. VX nerve gas production was done at an austere, grim-looking factory at Newport, Indiana.[7]

Dugway Proving Grounds, Utah, where open-air field tests of biological and chemical weapons were conducted and site of March 1968 nerve gas accident that brought CBW into public light. (US Army)

By the end of World War II, the army's biological warfare program had become "the perverted stepchild of medical science."[8] The same could also be said of CW; both programs were controlled by a triad of military, academia, and industry. The number of government contracts with these production and research facilities grew exponentially over the next couple of decades. By the time Nixon became president, over fifty colleges and universities had research, development, testing, and evaluation contracts with CBW facilities. While much of the research was conducted secretly, some was published in medical and academic journals. Additionally, a host of companies held government CBW contracts, which provided chemical compounds or other supplies and materiel. These included Associated Nucleonics, Dow Chemical Company, Arthur D. Little, Dupont, General Aniline & Film Company, Honeywell Regulator Company, Hooker Chemical Corporation,

Hyland Laboratory, Insect Control and Research, International Business Machines, Mine Safety Appliances Company, Monsanto Research Corporation, National Research Corporation, New Mexico State University, Northrop Corporation, Pfizer, Charles & Company, Ryan Aeronautical Company, Sharpley Laboratories, and US Rubber Company.[9]

Biological, or germ, warfare, as it was more often called, received almost no public attention during World War II or in the two decades thereafter, with the dramatic exception of the Korean War. Both North Korea and China accused the United States in a variety of international forums of spreading disease-infected insects over the North Korean countryside and over northeastern China. The United States vehemently denied the charges as propaganda; the Soviet Union vetoed a UN Security Resolution offered by the United States that would have permitted a Red Cross inquiry.[10]

Probably because so little was known about the extent of CBW programs worldwide, there was little domestic or international impetus for arms control measures for these weapons of mass destruction in the first decades after World War II. The first meaningful international discussion took place at the 1959 meeting of the Conference on Science and World Affairs, commonly known as Pugwash. A small group of scientists representing the United States, the Soviet Union, the North Atlantic Treaty Organization (NATO), and Warsaw Pact countries and some nonaligned nations came to general agreement that multilateral controls were needed, but the scientists quickly realized that verification measures would be the sticking point between the Eastern and Western blocs. Interestingly, their fears of terrorists getting hold of chemical or biological war agents or of state sponsorship of a clandestine CBW program prompted the consensus about the desire for international controls.[11]

Those multilateral controls were not on the horizon. Instead two wars in the 1960s brought chemical weapons out of the realm of the hypothetical and into actual wartime use. The US expansion of hostilities in Vietnam during the 1960s brought with it greater contemplation of military deployment of CW. The United States limited use of CW to riot agents, defoliants, and herbicides, all of which the military claimed were not chemical weapons. A less publicized conflict in the Middle East witnessed the use of nerve agents. In 1962 a civil war erupted in Yemen as dissidents overthrew the monarchy and declared a republic. Egypt, which recognized the new republic, provided military support to defeat the royalist troops supported by Saudi Arabia and later Jordan. The civil war raged most of the decade, and in 1967 Saudi Arabia charged Egypt with the use of nerve gas in Yemen, claiming that the gas was used in Egyptian and Yemeni rebel attacks against villagers who remained loyal to the Saudi-backed royalist regime in Yemen. The Egyptian use in Yemen marked the first definitive episode of gas warfare since Japan released it in China during World War II.[12]

Dawn of the Nuclear Era

With the first and only military use of atomic weapons at Hiroshima and Nagasaki in 1945 to end World War II, the focus of WMD concerns shifted dramatically away from CW and BW for the next several decades. The United States understood that its nuclear monopoly would not endure if other nations, particularly the Soviet Union, decided to develop their own arsenals. This held the frightening prospect of uncontrolled arms races and devastating future wars. The initial American impulse was for comprehensive nuclear disarmament through the international control of all aspects of atomic energy, coupled with an iron-clad verification regime to prevent cheating. The Soviet counterproposal was to do away with American nuclear weapons in the context of an agreement for general and complete disarmament.[13]

When the Soviet Union demonstrated its own nuclear capability in 1949, the US government pursued two paths. First, it embarked on developing an extensive nuclear weapons program. During the 1940s, the Manhattan Project and its peacetime successor originally included three primary government-owned, contractor-operated (GOCO) facilities: the laboratory at Los Alamos, New Mexico, which designed nuclear weapons; the Hanford Engineering Works near Richland, Washington, which produced plutonium; and major sites at Oak Ridge, Tennessee, which produced uranium enriched in the fissile isotope 235. The nuclear weapons complex also incorporated hundreds of smaller contractor-owned, contractor-operated facilities that allowed for rapid increases in production in the early years of the nuclear weapons program. During the early 1950s, the Atomic Energy Commission (AEC) consolidated many of these functions into a smaller number of large GOCO facilities constructed throughout the United States. To provide sufficient capacity to meet the needs of the rapidly expanding stockpile, some operations were performed at multiple facilities. These included plants at Savannah River, South Carolina; Oak Ridge, Tennessee; Hanford, Washington; Fernald and Miamisburg, Ohio; Rocky Flats, Colorado; Largo, Florida; Albuquerque, New Mexico; and Kansas City, Missouri. The nuclear weapons complex was downsized after the Cold War, and certain facilities were decommissioned (notably Hanford and Rocky Flats), but the structure remained basically intact.[14]

Responsibility for US nuclear weapons resided in both the Department of Defense (DoD) and the AEC. DoD developed, deployed, and operated the weapons that delivered nuclear warheads. It also generated the military requirements for the warheads carried on those platforms. During the Cold War, the US nuclear arsenal contained many types of delivery vehicles for nuclear weapons, including short-range missiles and artillery, medium-range missiles and aircraft, short- and medium-range systems based on surface ships, long-range missiles based on US territory and submarines, and heavy bombers that could threaten Soviet bloc targets from their bases in the United States. The longer-range systems became known collectively as the strategic triad. Each component had a different basing mode, which complicated Soviet attack planning, and each offered different military capabilities that ensured high confidence that US strike plans could be successfully executed.

According to unclassified estimates, the number of these long-range nuclear delivery vehicles (intercontinental ballistic missiles [ICBMs], submarine-launched ballistic missiles [SLBMs], and nuclear-capable bombers) in the US force structure grew steadily through the mid-1960s, with the greatest number of delivery vehicles, 2,268, deployed in 1967. At the same time, shortly before Richard Nixon entered office, the total US nuclear stockpile reached its peak of 31,255 weapons.[15]

Early Nuclear Arms Control as Theory

The second path the US government took regarding nuclear weapons was to find ways to control the superpower arms race. On the conceptual and intellectual front, the 1950s and early 1960s witnessed a veritable explosion of academic and think-tank literature on the impact of nuclear weapons on international politics and US security. This literature developed key notions that subsequently shaped expert views about nuclear deterrence, the technical factors driving the arms race, the character of strategic stability, and the threat posed by uncontrolled nuclear proliferation. A first wave of analyses from government-sponsored think tanks such as the RAND Corporation warned of the potential vulnerability of US nuclear forces to a surprise Soviet first strike. A second wave considered the problems that resulted from the interaction of the opposing strategic forces and their respective vulnerabilities. This body of work challenged many previous assumptions underlying US nuclear policy, such as the value of air and (particularly) ballistic missile defenses and the necessity of targeting enemy nuclear forces (counterforce). The danger of configuring strategic nuclear forces in this manner was that it resulted in the reciprocal fear of surprise attack. Each side would feel compelled to strike first during a crisis, if each thought that the other would gain war-winning (or even marginal) advantages by going first. Under this scenario, both sides could persuade themselves that they could destroy a substantial percentage of the enemy's nuclear forces in a preemptive attack and then mop up the residual, ragged retaliation with strategic defenses—but only if they went first.[16]

The solution was counterintuitive to traditional ways of thinking—to promote, or at least accept, mutual societal vulnerability and to encourage, or allow, each side to have secure retaliatory (second-strike) forces. Popularly known as mutual or mutually assured destruction, the concept was based on the assumption that strategic stability and deterrence were best preserved if both sides believed that the enemy could inflict unacceptable damage in response to a nuclear attack. Holding populations (the urban-industrial base) of the other side at risk was much less demanding and required much smaller forces than attempting to limit societal damage to an acceptable level through counterforce/strategic defense. The latter outcome was rapidly becoming a technical impossibility against a determined adversary like the Soviet Union, according to the "new thinking" about nuclear strategy and arms control that emerged from universities and think tanks in the late 1950s and early 1960s. Although mutual deterrence between the superpowers was attractive in theory, ongoing political conflict was bound to make each suspicious of the other's intentions and capabilities and to continue to drive an arms race. To counteract these pressures, the United States should seek tacit or formal agreements with the Soviets, guided by concepts such as second-strike stability and mutual societal vulnerability, which would at least moderate the strategic weapons competition and increase safety.[17]

Nuclear Testing

Meanwhile, public fears about nuclear war increased in part because of aggressive aboveground testing programs that spread radioactive fallout and that seemed to feed an ever-increasing arms race. Many believed that a ban on nuclear testing could also help curb the spread of nuclear weapons. Ostensibly nonnuclear nations that forswore all nuclear testing would find it difficult to build reliable nuclear weapons. Efforts to negotiate an international agreement to end nuclear tests began in May 1955 in the Subcommittee of Five (the United States, the United Kingdom, Canada, France, and the Soviet Union) of the UN Disarmament Commission. Over the next few years, the interested powers engaged unsuccessfully in technical discussions of whether a system of controls and inspections could ensure verification of a test ban, especially underground nuclear tests. Despite objections from many of his military and scientific advisers who were concerned about the resulting atrophy in US nuclear technology and clandestine Soviet activity, President Dwight Eisenhower agreed to a nuclear test moratorium in 1958.[18]

Renewed Soviet and US atmospheric testing in the early 1960s followed by the sobering Cuban Missile Crisis of October 1962 revived international interest in a test ban. Although negotiators agreed on the importance of a comprehensive test ban (CTB) treaty, they stalemated over the number of allowed on-site inspections (OSIs) and the number of unmanned seismic stations. In the summer of 1963, the United States, the Soviet Union, and Great Britain reached a less comprehensive prohibition with the signing of the Partial Test Ban Treaty, also called the Limited Test Ban Treaty (LTBT), which banned all nuclear explosions except for underground tests. Over one hundred nations adhered as parties to the treaty. The LTBT was the first major arms control agreement of the nuclear age. During the 1950s both sides had engaged in multiple large-scale nuclear tests, which raised public fears that the superpower arms race might spiral out of control as well as deep concerns about the environmental effects of radiation fallout. Between 1955 and 1963, in various forums, Washington and Moscow explored the possibility of negotiating a CTB, an objective particularly important to President John F. Kennedy, who assumed that a test ban would discourage nuclear proliferation, a priority for his administration. For arms control advocates, a test ban would prevent destabilizing modernization of the superpower nuclear stockpiles over time and would sufficiently degrade confidence in their performance to the point where neither side could contemplate their use for anything other than pure deterrence.[19]

Key elements in the US government were concerned, however, that verification technology was inadequate to the task of detecting covert underground nuclear tests without an intrusive OSI regime, which the Soviets rejected as a cover for Western espionage. The DoD and the AEC were concerned that a total test ban would prevent necessary modernization of the US arsenal and a loss of confidence in its effectiveness (precisely the effects that test ban advocates favored). Those agencies also felt that the Soviets would secretly find ways to work around the ban. In the end, the superpowers agreed to prohibit detonations for military and civilian purposes underwater, in the atmosphere, and in outer space, while permitting underground tests. The treaty was eventually joined by over one hundred signatories in addition to the original three parties. The hope among those who favored this line of arms control was that the Partial Test Ban Treaty would eventually serve as a bridge to a comprehensive ban. Discussions about such a ban continued in the Eighteen Nation Disarmament Conference in Geneva, but the administration of President Lyndon Johnson, Kennedy's successor, focused its attention mainly on obtaining a nuclear nonproliferation treaty.

The US Nuclear Umbrella and Nonproliferation

Opposition to nuclear proliferation lay at heart of the US approach toward the bomb as early as the Manhattan Project.[20] The United States tried unsuccessfully to discourage powers other than the Soviet Union from joining the nuclear club. Shortly after World War II, Washington ceased nuclear cooperation with its wartime ally, Britain. But in 1952 the United Kingdom tested its own nuclear device, demonstrating that proliferation was indeed technically possible and politically feasible. The US arms control agenda shifted from comprehensive formulas and unilateral options to limited agreements and indirect means of discouraging proliferation. The Dwight Eisenhower administration proposed the Atoms for Peace program in 1953, designed to satisfy other nations' interest in nuclear energy while diverting them from pursuing weapons programs. Although the program was never adopted in full, it did result in the creation in 1957 of the International Atomic Energy Agency, which became and remains a pillar of the international nonproliferation regime. Eisenhower also unsuccessfully proposed an Open Skies agreement, which aimed to reduce fears that the other side was preparing a surprise nuclear attack (a secret US reconnaissance satellite program would soon fill that purpose).[21]

From 1945 on, the US working assumption was that American nuclear superiority and willingness to use those weapons in defense of its allies against Soviet bloc conventional superiority was central to the defense of the "Free World." As the Soviet nuclear arsenal increased in number and sophistication, the credibility of American extended deterrence commitments was bound to come into question especially in its core interests, Western Europe and Japan. One possible solution was to encourage or permit other nations to develop their own nuclear forces to deter Soviet aggression. By and large, however, the United States followed the line it had adopted since 1945—general opposition to nuclear proliferation, even by its own allies. In what became known in arms control circles as the nth country problem to signify the unknown final number, US policy makers in successive presidential administrations grappled with how to slow nuclear proliferation. The number of countries that at one time or another sought a nuclear weapons program and then decided to abandon that pursuit (called "rollback" in nonproliferation terminology) is staggering: Norway, Sweden, Yugoslavia, Italy, Romania, Egypt, Indonesia, Argentina, South Africa, and Taiwan—to name only some.[22]

The indirect approach did not succeed entirely. As more nations possessed or sought to acquire nuclear weapons, international relations became far more complicated, and the likelihood of nuclear war seemed to increase proportionately. The United States might count on a friendly nation like Britain to behave responsibly, but what of a hostile, aggressive power with an erratic leadership like China? Communist China detonated its first atomic bomb in 1964, raising concerns that India would undoubtedly feel compelled to do the same and then Pakistan and so on in an uncontrollable proliferation chain reaction. In Western Europe, beginning in 1958, French president Charles de Gaulle followed a relentless path toward an independent *force de frappe*. The possibility of a West German nuclear force would not only cause a major counter-reaction by the Soviets but also alarm Bonn's democratic neighbors and threaten the NATO alliance. In fact, after the end of World War II, US policy toward Western Europe pursued the double containment of not only the Soviet Union but also of Germany. US policies were often a conundrum, a perilous balancing act between Atlantic partnership in promise and practice as the Western European allies, especially Gaullist France, called into question the US commitment to "trade Paris for Washington" in a nuclear exchange with the Soviet Union. One solution was a NATO seaborne medium-range ballistic missile (MRBM) force of Polaris submarines with mixed-manning and multilateral ownership—commonly referred to as the multilateral force. Under this arrangement, however, the United States would retain the sole finger on the nuclear trigger. For most of the 1960s the United States tried in vain to sell this proposal to its NATO allies.[23]

By the midpoint of the Johnson administration, the United States had shifted its approach on balancing the needs for nuclear sharing with allies with the impulse to avoid proliferation. Prompted by China's entry into the international "nuclear club," Deputy Secretary of Defense Roswell Gilpatric chaired an interagency committee charged with providing policy options. The committee studied the entire gambit ranging from preemptive strikes to alliance management to resignation to the realities of nuclear proliferation by accepting selective countries developing nuclear weapons programs. After more than six months of deliberations and reports, the president ultimately endorsed the recommendation for a full-blown US effort to negotiate an international nuclear nonproliferation agreement. That effort took another two years.[24]

The 1968 Nonproliferation Treaty (NPT) was hailed at the time as a landmark step toward curbing the spread of nuclear weapons. It remains today as the centerpiece of what is called the international nonproliferation treaty regime. The NPT was initially signed by eighty-five countries after being opened for signature on 1 July 1968. Yet only seven countries, including Great Britain, had ratified the treaty when Nixon assumed office. The NPT would not go into effect until the United States, the UK, the Soviet Union, and forty other countries deposited the instruments of ratification. Many of the key countries capable of developing nuclear weapons had not yet signed, including West Germany, India, Japan, and Italy. A number of the key nonsignatories were awaiting US ratification before they signed, and many of those that had signed wanted to see US action before they ratified. On 17 September 1968, despite the Czech crisis caused by the unprovoked Soviet invasion two months before, the Senate Committee on Foreign Relations voted to recommend Senate approval of the NPT. It fell to the Nixon administration in one of the first arms control decisions it faced whether to support the Nonproliferation Treaty by encouraging Senate ratification.[25]

Setting the Stage for SALT

The Nixon administration faced a second major dimension of US policy toward the control of nuclear weapons that had gained momentum during the 1960s. Efforts to limit the size and expansion of the respective superpower arsenals, what became the Strategic Arms Limitation Talks (SALT), would ultimately become the predominant arms control focus of the Nixon White House. Yet like most arms control issues confronted by the Nixon administration, SALT had antecedents in earlier presidencies. By the mid-1960s, "new thinking" on nuclear weapons began to influence strongly the American approach to its strategic posture and arms control policy. At first, the Kennedy administration, influenced by fears of a missile gap with the Soviets, had accelerated plans to deploy a large ICBM and SLBM force. The administration was also determined publicly to escape what it regarded as the straightjacket of President Eisenhower's "massive retaliation" policy, which seemed to lack the necessary political and military flexibility in an age of nuclear plenty, thus ceding the strategic initiative to the Soviets.[26]

In 1962 Secretary of Defense Robert McNamara, taking advantage of what was then significant qualitative and quantitative US nuclear advantages, introduced the idea of a "no cities" nuclear doctrine, at least as declaratory policy. The United States, in the event of less-than-all-out Soviet aggression, would target Soviet military forces, especially its nuclear weapons, while avoiding Soviet cities. The goal was to limit damage to the United States and its allies by destroying Soviet weapons before they were launched and leaving Soviet cities as hostages to follow-on strikes, thus discouraging Soviet attacks on American and allied cities. The object was not to fight and win a nuclear war but to deter Soviet aggression across the board by having greater flexibility, including, in the NATO context, more robust conventional forces to meet local contingencies.[27]

Within a few years, McNamara abandoned this approach, at least as a matter of strategic nuclear force planning. After the Cuban Missile Crisis, the Soviets began a major buildup of their ICBM force, including taking steps, particularly the hardening of silos, to protect the missiles against a counterforce attack. They also started deployment of an ABM system (the ABM-1 Galosh system) around Moscow, which perhaps presaged a future nationwide defense against ballistic missiles. McNamara's analysis showed that it would be inordinately expensive, and probably technically impossible, for the United States to maintain a damage-limiting counterforce capability especially as the bills for the Vietnam War became due. It therefore made sense to cap the size of American nuclear arsenal according to what became known as the "assured destruction" criterion. Assured destruction was generally defined as the ability to destroy 20 to 25 percent of the Soviet population and one-third of its industrial base. Such damage would surely be considered by any rational Soviet leader to be catastrophic, and efforts on the part of the United States to increase the damage beyond that point (the "knee of the curve") by building more missiles would not be cost effective. And major investments in US missile defenses also made no strategic sense, as the Soviets could easily overwhelm them sufficiently to destroy American cities. In the logic of the "new thinking," nationwide defenses might wrongly but dangerously convince one side in a crisis that it could shoot first and use its ABM systems to mop up the ragged retaliation of its opponent and thus to limit damage to an acceptable level. McNamara was determined to avoid an arms race that would be incredibly expensive yet leave the United States no better off.[28]

To be sure, McNamara, at least in public, was not then advocating what became known as minimum deterrence. The planned US nuclear force level (1,054 ICBMs and 710 SLBMs, plus over 400 strategic bombers) was more than sufficient to meet the assured destruction criteria under the worst possible contingencies. US nuclear targeting policy was essentially unchanged, as it continued to hold at risk Soviet military/nuclear assets as well as urban-industrial targets and was based on a massive, preplanned attack. In addition, the Defense Department envisioned a further round of modernization by adding multiple warheads (multiple independently targetable reentry vehicles [MIRVs]) to most of the ballistic missile force, thus considerably increasing the number of warheads. There were many impulses behind the MIRV program, but the most important was the felt need to penetrate through saturation a future Soviet ABM system and the belief that this increase in offensive capability might deflect political pressure to build a nationwide US ABM system.[29]

Early efforts by McNamara to bring about some flexibility in US nuclear weapons employment policy, such as the development of limited strategic nuclear attack options, went for naught. Those in the US military concerned with nuclear matters continued to believe that flexibility and limitations in a nuclear exchange were simply fantasies in the real world and counterproductive in maintaining deterrence. McNamara chose not to invest his time and effort in changing that part of the system. He probably came to agree with the military planners on this point, even if he reached that conclusion through a different route. At the very least, nuclear planning could be done only in the context of a specific contingency.[30]

Within this context of such strategic and economic logic, it made perfect sense to many within the Johnson administration to initiate a serious push to reach an arms control agreement with the Soviet Union that dealt directly with the offensive and defense weapons themselves. During 1964 and 1965, the administration pushed the concept of a strategic nuclear delivery vehicle "freeze" keeping both arsenals at their present size. The Soviets, still behind the United States in the nuclear competition, naturally were not interested. The urgency increased when the American intelligence community began to appreciate the rapid pace of the Soviet modernization program (even then, officials tended to underestimate the scale of that buildup). The White House found itself under pressure from the Joint Chiefs and Congress to deploy to an ABM system to counteract that buildup, drawing on the US Army's Nike-X program. Large segments of the Pentagon and Congress, as well as conservative politicians of both parties, had not bought in to the "new thinking." They were deeply suspicious of Soviet intentions and doubted that the Soviets embraced nuclear parity and mutual societal vulnerability as stabilizing. They still felt that US superiority at critical (if not all) levels of the strategic competition, including protection of the US population, was essential.[31]

McNamara tried to deflect these pressures by suggesting deployment of a "thin" ABM system while keeping open the option of an arms control agreement with the Soviet Union that would prevent an escalating arms race. In late 1966, the administration reached out to the Soviets to begin negotiations over ABMs; the Soviets expressed interest but insisted any talks must include offensive weapons. Johnson had a high-profile opportunity to tie down this commitment when he met with Soviet Premier Alexei Kosygin in Glassboro, New Jersey, in July 1967, where McNamara famously made his case to Kosygin about the need to head off an offense-defense arms race and especially the dangers posed by large-scale defensive systems. Kosygin seemed befuddled by the latter argument, wondering, "How can anyone object to defensive weapons?" He dodged Johnson's efforts to commit both sides to talks.[32]

The Johnson administration then believed it had no choice politically but to go forward with the "thin" ABM program known as Sentinel. The president announced the decision in September 1967. Sentinel was to consist of seventeen bases, each centered on a missile site radar and supported by a string of five long-range perimeter acquisition radars spread across the US-Canada border area and another in Alaska. The primary weapon was the long-range Spartan missile, armed with a high-yield nuclear warhead, with the shorter range Sprint missile providing additional protection. The system would initially have a total of 480 Spartan and 192 Sprint missiles. Officially, Sentinel was characterized as a defensive system against a future threat from the People's Republic of China (PRC) and accidental launches from the Soviet Union or other nuclear powers. The administration privately made the anti-Chinese orientation case to the Soviets, arguing that it therefore should not affect any future SALT negotiations.[33]

In mid-1968, as Soviet and American negotiators began to finalize the NPT, Johnson used the occasion again to appeal to Kosygin. He argued that an announcement of intent to enter into strategic arms talks might assist in obtaining the support of other nations for the NPT by countering the objections of nonnuclear states that the nuclear powers were promoting the NPT as a means of preserving their exclusive status. "I would hope that such a declaration, of primary importance in itself, would do much to ensure the successful completion of work on the Non-Proliferation Treaty," Johnson contended.[34] On 27 June 1968, Kosygin informed Johnson that the Supreme Soviet was willing to undertake an "exchange of opinion" with the United States on ABMs and ICBMs. At the NPT signing ceremony on 1 July 1968, both leaders announced that they had agreed to begin strategic arms talks in the near future.[35]

Johnson hoped arms control limitation negotiations would begin in August or September. A quick agreement might serve as a final historic landmark for his presidency, now deeply marred by Vietnam. A US interagency working group rapidly developed a negotiating proposal: (1) freeze construction of all land-based ICBM launchers except those already under way, up to a ceiling of twelve hundred launchers; (2) prohibit the construction of additional land-based intermediate-range ballistic missile (IRBM)/MRBM launchers; (3) ban deployment of all land-based mobile and inland waterway-based ICBMs, IRBMs, and MRBMs; (4) forbid construction of additional missile-launching submarines; and (5) restrict ABM defenses to one set of fixed, land-based launchers and radars. There would be no mobile ABM systems. These limitations would be verified by "national means." The Joint Chiefs, however, pressed for some sort of OSI. To compensate for possible verification failures, the Joint Chiefs called for an aggressive research and development (R&D) and modernization program that incorporated the latest technology, including MIRVs, into strategic weapon systems.

On 19 August 1968, Soviet ambassador Anatoly Dobrynin handed Secretary of State Dean Rusk a note expressing Moscow's willingness to host a summit visit in Leningrad early in October to discuss matters of mutual interest, namely strategic arms limitation talks. But then on the evening of 20 August, all hopes crumbled as the Soviet Union and several of its satellite nations invaded Czechoslovakia. This blatant and surprise act forced Johnson to place the summit announcement on hold indefinitely. Although behind the scenes Johnson remained highly interested in reviving the summit and strategic arms talks, that course was opposed by most of his high-level officials as signaling tacit acceptance of the Czech invasion. Through intermediaries, President-elect Nixon made it clear to Soviet leaders that he would not be bound by any arms agreements reached at a preinauguration summit. He also encouraged the Senate to go slow on NPT ratification. On 21 December 1968, Johnson decided against Secretary of Defense Clark Clifford's recommendation to develop a joint statement with the Soviets as the basis for future negotiations instead leaving the matter to the incoming Nixon administration.[36]

On the eve of his inauguration, then, the new president faced a rich but mixed inheritance in controlling and curbing all categories of weapons of mass destruction. Clearly arms control and nonproliferation matters had become an enduring feature of international politics. What remained unclear at the outset of the Nixon administration was just how arms control and nonproliferation initiatives would fit into his conception of national security as his presidency became part of the seminal decade of arms control agreements spanning 1963–73.

2

National Security Landscape and Arms Control Agenda

> I've got to get credit, I told [Secretary of State William Rogers], for anything that happens in arms control.
>
> —President Nixon, February 1971

The Landscape

President Nixon entered office in January 1969 facing what he regarded as a grave crisis in American national security policy. The United States was badly overextended by the war in Vietnam, but more fundamentally Nixon believed that the United States could no longer maintain the strategic order it had created after World War II to contain international communism. Washington did not possess the economic and military dominance that once allowed it, as President Kennedy had urged, to "pay any price, bear any burden, meet any hardship, support any friend, oppose any foe to assure the survival and the success of liberty." The US share of the global economy had dropped from roughly 50 percent in 1945 to a projected 25 percent in 1970. Japan and Western Europe, especially West Germany, had overcome the devastation of World War II and built modern industrial economies. They were, or would be, looking for their own places in the sun. So too would leading nations among the lesser developed countries as the Western colonial era finally passed the scene. American hegemony in the "Free World" was no longer assured. In Nixon's view, a new period of multipolarity, at least economically, seemed to be on the horizon.

That said, the bipolar Cold War was far from over. Although there had been something of a thaw in East-West relations since the Cuban Missile Crisis, the Soviet Union remained a serious threat to the American alliance system. The Soviets also preyed on the instability and strife in the so-called Third World, particularly the Middle East. China had

19

broken away from its alliance with Moscow, but its future course in the international system was uncertain. Domestically, the United States was roiled by racial strife and by a deepening popular resistance to American overseas military engagements, focused most notably through the anti–Vietnam War protest movement.[1]

Nixon and his new national security advisor, Henry Kissinger, entered office with well-defined views about national security if not a detailed blueprint for how to proceed. They were veteran Cold Warriors who viewed the world through the prism of superpower conflict. Nixon had served as vice president in the Eisenhower administration and during those eight years developed foreign policy expertise through numerous visits abroad and general exposure to national security issues. He is vividly remembered for his "kitchen debate" in Moscow with Soviet premier Nikita Khrushchev in which they argued the merits of their respective ideologies. Eisenhower, however, is purported to have kept his vice president at arm's length, and Nixon had not been intimately involved with decisions related to nuclear weapons and testing. Kissinger, a Harvard University professor turned government consultant, had participated in the intellectual and governmental development of nuclear policy and authored a major book on the subject, *Nuclear Weapons and Foreign Policy,* in the late 1950s. Initially a registered Democrat, Kissinger had advised the Kennedy administration during the protracted Berlin Wall crisis of the early 1960s but had gradually lost favor with then national security advisor McGeorge Bundy and gravitated increasingly toward the Republican Party. In 1965, Kissinger became a consultant to Governor Nelson Rockefeller and began what became a decade-long involvement in advising on the Vietnam War. During the 1968 presidential campaign after Rockefeller lost the Republican nomination, Kissinger placed personal ambitions aside to serve in a presidential administration above party and hedged on whom to endorse. Nixon's reasons for choosing Kissinger are less clear. Some biographers argue that Nixon did so less out of personal or political affinity and more from awareness that his academic national security adviser had been on what one biographer calls "the fringes of power." Another Kissinger biographer, however, makes an overwhelming case that Kissinger had a strong public reputation, appearing on televised shows such as *Face the Nation.* Regardless of Nixon's motivations, the future president fully intended to be his own secretary of state and would not permit anyone

Nixon walking with Kissinger on the grounds of the White House.
(National Archives)

to usurp his authority in the realm of foreign policy. Kissinger shared his
belief in centralizing control in the White House.[2]

As they were poised to take the reins of power, Nixon and Kissinger
prepared for what they regarded as an impending revolution in strategic
as well as geopolitical and economic affairs. Since the earliest days of the
Cold War, American national security policy had been underwritten by

nuclear superiority and long-range striking power to offset local Soviet conventional superiority and its geographic advantage of interior lines of continental communication. This offsetting asymmetry in military power allowed the United States to deter Soviet aggression at reasonable cost and to guarantee security relatively cheaply to its Eurasian allies, while they built or rebuilt their economies. "Extended deterrence" also reduced incentives by other nations to develop their own independent nuclear forces, which for decades Washington believed would be a dangerously destabilizing development. The United States had done its best diplomatically to discourage or limit nuclear multipolarity.[3]

American strategists had long been concerned about how to respond if and when the perception of US nuclear superiority was lost. Nixon and Kissinger believed this day had effectively arrived. The direction of technology, the sheer accumulation of numbers of nuclear weapons, and a determined Soviet nuclear buildup pointed to a situation of nuclear parity. Worse, it was possible that the Soviet Union would seek some degree of nuclear superiority of its own by developing the capability to threaten America's retaliatory forces. Nixon's choice for secretary of defense, Melvin Laird, came into office warning that the Soviets SS-9 heavy missile might already be placing US land-based Minuteman ICBMs at risk.[4]

The new administration's solution to this myriad of challenges was to accept the resulting shift in the global balance of power and use creative American diplomacy. Nixon dubbed this "an era of negotiation," complemented by a modernized military posture restructured after Vietnam, to create a new, stable international order termed "a generation of peace." All of this was a tall order requiring a new, stable working relationship with the Soviet Union—what became known as détente. The ongoing competition between the two nuclear superpowers would be moderated by a set of common understandings about acceptable behavior so that competition would not lead to direct confrontation or conflict.[5]

Other poles of power would be given their due. US allies in Western Europe and Japan would provide increased international influence and the means to better support their own defenses. China would be brought out of its isolation, though that vision was at best inchoate at the outset of the administration. The United States would maintain its security commitments in Asia, but there would be no more Vietnams. Allies would be expected to maintain their own local defenses, while the United States

SS-9 ICBM in Red Square, Moscow, 7 November 1970. (National Security Archive)

backed them against nuclear threats from outside powers—what became known as the Nixon Doctrine. The United States would support certain friendly states, such as Iran, to serve as "policemen" and provide stability in key regions. Whether this arrangement would allow these selective nations to develop their own nuclear capabilities was an open question. Nixon and Kissinger did not regard this as a strategic retreat but rather a necessary rebalancing of resources and commitments.[6]

Nixon's Early Conceptions of Arms Control

Part of this strategic rebalancing involved dealing with the problems and diplomatic opportunities presented by what were known collectively as weapons of mass destruction. The president and his administration would only use this term on occasion—instead speaking of the individual categories. As discussed in the preceding chapter, the new administration inherited a set of partial agreements covering nuclear weapons and immediately faced increased public awareness of other categories of WMD as well as widespread public expectations that more should be done. A number of layers of arms control and nonproliferation ideas and policies had accumulated over time—some technical, others diplomatic, domestic political, and utopian. The Nixon administration had to adjust to, build upon, and in some cases alter this very eclectic foundation—creating a new layer of policies to deal with WMD that have substantially set and perhaps limited the course for future administrations down to the present. The layers of previous WMD control policies and extant strategic and political pressures included

- the widespread assumption that strategic nuclear arms control talks with the Soviets should be undertaken but without any agreed-upon definition as to the content or specific objectives of those talks;
- aroused public awareness of dangers posed by CBW, stirred in part by publicized mistakes in CBW testing, US activities in Vietnam, and revelations or suspicions about aggressive foreign programs in these areas;
- the decision whether to ratify the NPT and then how to implement it, despite major residual concerns by key US allies; the administration also had to deal with proposals to advance nonproliferation through instruments such as nuclear-weapons-free zones as well as preventing the spread of WMD to the ocean floors;
- the apparently unfinished nuclear testing agenda, as it was generally assumed that President Kennedy's LTBT would be succeeded by a complete test ban or at least further restrictions on nuclear testing;
- deepening public opposition to military spending in general and specifically to nuclear weapons modernization programs and activities, including ballistic missile defenses;
- intelligence assessments (speculative when Nixon first took office) suggesting that the Soviets might be seeking to overcome the strategic advantage in nuclear weapons that the United States had possessed since 1945 to support at least a partial first-strike capability.

At the heart of Nixon's (and Kissinger's) strategic thinking was skepticism about the efficacy of arms control. They approached arms control with the fundamental belief that political differences caused arms races and not that arms races caused political differences. As the new president put it: "The adversaries in the world are not in conflict because they are armed. They are armed because they are in conflict, and have not yet learned peaceful ways to resolve their conflicting national interests."[7]

Nuclear arms races, or other issues involving WMD, were not fundamentally different in this respect, and the United States could not afford to fall behind in the belief that arms control alone would solve its problems.[8] And throughout his presidency Nixon's White House tapes would capture him making comments such as the following about the role of arms control generally in international affairs: "The main thrust of my remarks is far more fundamental than 'arms control doesn't mean peace.' It's not an end in itself. You see, that's directly contrary to what the Gerry Smiths and the others and the [William] Bill Fosters—they all look upon arms control as an end in itself. That's the Soviet line. It is not an end in itself. The purpose of arms control is the means to the end and the control of war."[9]

Nor were Kissinger and Nixon nuclear proliferation alarmists. Rather, they took a somber view of the grim global reality that the diffusion of nuclear weapons to new states was likely and not necessarily unwanted with regards to certain allies. They well understood the political realities that nuclear weapons were seen by many foreign governments as instruments to achieve related domestic and international objectives, namely international prestige and status as well as the deterrence of regional threats. Kissinger evidently intimated as much when he met Israeli ambassador to the US Yitzhak Rabin in December 1968. Rabin writes in his memoirs that Kissinger told him "that the Republican administration would be more relaxed on the nuclear issue." Also before Nixon's inauguration, when Spurgeon Kennedy and Morton Halperin of the National Security Council (NSC) staff approached Kissinger to press for NPT ratification, they were told that any country with national security problems would seek nuclear weapons and it was not the place of the United States to interfere.[10]

Nixon's and Kissinger's preinaugural views regarding controls of chemical and biological weapons were less well known. Yet in one highly publicized venue during the 1960 presidential campaign, while participating in a Harvard forum on CBW with his opponent John F. Kennedy, then candidate Nixon declared that "because of rapid technological progress in many fields of science, the country cannot afford to neglect investigation of any area which might be exploited by a ruthless enemy in time of war. . . . Our program of research and development in biological and chemical warfare is essential to provide our armed forces and our civilian populations with the necessary information for their own protection and defense."[11] Some have speculated that Kissinger's early views on chemical and biological weapons were shaped by his association with Cambridge neighbor and Harvard molecular biologist Matthew Meselson, who actively protested US use of CW in Vietnam and had been a consultant to the Arms Control and Disarmament Agency (ACDA). None of Kissinger's pre–Nixon era writings or public statements addressed those two categories of WMD.[12]

Nixon and Kissinger were inherently skeptical that arms control if pursued apart from a stable balance of power would contribute usefully to national security. Arms control should be integrated into US strategic and defense policy, not the other way around. A key litmus test of an arms control proposal or agreement was whether it increased or at least did not harm American security, defined ultimately as the ability to wage war successfully, or at least prevent its adversaries from doing so, and hence to credibly deter war. There were other critical tests, such as whether arms control reassured allies, but Nixon insisted that diplomatic accommodation and peace must reflect an underlying military balance of power. As Francis Gavin has aptly noted, "Their belief in the supremacy of geopolitics influenced Nixon and Kissinger's skepticism of arms control."[13]

For Nixon, arms control and especially strategic arms limitations were necessary in part because domestic and international opinion demanded it. As Kissinger put it, "The worst posture was to be dragged kicking and screaming into a negotiation by outside pressures; a statesman should always seek to dominate what he cannot avoid."[14] Yet Nixon was perhaps motivated less by noble aspirations of statesmanship and more, or at least as much, by a political agenda and an all-consuming preoccupation with obtaining single-handed policy successes while denying others credit. His secretly recorded Oval Office conversations capture him repeatedly declaring the same refrain about the necessity of receiving credit: "I've got to get credit, I told [Secretary of State William Rogers], for anything that happens in arms control, and I said it can't be [ACDA director Gerard] Smith that's going to get the credit."[15]

Nixon's overwhelming desire to be reelected in 1972 was intimately tied to his desire to be regarded as a peace president. Peace abroad—a goal he set as being in the national interest—would also pave the way to political victory. As Nixon calculated, if he were to bring about improvement in relations with the Soviet Union with a capstone nuclear arms control agreement as well as end the Vietnam War and "open" China, his "era of negotiation" strategy would be validated fully in the eyes of the American voter. More limited arms control measures, such as nuclear-weapons-free zones or a seabed treaty prohibiting WMD on the ocean's floor might likewise contribute to this perception. His liberal critics would be disarmed. He was convinced that the success of his administration would be a turning point for the nation and the world.[16]

Détente would not succeed if there was not some sort of negotiated agreement or understanding on strategic arms. The administration's working assumption was that the Kremlin was no longer driven by revolutionary, ideological imperatives that made agreements impossible, although great-power competition would undoubtedly continue. History had shown that Soviet behavior could be restrained by America's willingness to show strength and close opportunities for expansion. But détente had to have a positive dimension as well, offering incentives for the Kremlin to cooperate and to adhere to its agreements. For instance, Nixon and Kissinger felt that the Soviet economy had stagnated and that Kremlin leaders would welcome a negotiated respite in the arms race. The prospect of increased trade with the West, especially in agricultural goods and high technology, offered an especially attractive carrot that might be brought to bear in arms control negotiations.[17]

Nixon believed that his best chance to ensure reelection and secure his place in history was through what he called the "big play"—a sudden, unexpected policy development that seemed to change the course of history, capture the public imagination, and undercut his critics. For the "big play" to have maximum effect, he sought the element of surprise, which in his view necessitated secrecy, and he needed full credit to be attributed to the president and to him alone. He could not tolerate claims that foreign policy achievements came from the bureaucracy or that he had been pressured into action by the establishment. Arms control, especially involving agreements with the Soviet Union, offered glittering opportunities for the "big play." Under this formula, arms control agreements must not be seen as the result of painstaking negotiation by professional diplomats but the result of a breakthrough that could only be brought about at the highest levels.[18]

The president's national security advisor was certainly in tune with Nixon's way of strategic thinking but focused on the detailed problems of arms control in a way that Nixon eschewed (although the president was certainly aware of the significance of the details). As the three thousand hours of secret presidential recordings reveal, Nixon loved to develop his ideas about foreign policy, including arms control, in colloquy with others. He found in Kissinger someone whose intellect, knowledge, and conceptual capacity were ideally adapted to serving as his interlocutor. And perhaps equally important, Kissinger provided almost a sycophant's ear for the president to express viscerally his foreign policy ideas and explore the implications of various possible approaches to dealing with the problems of arms control, Vietnam, and all the interlocking foreign policy issues of the times.[19]

Kissinger was well aware of the "new thinking" on deterrence, coercion, and arms control that had emerged from academia and think tanks over the past decade. He acknowledged the important insights, many of them counterintuitive, that this community had produced. Above all, he stressed the unprecedented fact that in the age of nuclear plenty, beyond a certain point, the additional accumulation of military, even nuclear, power no longer added to a nation's security. He felt that his conservative critics failed to recognize this revolution and continued to yearn for a superiority that was no longer possible or meaningful. Kissinger's strategic logic pointed to the substantive value of seeking to negotiate nuclear arms control, beyond that of accommodating political pressures. But here the case for arms control became more complicated.[20]

Kissinger believed that abstract academic theory about nuclear deterrence and arms control did not account for "real world" political and psychological factors that impinged on governments and their publics. In a crisis, assured destruction, for example, would hardly be a guide to statecraft. At the height of the Cold War, Kissinger noted, the Soviets had advanced various arms schemes as instruments of political and psychological warfare, to frighten Western publics and divide the allies. There was no assurance that they would not continue to do so in the future. America's allies—the NATO nations in particular—might hanker for arms control agreements to ease East-West tensions, but Kissinger believed that they had not yet fully thought through the implications of superpower nuclear parity, especially once codified through arms control. Once they did, he felt they were bound to fear the loss of the US security guarantee and the specter of a superpower condominium erected over their heads. He had to find means to reassure them this was not the case and deal with lingering resentments over US efforts to dictate NATO nuclear policy during the 1960s, especially over the creation and control of some sort of allied nuclear force and pressure to accept a nonproliferation agreement on Washington's terms.[21]

There was an additional complication: the United States could not expect to pursue successfully an opening to Beijing if the Chinese concluded that bilateral arms control negotiations represented a Soviet-American conspiracy against them or if other agreements (e.g., on nonproliferation and nuclear testing) were seen as explicitly anti-Chinese. Nixon's vision of a new world order postulated some sort of normalization of relations with Beijing, bringing the sleeping giant of 600 million people out of its self-imposed isolation. In January 1969, it was unclear what exactly "normalization" would mean, but Nixon and Kissinger's basic geopolitical instinct was to find ways to exploit the Sino-Soviet split and to tilt toward China if its security was threatened. As Kissinger put it: "History suggested to him that it is better to align yourself with the weaker, not the stronger of two antagonistic partners."[22]

But would the Chinese go along? The United States had well-established channels of communication with its major allies and shared with them basic concepts of security, so there were ready means for Washington to offer reassurances that arms control would not affect allied security. That was certainly not true in the case of the Chinese leadership. To be sure, in the early days of the administration, Nixon and Kissinger were focused on the Soviet nuclear relationship and did not systematically figure the China factor into the equation. As events showed, however, when channels of diplomacy became available, Kissinger was prepared to offer explicit reassurances to Beijing.[23]

Other Poles of Influence in the Administration

The Nixon administration's general approach to arms control reflected the realist outlook of the president and his national security advisor. The White House, however, quickly found the greatest challenges to be domestic and not with the allies, the Chinese, or the Soviets. As Kissinger later characterized the situation, he had to deal with two opposing camps, the "psychiatrists" and "theologians." Broadly speaking, the first camp consisted of what might be called the diplomatic, or arms control bureaucracy in the State Department, ACDA, and parts of the intelligence community. These officials had close intellectual and often personal ties with outside experts and congressional staff who had developed and generally embraced the arms control and deterrence theories of the 1960s. In dealing with the arms control die-hards Nixon had to account for the views of two particularly important figures. Secretary of State Rogers had served with Nixon in the Eisenhower administration as attorney general, and Nixon considered him to be a personal friend. Nixon was determined to run foreign policy from the White House—hardly an unprecedented choice, but rarely if ever would it be taken to quite this extreme. In doing so, Nixon ran the risk of alienating Rogers, a relative novice in diplomacy, who in the view of Nixon and Kissinger essentially reflected the views of the arms control bureaucracy. To make matters worse, Kissinger developed an intense rivalry with Rogers and frequently threatened to resign over perceived slights. Nixon hoped that he could propitiate Rogers by nominally giving him the diplomatic portfolio for the Middle East, but by virtue of his position as secretary of state Rogers could not easily be denied a seat at the table in the formulation of arms control policy, especially the SALT policy process.[24]

An even more important figure in terms of his potential influence on the substance and process of arms control negotiations was Gerard Smith, whom Nixon appointed as ACDA director and soon thereafter as chief SALT negotiator. Smith, nominally a Republican, had served administrations of both parties in disarmament negotiations. He was widely respected among liberals and moderates in Congress and could claim technical arms control expertise that surpassed that of Kissinger. Smith and his allies in the arms control community in government, academia, and Congress believed that arms control should primarily be about that—controlling the arms race by breaking the technological momentum created by the deployment of destabilizing weapons systems. In Smith's view, the argument that Washington should exploit its technological superiority to stay ahead in the arms competition was a chimera—the United States might gain short-term advantages, but history had shown that a determined adversary like the Soviet Union would soon catch up, leaving both sides worse off.[25] Smith's interest in arms control went well beyond SALT. He believed that the successful negotiation of an agreement with the Soviets would have an impact on what he regarded as the greatest danger, nuclear proliferation. He also verbalized fears of state-sponsored use of CBW. Writing to Kissinger just a few weeks into the new administration summarizing the status of various arms control issues, Smith cautioned that "CBW technology may soon offer 'a poor man's alternative' to nuclear weapons."[26] Certainly at the outset of the Nixon administration, Smith essentially stood alone in thinking about WMD problems outside the nuclear arena.

Nixon hoped that Smith would use his prestige on Capitol Hill to support the White House's position and that he would be a good soldier as SALT chief negotiator and simply stick to the script spelled out for him by the White House. Yet the president feared that Smith might depart from White House directives, especially by freelancing with Soviet negotiators or diplomats from other nations in multilateral forums and by suborning leaks that undercut the administration's official position. Smith also possessed the option of resigning in protest, which could energize political opposition to Nixon.[27]

The "psychiatrists" denied the charges of their critics that they sought arms control agreements merely for agreement's sake. They argued that the nuclear arms race was at a critical juncture, which compelled the United States to seek agreements in its own best interest. The Soviet Union had or shortly would achieve strategic parity with the United States, which provided opportunities for an equitable agreement that had not existed when the United States had superiority and would not long exist if the aggressive Soviet offensive building program continued. In addition, both superpowers were on the verge of deploying new technologies, specifically, MIRVs and ABMs, which threatened to destabilize the strategic relationship. Once those technologies were deployed, there was no putting the genie back in the bottle. Of particular importance was the need to prohibit nationwide strategic defenses, the pursuit of which promised to undermine both the arms race and crisis stability. Furthermore, America's technical verification capabilities had improved to the point where the United States could detect strategically significant violations of an agreement in critical areas, thus obviating the need for OSIs and other intrusive measures that the Soviets had consistently rejected.[28]

The arms control community also pushed hard for a strict commitment to follow the legal and moral-political framework of the newly agreed-upon Nonproliferation Treaty and to seek out other opportunities to prohibit or limit other WMD-related activities such as through a comprehensive nuclear test ban. Interestingly, the "psychiatrists" had no preconceived notions about CBW controls, though as those issues emerged early in the administration they became staunch advocates.

The "theologians" as Kissinger later dubbed the second camp centered in the DoD, the AEC, and the nuclear weapons laboratories. They were willing to explore arms control as a possible means of enhancing US security or, perhaps better put, as a necessary means to accommodate political pressures to cut defense spending. Some civilian specialists in the Office of the Secretary of Defense (OSD) and elements of the Joint Chiefs, were particularly skeptical of arms control, and in some cases, outright opponents.

DoD corporately was hesitant to accept constraints on qualitative improvements such as MIRVs. The military collectively was clearly reluctant to forgo any technology or program, even if it presently had operational deficiencies and even if the adversary seemed likely to respond. The Joint Chiefs preferred to preserve its options. Keeping programs in R&D status or halting them altogether in the expectation that they could be restarted if a greater than expected threat emerged was tantamount to killing them or at least putting the United States at a competitive disadvantage. History demonstrated that it was imprudent to make sanguine assumptions about threats and that it was imperative to stay ahead of the military-technical curve with actual, not virtual, capabilities. It was impossible to anticipate how technology might develop over time, and breakthroughs by an opponent were often immediately invisible. Banning one type of technology often pushed military developments into other, unpredictable directions (the 1922 Washington Naval Treaty did not anticipate the importance of aircraft carriers, for instance).[29]

The Pentagon also judged arms control proposals based on its collective experience with the Soviets since World War II. Defense officials tended to emphasize the basic asymmetry between the two societies, the one democratic and open, the other totalitarian and closed. The Soviet Union could practice strategic deception on a scale impossible for the United States, which made intelligence assessments of current and future Soviet capabilities difficult. The Soviets misled the United States about the size of its bomber force in the mid-1950s (it was much smaller than believed) and encouraged the perception of a missile gap in their favor toward the end of the decade. Khrushchev attempted secretly to install Soviet medium- and intermediate-range missiles into Cuba in 1962 despite previous public and private assurances that the USSR would not place "offensive weapons" on the island.

The incident freshest in the minds of the arms control skeptics was the 1958–61 nuclear testing moratorium. Both sides were under political pressure to end at least atmospheric testing because of its adverse environmental effects. In 1958, the Soviets proposed a testing moratorium, subject to agreement by other powers. The full story is a complicated one, but after considerable wrangling and further nuclear testing, the United States and Great Britain, along with the Soviet Union, ceased testing and entered into negotiations for a more permanent arrangement. Three years later, Moscow suddenly resumed testing with a very large series of atmospheric explosions. The United States eventually followed suit but at a lesser level. In 1963, the three powers agreed to a LTBT, prohibiting such tests, while permitting underground programs. As the American arms control skeptics remembered the event, the Soviets clearly had preplanned their testing breakout to achieve the maximum results in a short period of time; indeed, Moscow had probably proposed the moratorium in order to lull the United States into complacency. As a result, the Soviets had gained valuable data, primarily about nuclear weapons effects, that the United States now lacked and, with the LTBT in place, it could never duplicate.

As a price for supporting the test ban, the US defense and nuclear weapons communities had insisted on a series of safeguards that would prevent the United States from being caught off guard in the future, including support for a vigorous underground nuclear program and continued readiness to resume atmospheric testing. And there was deep opposition to any further testing constraints, especially a comprehensive ban.[30]

From the standpoint of many arms control skeptics, however, this was a case of locking the barn door after the horse had left. For agreements such as SALT to succeed in their basic purpose—to enhance American military security and not merely to control nuclear weapons—the barn door needed to be locked in advance. The United States must have the necessary flexibility to deal not merely with Soviet cheating but with Soviet secrecy and deception in areas not formally covered by an agreement. The same was true of other nations in multilateral arms control agreements.

Nixon and Kissinger recognized the critical role that Defense Secretary Melvin Laird would play in the bureaucratic and political process surrounding SALT and the ABM Treaty. Yet they did not anticipate the even more integral role Laird would assume concerning chemical and biological weapons. Laird had not been Nixon's first choice for the position, initially preferring prodefense Democratic senator Henry M. "Scoop" Jackson. But Laird brought to the table years of service in the House of Representatives, with particular expertise in matters of defense and health and human services (which would have bearing on CBW issues). A cigar-chomping politician known for his maverick proclivities, Laird had demonstrated throughout his time as a congressman his willingness to confront controversial issues and his ability to work both sides of the political aisle. Nixon expected him to provide critical assistance on Capitol Hill in promoting controversial programs such as the ABM Treaty and to support a future SALT agreement, reassuring conservatives that Nixon had not given away the store. He was also to keep the Joint Chiefs in line. In a broader sense, Nixon also needed Laird to make Vietnamization succeed and to reorganize the defense establishment for the post-Vietnam era. This made the president even more anxious to satisfy Laird on arms control. Laird's collegial standing with Congress and his ability to "work" the bureaucracy quickly made him an independent force to be reckoned with—something that Nixon barely tolerated. The president could be reasonably confident that Laird would not openly oppose the administration on arms control, but he had many other subtle ways to influence matters.[31]

For his part Laird relied heavily on the SALT analysis provided by his civilian experts, who constantly warned about an immediate or growing threat to the US retaliatory force. These concerns were channeled into the arms control policy process and the formal negotiations by Paul Nitze, who had long been a stalwart of the Democratic Party's hawkish national security wing. As the principal author of NSC-68 (1950), which became the blueprint for globalized containment, Nitze went on to serve in high-level positions in the Kennedy and Johnson administrations and played a major role in formulating the latter's abortive SALT approach in 1968. Nixon had considerable respect for Nitze and originally planned to appoint him to a high post in OSD, but Republican senator Barry Goldwater opposed Nitze's confirmation because of his Democratic Party affiliation. Nitze, however, proved willing to serve as OSD's representative on the SALT delegation. His political connections and national security expertise gave him a gravitas that far exceeded this modest position—making him a critical ally or potentially a dangerous adversary as SALT moved forward.[32]

Nixon also had to account for views of the Joint Chiefs and their chairman, Army General Earle Wheeler, succeeded by Admiral Thomas Moorer. The Joint Chiefs would eventually have to sign off on any arms control agreement or unilateral action involving WMD, and Nixon, as a congressman, had witnessed a number of unpleasant occasions of implicit and overt military opposition to civilian decisions, such as the Revolt of the Admirals in the late 1940s and General MacArthur's insubordination during the Korean War. He had been present during Eisenhower's battles as president against military resistance to the restructuring and reduction of the US armed forces. He had a low opinion of the military "brass," complaining in private about their swanky golf courses and their resistance to eliminating expensive anachronistic capabilities, such as continental air defense.[33]

On the other hand, with antidefense pressures so severe in Congress, Nixon believed that the Joint Chiefs would be pliable on arms control if certain basic concerns were met. In that circumstance, the Joint Chiefs' support for SALT and other arms control agreements could be used to counter any bitter-end civilian opposition in OSD as well to assure prodefense congressmen and conservative commentators. The White House would also face Joint Chiefs intransigence, especially from the army, in tackling control of the US CBW program. Not anticipated at the outset of the administration, those "lesser" WMD posed a potential distraction to a White House that wanted to focus on SALT.

For Kissinger, the bureaucratic trick was to break down or work around opposing viewpoints, build upon or create areas of common agreement, preempt arguments that might cause the policy-making process to gridlock, and prevent the formation of politically effective coalitions inside and outside government that opposed the developing Nixon-Kissinger arms control policy.

On the eve of Nixon's presidency it was abundantly clear that arms control, especially strategic arms negotiations, was going to be an extremely complicated enterprise for the White House aside from the obvious challenges of dealing with the Soviets across the negotiating table. How well Nixon and Kissinger managed their domestic bureaucratic and political processes would in large part determine whether arms control would succeed or fail as an integral foundation for their general restructuring of the US national security posture for a new, stable geopolitical era. Ultimately, despite the controlling efforts of the White House, the Nixon administration did not speak with one voice or act in a cohesive way in arms control and nonproliferation matters. Even Nixon and Kissinger, whom many historians regard as "partners in power" or speak of "Nixonger" foreign policy, were not always of the same mind. Their high-strung personalities, individual quirks, and some might say doubtful moral standards complicated matters even further.[34]

Under this host of circumstances, national security policy and arms control required a great deal of improvisation under the relentless pressure of events, many outside of White House control. Of the panoply of arms control issues the administration would tackle over Nixon's five-and-a-half-year presidency, SALT was the expected focus. Instead, biological and chemical weapons intruded as an early distraction for an administration that already lacked a blueprint for arms control.

3

Two Paths

BIOLOGICAL AND CHEMICAL
WEAPONS CONTROL

> We've got to do something about our chemical and biological weapons
> policy. You know, we've got a nightmare growing here, and we've got
> differences between State and ourselves.
>
> —Secretary of Defense Melvin Laird, 1969

TO APPRECIATE the Nixon administration's arms control measures to combat CBW requires embracing the ironic and ultimately the paradoxical. In sharp contrast to nuclear arms control policies, especially SALT and the ABM Treaty, President Nixon and his national security adviser spoke infrequently about CBW. Of the over three thousand hours of Nixon White House recordings, few substantive conversations arose about those programs, and when they did, they were often dismissive about arms control measures related to them. The president's handful of public remarks and speeches surrounding the renunciation of the BW offensive program were likewise minimal and given almost grudgingly as his White House recordings indicate. Neither the President nor Kissinger mention CBW in their memoirs.

A related irony is that the offensive BW renunciation and resultant multilateral treaty, the 1972 Biological Weapons Convention (BWC), which banned the development, production, and stockpiling of biological and toxin weapons, came about quickly and relatively easily compared to the SALT and ABM agreements that engaged the White House for the entire presidency. And even though it was primarily a series of CW incidents that aroused congressional, scientific, and general public outrage that led to the offensive BW renunciation and then the BWC, ironically, it took another two decades for an international agreement to be reached on CW.

What led to the abrupt cancellation of the US biological weapons program that had its origins in World War II and had continued in covert
fashion for over thirty years? And what caused an unexpected end to
one of the long-standing assumptions that had provided the foundation
of American CBW policy for decades—the coupling of chemical and
biological weapons? The president's decisions regarding BW were the
culmination not of the mere seven months of NSC deliberations that his
administration undertook but of over a decade of pressure from outside
forces that revealed the limitations of BW and CW to the US strategic
arsenal. As Kissinger once remarked, "Most ideas that masquerade as
new ideas in Washington have been around a long time."[1]

Vietnam War as Backdrop to Public Awareness

At the center of those fierce internal and external deliberations was the
Vietnam War, as it was with so many contentious policy issues of the
period. The Nixon administration and especially its civilian leadership
at the Pentagon stepped into Southeast Asian quagmire amid intense
public controversy over the use of chemical agents in that war. Growing protests over the US Army's use of napalm and defoliants in the
jungles of Southeast Asia had brought increased public awareness of the
horrors wrought by chemical weapons. Napalm, often described as jel-
lied gasoline, is an incendiary gel that congeals to skin until it burns
to the bone. Concocted in 1942 in a secret Harvard University laboratory for use during World War II, the US military employed napalm
to great effect against Imperial Japan—killing over eighty-seven thousand in one bombing of Tokyo alone on 9 March 1945. And in America's
next major war in Korea, the US chairman of the Joint Chiefs of Staff
touted napalm as instrumental to the 1950 counterattack from Inchon
that turned the tide of the war. By 1966 when US engagement in Vietnam was in full throttle, the use of napalm had become central to its
war effort. While about 16,500 tons of napalm had been used against
Japan during World War II and 32,357 tons on Korea, about 4,500 tons of
napalm was dropped over Indochina monthly. By 1967, that average had
increased to five thousand tons. The strategic value of this potent fire-
bomb was rarely articulated by those in high command, but as one pilot
responsible for dropping this chemical weapon stated, "People have this
thing about being burned to death."[2]

US Air Force crews sprayed defoliants to clear jungle hiding places around air base perimeters. (US Air Force)

In unprecedented ways not witnessed during World War II or the Korean War, the media brought home to the American public the atrocities caused by napalm in the Indochina conflict. As one historian has written, "Seeing is believing," and three major magazines—*Ladies Home Journal* (circulation of 6.8 million), *Redbook* (circulation of almost 5 million), and *Ramparts* (circulation of over 4 million)—carried article after article with gripping full-color photographs of burn victims that visually chronicled the cruelty of napalm against the Vietnamese civilian populations. One children's hospital director was quoted as saying, "Torn flesh, splintered bones, screaming agony are bad enough. But perhaps most heart-rending of all are the tiny faces and bodies scorched and seared by fire."[3] US military use of napalm became central to the mobilization of the antiwar movement. The October 1967 demonstrations at the University of Wisconsin prompted by the atrocities committed during the Battle of Ong Thanh showed this public outrage. The antiwar movement compared napalm to the Nazi use of Zyklon B in its concentration camps.[4]

Use of another highly toxic chemical agent in Vietnam initially drew less attention to the US arsenal of CBW agents than napalm. Commonly known as Agent Orange, 2,3,7,8-tetrachlorodibenzo-p-dioxin was one of several color-coded highly toxic herbicides that US forces began spraying over the Vietnamese rural landscape to eradicate the forest cover for the Vietcong and the crops that fed them. By 1966–67, however, its use added to awareness of America's hitherto largely secret CBW programs. Additionally, use of riot control agents both in Vietnam and on protestors at home fueled further domestic outrage. Images of US military forces donning protective masks as they used tear gas to clear enemy tunnel complexes made it difficult to disguise the use of this chemical agent even though the US government insisted tear gas was a nonlethal agent. But as that same CW agent was being unleashed on protesting Americans in city streets, the national awareness of the definition, legality, and ultimately morality of CBW continued to heighten.[5]

In 1968 investigative reporter Seymour Hersh published a telltale book, *Chemical and Biological Warfare: America's Hidden Arsenal,* highlighting US use of herbicides and tear gas in Vietnam. Additionally, he provided a comprehensive review of the US CBW capabilities, stockpiles, and policies. His sources, all unclassified, were provided primarily by Harvard scientist (and incidentally a former Harvard colleague and neighbor of Kissinger when they lived in Cambridge) Matthew Meselson, who actively protested US use of CW in Vietnam and had been a consultant to the ACDA.[6]

Series of CBW Accidents

Chemical and biological weapons were one and the same in the minds of most people, including inside the government. A series of non-combat-related chemical accidents from the late 1960s particularly roused congressional reaction to CBW programs. The army's practice (through a poorly named program called Operation CHASE, or "Cut Hole and Sink 'Em,") of secretly dumping leaking surplus munitions at sea after transporting them across the country by train began including chemical weapons in 1967. Over the course of the next two years, Operation CHASE disposed of mustard agents, sarin, and VX rockets.[7]

Another prominent CW accident occurred in March 1968 in Skull Valley, Utah, next to Dugway Proving Ground's open-air testing site. Early in the morning of 12 March 1968, the general manager for a livestock company telephoned the director of the University of Utah's ecological and epidemiological contract with Dugway Proving Ground. The outraged livestock manager was rightly convinced that sixty-four hundred sheep had not simply dropped dead by an accident of nature. The army made no admissions of culpability. However, despite public statements that no testing had occurred, the army paid for the sheep. Those denials of responsibility would unravel a year later as Congress pieced together information.[8]

Congressional Responses

The initial governmental impetus for opening a review of CBW programs came not from the executive branch but from Capitol Hill. Following growing awareness of chemical weapons program hazards and accidents, congressional opposition to CBW agents intensified. Congressman Richard McCarthy (D-NY), himself a former reporter for the *Buffalo Times,* led the charge. On the evening of 4 February 1969, after watching the NBC television airing of the documentary *First Tuesday,* which discussed American CBW activities including the nerve gas mishap near Dugway Proving Ground, he decided to spring into action and eventually published *The Ultimate Folly: War by Pestilence, Asphyxiation, and Defoliation* in late 1969. In the process of informing himself about the US CBW programs and writing his book, McCarthy and several colleagues on Capitol Hill ensured that Congress became a "transmission belt" by holding investigative hearings, introducing legislation limiting CBW activities, and generally prodding executive branch officials.[9]

On 4 March, McCarthy arranged for a closed briefing by the army for three senators and eighteen congressmen on the US CBW program. For the first time, they learned about Operation CHASE. The following day, the *Washington Post* quoted McCarthy: "There is a cloak of secrecy without any strong reason for it. I think it can be said that we have the capability to retaliate (with CBR [chemical/biological/radiological]). But what is our policy? Would we want to retaliate in kind? It has never been stated." The *Post* further reported McCarthy's intention to pursue questions with Secretary of Defense Melvin Laird.[10]

McCarthy did indeed pursue follow-on with Laird as well as with Secretary of State William Rogers, director of ACDA Gerard Smith, United Nations Ambassador Charles Yost, and Kissinger. Between 7 and 13 March, he sent each of them variants of the same questions covering different aspects of US CBW policies, including the state of offensive and defensive capabilities, US retaliatory stance, measures taken to protect public health against testing accidents, and use of chemical agents in Vietnam.[11]

Pentagon Enters

On 13 March, at a congressional reception held at the White House, Laird came up to McCarthy (they had served four years in the House together) and exclaimed, "Well Max [his middle name as called by colleagues] you sure stirred up a storm over chemical warfare!" Laird then put his arm around the congressman and began to inquire about the congressional briefing that had occurred the week before. McCarthy recalls, "I told him firmly and pointedly that my concern was entirely serious and sincere, that I was not at all satisfied with the Army's performance, that I was addressing a series of questions about CBW to him and that I wanted answers. His broad smile vanished as he walked off."[12]

Nixon's secretary of defense would later cast himself as the chief protagonist in the administration's efforts to end the US offensive BW program. Laird may not have been the original advocate for a governmental review of CBW programs, but he certainly was an eager convert. Not long after and less than five months into the administration, Laird decided to tackle head on the series of controversies that had engulfed the army's CBW programs. His decision to address the government's CBW programs was no doubt prompted by several mutually reinforcing factors. As the former chair of the House Heath, Education, and Welfare Committee, he continued to care about national issues that could negatively impact public health. Yet ever the politician, he also wanted to curry favor with his former congressional colleagues to obtain their support on the upcoming ABM vote in return for his taking control of CBW issues. Lastly, he was politically savvy and knew that pressure from Capitol Hill could create a political firestorm the White House did not need.[13]

On 30 April 1969, in a brief and to-the-point memorandum to Kissinger, Laird asked that the president direct the NSC staff to initiate an

immediate interagency review of US CBW policies and programs. The
secretary of defense recognized that "the administration is going to be
under increasing fire as a result of numerous inquiries, the more notable being Congressman McCarthy's and Senator [James W.] Fulbright's
[D-AR]."[14] Indeed on 21 April, McCarthy entered into the *Congressional Record* the answers he had received from the Pentagon, State, and
ACDA to his March queries about CBW policy. The contradictions
between those agencies' statements and public pronouncements presaged the inconsistencies, debates, and divergent views that unfolded
during the NSC review process.[15]

NSC Review of CBW Policy

Kissinger did not respond to or act immediately on McCarthy's inquiries
or Laird's suggestion. The national security advisor rarely relinquished
control over any aspect of foreign policy, even those that he knew little
about, such as the status of the country's CBW programs. At the outset
of the administration, with Nixon's blessing he had structured the NSC
to harness the interagency to bend to his will. He used a variety of mechanisms—National Security Study Memoranda (NSSM) and National
Security Decision Memoranda and (NSDM) as well as various sub-NSC
review groups—to centrally coordinate interagency policy reviews. In
the first five months of the Nixon administration fifty-eight NSSM were
commissioned. The NSSM process involved a comprehensive (many
described it as convoluted) examination of all key areas of a given US
national security policy. Each study resulted in a paper, prepared by
the major national security agencies and coordinated by the NSC staff,
that provided a broad set of options in an issue area and identified the
pros and cons of each. The NSC principals—the secretaries of state and
defense, the director of ACDA, the chairman of the Joint Chiefs, and
the director of the Central Intelligence Agency (DCI)—typically met in
weekly sessions to discuss the various issues under review. During these
meetings, each principal orally defended his agency's preferred policies
for the president's consideration.[16]

On 9 May 1969, ten days after receiving Laird's recommendation,
Kissinger promised him that he would initiate a review process. NSSM
59, sent out on 28 May, directed an interagency review of CBW policies. The thrust of the policy review centered on several key issues

and options: Should the United States maintain a lethal biological and chemical weapons capability? Should the United States maintain a capability for the use of incapacitating biologicals? Should the United States maintain only an R&D program either in both offensive and defensive weapons, or just in defensive areas? Should the United States ratify the Geneva Protocol of 1925 prohibiting the use in war of chemical and biological weapons?[17]

Kissinger initially assigned the task of drafting and vetting the papers for NSSM 59 to the Interdepartmental Political-Military Group (IPMG), a standing interagency committee made up of representatives of nine agencies, including the Department of State, the OSD, the Joint Chiefs of Staff, ACDA, and the intelligence community. To address the various questions posed in the study memorandum, the IPMG divided up the analytical work among three subcommittees called interdepartmental groups (IGs). The first subcommittee assessed intelligence on foreign CBW capabilities, the second analyzed military options for employing CBW, and the third explored diplomatic options open to the United States with respect to the ratification of the 1925 Geneva Protocol and the negotiation of additional CBW arms control agreements. Once the three IG papers were drafted, the IPMG combined them into a summary report that would be submitted to the NSC review group, a committee chaired by Kissinger and made up of officials at the deputy secretary level. The review group prepared the meetings of NSC principals and made sure that the president was presented with genuine choices among well-defined policy options and not with prepackaged decisions.[18]

Status of Soviet BW Program

The IG tasked with assessing intelligence on foreign CBW capabilities had little specific information about Soviet CBW capabilities to use as a baseline. Michael Guhin, the young NSC staffer whom Kissinger tasked with overseeing the review, later recalled: "That review, unbeknownst to a lot of people, basically challenged the whole way the intelligence community had looked at assessments. I remember [we] spent a whole week out at the [Central Intelligence] Agency trying to figure this out. In the end, we didn't understand how to compute something from zero, and that was our problem."[19] One rare article on Soviet CBW capabilities that appeared in the *Washington Post* in the midst of the NSC policy review espoused skepticism about Soviet work in that field: "One [US] Government man familiar with the intelligence for years says the classified materials 'really tell you no more' than the published materials, which—in the specifics—amount mostly to assertions from sources with an ax to grind, such as the Army Chemical people or anti-Soviet emigres."[20]

For the US intelligence community, the years 1947–72 were known as the dark period for knowledge of Soviet capabilities in biological weapons. The only National Intelligence Estimate (NIE) generated in the late 1960s by the CIA was an overly generalized ten-page estimate released on 13 February 1969 that covered both Soviet chemical and biological capabilities in the same brief summary. Interestingly, the agency determined that the USSR grouped chemical, but not biological, weapons with nuclear as "weapons of mass destruction." For both categories, however, it opined that the Soviets would not hesitate to employ CBW in the event of a general nuclear war. Yet in terms of specifics about either program, the NIE was skewed heavily toward analysis of CW. The intelligence assessment devoted a mere page and a half to the Soviet BW program, describing "a high degree of political control and restraint" seeming to govern it. "We believe it highly unlikely that the Soviets would employ BW in an initial strategic attack," the NIE set forth. Its conclusion about "availability of biological agents" was nebulous, stating that "we have insufficient evidence on which to base an estimate of the types and quantities of BW agents which might be available to the Soviets for offensive use."[21]

What is now known about Soviet military doctrine for the use of biological weapons comes primarily from interviews with former scientists who worked on the Soviet program. The Soviet doctrine devised in the 1940s that continued for decades thereafter followed the triad of strategic, operational, and strategic-operational biological weapons. Because highly contagious agents such as smallpox and plague could potentially blow back and infect the attacker's own troops, these were intended for long-range, strategic attacks against the territories of the United States, Great Britain, and some other European countries; operational biological weapons such as tularemia and glanders, which tended to incapacitate but not typically kill, were intended for use against military targets about 100 to 150 kilometers behind the front lines; finally, strategic-operational biological weapons, primarily anthrax, were meant to be used against both strategic and operational targets. This level of detail was never more than speculation, however, among the US intelligence community.[22]

Role of Scientists in the NSC Review

To inform and assist all three IGs preparing reports for the NSC review group and principals, Kissinger encouraged the president to permit advice from nongovernment scientific experts. The overt rationale was the highly technical nature of CBW issues, but the White House also sought to defuse criticism from a scientific community that had grown increasingly critical of CBW policies, especially with regard to Vietnam. Several prominent members of the President's Science Advisory Committee (PSAC), whom Kissinger would have convene to write a separate report on chemical and biological weapons, had already contributed to the growing public consciousness about CBW policies during the last years of the Johnson administration. Meselson had led an effort to collect the signatures of five thousand members of the American Federation of Scientists on a petition calling for a top-level review of US CBW policies, which was presented to the White House in February 1967. And by sheer coincidence, on 4 March 1969, as Congressman McCarthy and his colleagues were receiving an army briefing on US CBW policies, Meselson was speaking at MIT as part of an open discussion about the misuse of science by the government. The day had been set aside by several universities nationwide for the designated discussions.[23]

Additionally, on 30 April, Meselson had received an invitation from Senator Fulbright to speak before a closed session of the Senate Foreign Relations Committee to "educate" the members about chemical and biological weapons. Ivan Bennett, the dean of the New York University School of Medicine, chaired the panel for PSAC, which also included Meselson, Harvard chemistry professor Paul Doty, IBM physicist Richard Garwin, and others.[24] In reflecting on his involvement with preparing a report on CBW for PSAC, Meselson later recalled that "one of the principal national security arguments was that here we were, never having carefully reviewed this program for more than 15 years, pioneering the development of weapons that would make it possible for a multitude of other states, and even non-state entities, to destroy the United States when we had no need for such a weapon because we had the nuclear deterrent."[25]

Congressional Hearings

In early May 1969, the same week that the NSC review commenced, Congress began to penetrate the secrecy surrounding the US CBW program through a series of hearings. The first set highlighted the environmental and safety hazards posed by Operation CHASE. On 13 May, Congressman McCarthy learned from the Federal Railroad Administration that the army intended to ship twenty-seven thousand tons of obsolete but still lethal nerve and mustard gas from its Rocky Mountain Arsenal to Earle, New Jersey, where it would be dumped off the coast of Atlantic City. The House Foreign Affairs Subcommittee on International Organizations, Human Rights, and Oversight held three days of hearings on the effects of dumping poisonous gases into the oceans.[26] Only a week later, also largely at McCarthy's instigation, the House Government Operations Subcommittee on Conservation and Natural Resources held hearings on the dangers posed by open-air testing of lethal CBW agents. During those hearings the sequence of events that led to revelations about the army's disastrous testing mishap involving six thousand sheep deaths at Dugway Proving Grounds fifteen months before came to light.[27] As the *New York Times* reported the day after the hearings concluded, "The Army spokesman confirmed, after much verbal jousting, that the public information officer at Dugway had not told the truth when he told reporters last March that Dugway had done no testing that could have caused the sheep to die."[28]

Another embarrassing chemical weapons accident came to policy makers' attention with a telephone call from the field. On the night of 9 July Laird was dressed in a tuxedo and ready to attend a state dinner for the emperor of Ethiopia when he received word of "rabbit dead at Chibana." The cryptic message referenced the secret Chibana Army Ammunition Depot next to the US Air Force Base on Okinawa, where in the absence of chemical agent detectors to detect chemical leaks, rabbits were used. Unbeknownst to the Japanese government, let alone its populace, Laird's predecessor, McNamara, had ordered the storage of some eleven thousand tons of mustard and sarin gas munitions on Okinawa in the event of war in the Pacific. Since the United States still had legal and jurisdictional control over Okinawa, the US Army informed Laird that public disclosure was not required. Still, the revelation of twenty-three soldiers and one civilian hospitalized could not easily be kept quiet. On 18 July 1969, the *Wall Street Journal* reported that the victims had been exposed to low levels of nerve gas involving sarin-filled bombs.[29]

The White House was furious at the Pentagon for the embarrassment and failure to inform. The day before the *Wall Street Journal* broke the story and contacted the White House for comment, the president was in the dark. Kissinger spoke with Laird, who claimed he sent a memorandum to the president right after the incident occurred. Kissinger said they never received it and that he and his staff had scrambled furiously to present the facts to Nixon. In the end, Laird agreed with Kissinger that "Defense should take the rap for it rather than the White House."[30]

Even with the Pentagon agreeing to make a public announcement acknowledging the storage of the weapons, the timing of the accident could not have been worse from a diplomatic standpoint. Days before the incident hit the newspapers as a front-page story, Kissinger had begun secret talks with the Japanese government on the reversion of Okinawa to Japan. And Rogers was preparing for a visit to the pro-American government of Japanese premier Sato to discuss continued US use of Okinawa as the main American strategic base in Asia. Massive riots broke out in Japan over the Okinawa revelations. On 22 July the Department of Defense announced that preparations were being made to remove lethal chemical agents stored on Okinawa. However, no immediate action to implement the directive was made. It took the Pentagon months to figure out a place that would accept the CW agents. The selected location—Umatilla Army Depot in Oregon—met with public resistance. A series of lawsuits to prevent the move aroused congressional attention and resulted in passage of Public Law 91–762 in 1972, which prohibited the army from transferring the weapons from Okinawa to anywhere in the continental United States. Ultimately, Operation Red Holt moved the stockpile to Johnston Atoll in the South Pacific, for long-term storage and eventual demilitarization.[31]

Decoupling Chemical and Biological Weapons Policy

The great conundrum that went without public comment at the time and by scholars since then is how the death of thousands of sheep at Dugway from nerve gas, the hazards posed by Operation CHASE, and the disclosure of chemical weapons storage on Okinawa led not to the abrogation of US *chemical* capabilities but to the renunciation of the country's offensive *biological* weapons program. This shrewd maneuver was the result of a series of not always linear machinations by Laird, with the ultimate outcome resonating with the president and his national security adviser. The defense secretary knew well that the White House sought to draw attention away from the longer established and proven US chemical weapons capability recently used in Vietnam and that it also needed to placate congressional, national, and international critics.

Yet the defense secretary, ever the pragmatist, was under constant pressure from the Joint Chiefs and the services, especially the army, to maintain full capacities for both CW and BW. Laird, however, faced stronger military resistance to curbing the army's CW program than the BW one because the former centered on chemical herbicide usage in Vietnam. The Joint Chiefs maintained that CW provided operational benefits through the defoliation of jungle vegetation, which was supposed to prevent ambush along key travel routes and destroy field crops grown by insurgents in remote areas. Laird's decision to argue for the separation of chemical and biological weapons was the outcome of a slow, circuitous journey. In numerous interviews after leaving the Pentagon, Laird readily claimed credit for the administration's BW decisions but never mentioned the strategic decision to decouple CW.[32]

Laird ultimately believed the abnegation of the US offensive BW program would not adversely affect or undermine national security. Given the unpredictability of BW, the defense secretary was convinced that conventional, chemical, and nuclear weapons were far more reliable components of the US strategic arsenal. The secretary pitched his case most strongly at an 8 August 1969 meeting of the DoD staff by arguing that biological weapons and chemical weapons programs "should be broken down to two separate programs—one for chemical and one for biological research. There are a number of differences between these programs on what we are trying to accomplish."[33] In his politician style, he spent the next several months privately working within the bureaucracies to decouple the two WMD agents.[34]

Part of his maneuvers required talking out of both sides of his mouth while the review process unfolded. Though the Okinawa debacle may have caused Laird privately to take stock of the possible folly of maintaining a full US CBW program, he publicly came out staunchly defending the status quo. "We do not have the capability of the Soviet Union in this area," Laird was quoted as saying in the press. He declared that the United States must possess CBW capabilities to deter other nations from using them against American cities. The failure of the intelligence community to analyze Soviet CBW capabilities adequately unfortunately led to widespread acceptance among policy makers of inflated claims of its programs.[35]

Interagency Debates Continue

The interagency review process overseen by the NSC was convoluted, often turgid, and initially resulted in divergent agency positions. In early August 1969, the NSC review group received the full report of the PSAC along with two papers on CBW policy prepared by different offices at the Pentagon, which came to diametrically opposite conclusions. The scientific experts on the PSAC concluded that biological weapons had serious drawbacks from a military standpoint. Biological pathogens were slow acting, unreliable in the field, unpredictable in their effects, and had a short shelf life in storage. Because biological weapons caused acute symptoms only after an incubation period of several days, they had little utility on the battlefield and were best suited for attacks against population centers. Yet the effectiveness of BW for strategic deterrence and retaliation was limited because retaliatory use would entail lengthy delays to detect an enemy attack and deliver a counterattack to sicken the target population. Moreover, biological weapons would presumably be redundant in a nuclear exchange. The PSAC also worried that microbial pathogens released into the environment could create hazards that would remain long after a conflict ended. For example, an infectious agent might mutate into a more deadly strain or could infect wild animals, creating persistent foci of infection that would pose a serious threat to public health. Given these liabilities, the PSAC recommended halting the US production and stockpiling of biological weapons, while retaining a strictly defensive R&D program as a hedge against "technological surprise," meaning the possibility that an enemy might develop a new BW agent against which the United States had no medical countermeasures, such as vaccines or antibiotics. At the same time, the PSAC favored keeping BW production facilities in a standby state of readiness and continuing research on the chemical synthesis of toxins.[36]

Meanwhile, the two contradictory Pentagon papers on CBW policy left Laird frustrated by bureaucratic parochialism and compelled him to take an even more hands-on approach to the review process. The first paper, written by the Office of Systems Analysis within the civilian OSD, was critical of BW agents as combat weapons and questioned their politico-military utility as instruments of deterrence and coercive diplomacy. The military options paper, prepared by officials from Joint Chiefs and the State Department's Bureau of Politico-Military Affairs, came to diametrically opposite conclusions, arguing that biological weapons were reliable and controllable in the field and that US offensive BW capabilities should be preserved and even expanded.[37]

Laird withdrew the military options paper and instructed the Office of the Assistant Secretary of Defense for International Security Affairs to coordinate a new, more balanced document that reflected the views of the Joint Chiefs, the individual military services, and civilian offices within OSD such as the Office of Systems Analysis and the Office of Defense Development, Research, and Evaluation. Laird saw to it that the Army staff, which as the parent service of the Chemical Corps, had an institutional interest in retaining biological weapons, was not represented on the IPMG and remained largely shut out of the interagency deliberations. In fact, on 15 August, Laird ordered the army to halt all production of BW agents until the NSSM 59 review had been completed. Army historian David Goldman best describes the army's role in the review process as "its mismanagement of the programs, particularly the public relations aspect." Those embarrassing revelations helped unravel congressional and executive branch support.[38]

Mounting Congressional and International Pressures

Laird also prevailed upon Kissinger to ensure all NSC principals be given an opportunity to review IPMG papers prior to formal submission (counter to NSSM procedures) and to extend the review process until October 1969. The White House initially resisted delay because congressional and international pressure made it feel like it was forever swimming against the tide of public opprobrium. Capitol Hill shifted tactics from mere hearings to defense procurement actions affecting purse strings for CBW programs. On 3 July, the Senate Armed Services Committee cut $16 million from the fiscal year 1970 DoD budget request. A month later, on 11 August, Senator Thomas McIntyre (D-NH), working to bring together multiple amendments that would restrict CBW programs, offered a compromise amendment to that authorization bill. Most surprisingly, Laird's staff worked hand in glove with McIntyre's to draft those restrictions, which strove to meet many of the objections that had come to light through Congress: DoD would be required to submit semiannual reports to Congress; funding would end for delivery systems of lethal agents; standard operating procedures would be established with other federal agencies, congressional committees, and state and local governments for the reporting of CBW material transportation; detoxification of CBW would occur before domestic transporting; surgeon general certification of open-air testing would be mandated; and the secretary of defense would be required to declare testing beforehand.[39]

Two days before the amendment vote, on 9 August, Laird released a public statement endorsing the amendment. Yet as the *New York Times* reported, "It appeared to be a case of the Defense Department acknowledging the inevitable." And the *Times* also captured Laird's thinking on separating the CW and BW, as he was quoted praising the deterrent value of chemical warfare while opining that "the deterrent aspects of biological research are not as sharply defined."[40]

Abroad as well as at home, developments galvanized the administration's internal deliberations over CBW policy. In July 1969, the secretary general of the United Nations bolstered this by issuing a scathing, extensive report on the necessity of banning chemical and biological warfare. In the fall of 1969, twelve nonaligned countries in the United Nations drafted a resolution affirming that the 1925 Geneva Protocol banned the use in war of tear gas, herbicides, and other nonlethal harassing agents. Because the United States continued to employ tear gas and herbicides in Vietnam, it was in the small minority of dissenting states. Then on 19 September 1969, Soviet foreign minister Andrei Gromyko gave a major speech on CBW policy to the United Nations General Assembly in which he proposed a draft convention that called for the simultaneous disarmament of both BW and CW.[41]

The British government, which continued to be the primary proponent in international bodies for a BW ban led the Western opposition to the Soviet draft. Solly Zuckerman, the chief scientific advisor to the British government and member of the UN secretary general's group of consultant experts on CBW, convinced the prime minister that the distinctions between the two categories of WMD were too great to lump them together. As he argued, "Biological agents depend for their effect on their ability to reproduce themselves in the target and that this is something no chemical weapon can ever do. No chemical agent is contagious." The British government put forth numerous reports and draft resolutions in UN forums. Despite some allies endorsing the separation of BW and CW, it was clear that the White House struggled throughout the spring and summer of 1969 to stay ahead of news revelations and diplomatic efforts taking place in the United Nations that put continuous pressure on the Nixon administration.[42]

Coming to a Decision

The interagency review process inched forward in October and early November 1969. The papers became more voluminous, but the positions evolved only incrementally from where they stood during the summer. Yet from the NSC review meeting on 30 October, which convened to prepare for a full NSC discussion on 18 November, the nucleus of likely administration policy options emerged. The decoupling of CW from BW with the concerns over Vietnam was reflected in the decision to rework the final IPMG paper "into three categories: biological warfare, chemical warfare, and the question of the Geneva Protocol with respect to tear gas and herbicides." The "summary of decisions" from the NSC review group meeting showed just how sticky CW policies remained: "State the arguments for and against briefing the German government on deployment of CW stocks in Germany; define an adequate CW retaliatory capability; state the pros and cons for ratification of the Geneva Protocol including the question of reservation on tear gas; and raise the issue of a requirement for a Presidential decision to use tear gas in conflicts other than Vietnam." BW issues remained less thorny: "Clarify the distinction between offensive and defensive R&D; include a specific policy issue on the UK draft convention on BW."[43]

Because Nixon did not begin recording his Oval Office conversations until February 1971 and was not intimately involved in the NSC review process until the end, there is little in the documentary record of his personal comments and views. It is therefore illuminating to include many of his statements from the decisive NSC meeting of 18 November, a week before his landmark announcement. The president's opening comment

expressed his chagrin at the paucity of US intelligence about Soviet capabilities. After DCI Richard Helms evidently provided a vague briefing,
the president quipped, "I hope we know more about ours than about
theirs." When the discussion turned primarily to the chemical weapons
program, the president shifted to listening mode as Joint Chiefs chairman
Earle Wheeler expressed the position for retaining both offensive and
defensive CBW programs and opposing US ratification of the Geneva
Protocol. Laird, who had maneuvered all summer and fall to bring the
Joint Chiefs on board, realized Wheeler was speaking for the record and
would retreat on his BW position. The secretary of defense contended at
one point that "CW and BW should not be put together. . . . These are two
entirely different subjects. We need to clarify what CW and BW mean."[44]
The president concluded, "We have mixed CW and BW together and
should get them separated." As the NSC meeting drew to a close, the
president reinforced his concern to cover the "public relations" aspects,
including informing the Senate Armed Services Committee.[45]

President's Announcement

A week after the NSC meeting, on 25 November 1969 President Nixon
announced before a group of reporters in the Roosevelt Room of the
White House a major policy decision on the US chemical and biological warfare program. With rhetorical flourish, the president declared,
"Mankind already carries in its own hands too many of the seeds of its
own destruction. By the examples we set today, we hope to contribute to
an atmosphere of peace and understanding between nations and among
men." Nixon decided that henceforth there would be two distinct programs, chemical and biological, rather than one combined program,
given the important differences between the two. With respect to CW,
he renounced the first use of lethal and incapacitating chemicals, and
he stated that he would resubmit the Geneva Protocol to the US Senate
for ratification. With regard to the BW program, Nixon renounced the
use of lethal bacteriological agents and weapons and all other methods
of biological warfare, and he directed the Defense Department to make
recommendations for the disposal of existing BW. He further stated that
the United States would confine its biological research to defensive measures such as immunization and safety measures.[46] The next day when
Kissinger informed Nixon of all the congratulatory telegrams coming

from Harvard for the renunciation of germ warfare, Nixon retorted tongue in cheek that "the wires would really pour in from Harvard if I surrendered the United States to Kosygin."[47]

Toxins Decision as Afterthought

After the president's announcement questions remained, however, on whether the policy applied to biological toxins. The significant omission of the category of toxins opened Nixon's unprecedented BW executive decision to additional congressional pressure. McCarthy wrote the president in December 1969, describing the offensive BW abnegation as potentially hollow: "In your statement of November 25, 1969 you announced that the United States would not use bacteriological or germ warfare. Yet on Friday, Mr. Jerry Fiedheim, Department of Defense spokesman said that your decision did not apply to biologically produced toxins such as the deadly botulinus. . . . The same men who have been working on anthrax and 'Q' fever will now be working on biologically derived toxin."[48]

Toxins fell in a somewhat nebulous category somewhere between chemical and biological weapons. Toxins, unlike biological weapon agents, do not replicate; in some respects, toxin weapons could best be described as a type of chemical weapon produced by biotechnological means. Given the confusion both inside and outside the federal government over the US policy on toxins, Kissinger encouraged Nixon to authorize an expedited interagency review of the issue through another NSSM, "Review of Toxins Policy." Issued as NSSM 85 on New Year's Eve, the NSC staff gave the interagency a mere two weeks for the study so that the administration could quickly quell the growing concern that the controversy was sowing doubts about the president's earlier BW decision.[49]

The same IPMG that handled the CBW review earlier in the year was now tasked with coordinating a toxins policy review. It met twice, on 7 and 10 January 1970, to discuss the draft options paper. In sharp contrast to his stance during the CBW review in the summer, during this interagency debate Laird sided with the military in defining toxins as CW agents. State Department officials countered that most toxins of military interest, such as botulinum toxin and staphylococcal enterotoxin B, were produced by bacteria, which were grown in large fermentation tanks that were identical to those used to produce microbial agents such as anthrax spores. Maintaining the toxin production facilities at Pine Bluff Arsenal would seriously undermine the credibility of the US renunciation of BW and might forfeit the international goodwill that the president had reaped from his decision. On 29 January, the NSC review group met to discuss the IPMG's options paper, a process and paper that very much mirrored that of the larger CBW policy review.[50]

The positions of the representative agencies also mirrored those taken during the earlier CBW review. The State Department and ACDA representatives supported renouncing offensive toxin capability while maintaining a defensive program on the grounds that a capability to retaliate with toxins was not essential to US national security. Because most toxins could not penetrate the skin, they were easier to defend against than chemical nerve agents and would not add any significant capability to the existing US chemical arsenal. Although renouncing an offensive toxin warfare capability involved some risk of raising questions about the continued US retention of chemical weapons, inasmuch as toxins were classified as chemical agents, the State Department regarded this risk as low.[51]

The Department of Defense was divided on the toxins issue as it had been on CBW generally. The Pentagon's civilian leadership, namely Laird and Deputy Secretary David Packard, took a position congruent with the decoupling of CW and BW; they supported banning toxins produced by bacterial fermentation but permitting those made by chemical means. The Joint Chiefs favored retention of toxin development and stockpiling produced either by biological processes or by chemical synthesis as a way to maintain maximum military flexibility.[52]

Unlike the previous larger CBW review, the NSC review group added a public affairs modification to the toxins debate. The administration was intent upon muting the embarrassment this oversight of toxins had created. Director of the US Information Agency (USIA) Frank Shakespeare cautioned that toxins were a "sleeper issue" that could potentially damage the president's reputation at home and abroad. He explained, "The repugnance with which the public regards such agents—whether they are classified as chemical or biological—is so great that technical explanations and attempts to justify rationally their possible military use would fall mainly upon deaf ears." For this reason, USIA endorsed the option of giving up toxin weapons entirely, whether produced by biological fermentation or by chemical synthesis, and permitting work only on defensive measures.[53]

In presenting a decision memorandum to the president that summarized the various agency positions on toxins, Kissinger put forth the Laird recommendation that Nixon approve the middle-ground recommendation of continuing offensive and defensive research on toxins produced by chemical synthesis and defensive-only research on those produced by biological fermentation. Kissinger endorsed this position for the same reason as OSD, and that was to avoid exposing the US chemical weapons program to possible political attack while retaining the possibility that toxins might have future military utility. In discounting the USIA argument about the repugnance with which the general public viewed toxin weapons, the national security adviser worried that the greater public relations concern was the public's tendency to lump toxins together with classical chemical weapons. If the United States therefore abandoned the toxins outright, critics at home and abroad would call into question the continued existence of chemical weapons, which the entire CBW review process had succeeded in separating with minimal public backlash.[54]

In the end Kissinger was persuaded privately by Meselson to abandon toxins. The scientist was preparing for testimony he would give before a congressional committee in which he stated: "Whether toxins were made by living organisms or by chemical synthesis, keeping them as a military option would soften the hard line against biological weapons that the President's decision intended to communicate."[55]

Rather than hold an NSC meeting as he had in November before those executive decisions, the president simply read Kissinger's summary memorandum, discussed it while they were in Key Biscayne, Florida, and quickly came to a final decision. Nixon overrode Kissinger's initial recommendation and decided that he would limit the US toxins program to defensive R&D. Nixon went with his political instincts; he realized that the public would lambast his administration for renouncing biological weapons but retaining toxins produced by biological or chemical means. He also did not want to risk hampering progress in the SALT talks, which had begun in November 1969 and which remained the administration's top arms control priority.[56]

On 14 February 1970, the White House press secretary released a statement in Key Biscayne that clarified the president's earlier decision to renounce biological weapons by declaring that the United States would henceforth abandon "offensive preparations for and the use of toxins as a method of warfare." The administration tacked on provisions to include toxins with NSDM 44, issued on 20 February 1970. By extending the unilateral ban on biological weapons to cover all toxins, regardless of their means of production, Nixon's decision closed the potential loophole that would have been created by the future chemical synthesis of toxin agents and resulted in a US policy that was cleaner and less ambiguous.[57]

From Unilateral Renunciation to BWC

Like the decision on toxins, the negotiation of the Biological Weapons Convention was regarded by the White House as somewhat of an annoying afterthought and has been underexamined in the scholarship on this topic. Gerard Smith evidently had to persuade Kissinger first by telephone and then more formally by memorandum to convince the president to attend the signing ceremony for the BWC: "I think that his absence would be taken by the Soviets as a sign that the President is for some reason less interested in lending his prestige to this latest instance of US-Soviet agreement than was the case when he attended the signing of the Seabed Treaty."[58]

While the president's offensive BW program renouncement in November 1969 had been a bold rhetorical stroke, it did not necessarily facilitate a firm negotiating position for the US delegation in Geneva for a multilateral treaty. Ironically, the president's unilateral decision to renounce US offensive BW capabilities removed leverage for US and Western allied negotiators to push for verification measures. The Kremlin resisted, as it did in all arms control negotiations, the principle of OSI, which it maintained was a guise for espionage. Additionally, the president's unexpected November renouncement of the US offensive BW program was met with mistrust by the Soviets. They received no indication beforehand, and after all, Kissinger typically used his back-channel conversations with Dobrynin to keep as much of a pulse on Soviet thinking about bilateral relations as possible. Yet during their last conversation, which was nineteen days before Nixon's executive decision, no mention was made of a possible decision on BW.[59]

The administration did inform the British in advance of Nixon's executive decision and promised to champion the UK proposal in the UN. The American and British decoupling of BW and CW, however, became a major sticking point for the Soviets in negotiations for a treaty banning the two categories of WMD. Little initial progress was made in negotiations for what ultimately became the BWC. The White House instructions to James Leonard, the US chief negotiator in Geneva, "were to stall for all of 1969; don't let it go one way or the other."[60] In his "First Annual Report to the Congress on United States Foreign Policy for the 1970s," the president gave himself great kudos for his November 1969 executive decision and continued to endorse the British UN proposal that called for an international treaty to ban biological weapons but reported no substantive progress. Negotiations for the BWC, as for any major international arms control agreement, was a complex affair. Certainly political motivations to keep riot agents and herbicides out of negotiations motivated US positions, but there were a host of highly technical issues as well. For instance, US and UK negotiators realized that dual-use capabilities of BW and CW agents were different and required separate measures to keep dual-use goods from nefarious purposes. One operating rationale for biological weapons negotiators was a desire not to inhibit vaccine production and commerce in biotechnology products.[61]

The US-Soviet stalemate over whether to separate CW from BW in an international convention finally broke at the end of March 1971. Suddenly the USSR changed course by presenting a draft prohibiting BW alone. Why the Soviets suddenly dropped their insistence on negotiating both categories of WMD together remains a mystery. Some insight was offered by Arkady Shevchenko, a confidante of Gromyko, who served as a UN under secretary general and later defected to the United States. Shevchenko has stated that Gromyko "felt it necessary for propaganda purposes" that the Soviet Union sign the BWC especially after "the [Soviet] military's reaction was to say go ahead and sign the convention; without international controls, who would know anyway?"[62]

To the consternation of the British delegation, which had previously taken the lead on Western BW proposals in the United Nations Eighteen Nation Committee on Disarmament (ENCD), the remaining six months of negotiations became largely a US-Soviet affair, with the American delegation giving in on the question of verification of compliance. The British relented on grounds that the BWC was a worthwhile arms control agreement on its own. In one of the rare instances of SALT considerations influencing BW issues, Leonard informed his British counterpart that the experience of the US SALT delegation in Geneva

showed that it was futile if not "counterproductive to insist on a procedure for investigation of or complaints of misuse."[63] The two superpowers, largely excluding their allies from final deliberations, agreed to a
draft treaty on 5 August 1971, and after another round to iron out specifics, the Convention on the Prohibition of the Development, Production,
and Stockpiling of Bacteriological (Biological) and Toxin Weapons and
on Their Destruction, commonly referred to as the Biological Weapons
Convention, was concluded on 28 September 1971. By unanimous vote,
the UN General Assembly adopted a resolution endorsing the treaty on
16 December 1971, and the final treaty was open for signature on 10 April
1972; ninety-nine nations had acceded to the convention by the end of
1972. Thus, in a relatively short period, especially compared to the protracted SALT negotiations, the BWC was agreed upon within a mere
sixteen months.[64]

At the signing ceremony hosted in the main conference room of the
US Department of State, Nixon spoke eloquently before representatives
from the United States, Great Britain, and the Soviet Union, the three
countries designated as treaty repository states. And he made refer-
ences to other arms control and nonproliferation agreements but failed
to expound on linkages among the agreements because no efforts had
been made to establish any:

> As has already been indicated, we have been here in this room before.
> We recall the nonproliferation agreement ceremony which occurred
> in 1970. We recall also the seabed ceremony, and that treaty will soon
> come into force [see chapter 5]; and now we have this ceremony today.
> The Soviet Ambassador has referred to the negotiations with regard to
> the limitation of strategic arms [see chapter 4]. . . . As far as these agree-
> ments are concerned, they are basically not an end in themselves. They
> limit arms, but they do not mean the end of war. They are means to an
> end, and that end is peace.[65]

In private, however, Nixon spoke derisively, even crudely, about the
multilateral treaty, which in his view had little strategic value vis-à-vis
the Soviet Union. He confided to Kissinger: "I'll bet you that the disarmament boys at ACDA are probably just shitting their pants because of
this thing [BWC] because we should have kept the emphasis on peace
and all that. The hell with them. That was senseless to make us sit there

with the Soviet Ambassador at a time when they're raping South Vietnam and say that they have made a great contribution to peace by signing this silly biological warfare thing which doesn't mean anything. Now
you know it and I know it."[66]

Consequences

Nixon's unilateral abnegation in November 1969 of biological and toxin
weapons was the first time that a major power unilaterally abandoned
an entire category of armament. The signing of the BWC just two years
later seemed to cap the administration's accomplishments in BW arms
control. Initially few questioned the wisdom of Nixon's decision, and the
Western allies lauded it. Yet the president's decisions were rather hastily
made, which was immediately evident with the overlooking of toxins.
Even the supremely confident Kissinger admitted in a press briefing
several months after the president's November 1969 executive decisions
that the initial exclusion of toxins had been a "slip up."[67]

The lack of presidential interest, or at least intimate involvement, in
CBW policy review may have stymied what was accomplished in the
area of biological arms control. Although the BWC was signed in 1972, a
verification regime was minimal to nonexistent. The resultant multilateral agreement therefore did not include mechanisms for monitoring or
enforcing compliance with its prohibitions. Neither did it provide for an
associated international organization to assist treaty signatories to fulfill
their obligations as the Chemical Weapons Convention's Organization
for the Prohibition of Chemical Weapons provided the Chemical Weapons Convention (CWC) when signed in 1992. As one BW expert has
written, "Without formal verification measures, the BWC was reduced
to little more than a 'gentleman's agreement.'"[68]

Soviet cheating in the BW realm began almost immediately after the
signing of the BWC and continued until at least 1992. Meselson, who
was an ardent supporter, later conceded, "Now, there is a loophole in the
Biological Weapons Convention. It prohibits the development in production of and stockpiling of biological weapons, but it doesn't prohibit
the construction of facilities to make them. That was left out and, so,
that's what they did. They were in a position to catch up and probably
in terms of research and development did catch up with us."[69] Former
Soviet biologists from the state covert program, code-named Ferment,

worked for decades at an allegedly civilian organization named Biopre-parat that in actuality existed to apply genetic engineering to produce strains of pathogens that previously never existed in nature. During the 1980s, Soviet scientists at Biopreparat genetically engineered antibiotic-resistant strains of plague, anthrax, tularemia, and glanders. One for-mer Soviet biologist conceded in an interview after 11 September 2001: "We came closer and closer to developing so-called 'absolute' biological weapons. The 836 strain of anthrax, for example, was extremely viru-lent, stable in aerosol form, and persistent in the environment. The high virulence of this strain was based on several factors, including a thick protective capsule and an ability to produce large amounts of toxin. In 1985 I compared the 836 strain with strains of anthrax obtained from all over the world, and nothing was better."[70]

The US government's record on continued BW program work was likewise not without blemish. Nixon's executive order implementing his November 1969 unilateral declarations was contained in the then top secret NSDM 35, which was issued on the same day as the president's public pronouncements. His rhetoric was at odds with the instructions for implementation and wound up providing a good deal of flexibil-ity for the US biodefense program. For example, NSDM 35 included a provision authorizing research into "those offensive aspects of bacterio-logical/biological agents necessary to determine what defensive mea-sures are required." The omission of precise definitions or guidelines for defensive R&D provided great latitude down the road for individual agencies to make their own determinations. The Church Committee investigations into the activities of the CIA in 1975 revealed that the agency, in violation of Nixon's executive order, had kept a small stockpile of biological agents and toxins capable of sickening or killing millions of people, including anthrax, smallpox, Venezuelan equine encephalitis (VEE) virus, salmonella, and botulinum.[71]

It is unfair to equate the relatively small-scale, isolated "infractions" committed by some elements of the US government with the large-scale deception perpetrated by the Soviets. The Soviet government not only retained but built up on a massive scale its BW production facilities in the decades after the signature and ratification of the BWC. Nixon's uni-lateral renunciation of the American offensive program carried with it two monumental undertakings—the demilitarization and conversion of offensive BW facilities to peacetime or defensive only applications.[72]

Demilitarizing and dismantling the BW program was no small or easy feat. The two major installations involved were the US Army Laboratory at Fort Detrick, Maryland, and the production facilities at Pine Bluff, Arkansas. It took well over a year for plans to be developed and approved under the auspices of not only the Department of Defense but the Department of Agriculture and the Department of Health, Education, and Welfare (HEW). Additional requirements for safety were placed by the 1969 National Environmental Policy Act that required written compliance with environmental safety standards.[73] Despite the initial delays, between May 1971 and February 1973, the destruction and conversion of BW offensive programs unfolded. The army transferred its facilities at Fort Detrick to the HEW and its Pine Bluff production program to the Food and Drug Administration. The army established the US Army Medical Research Institute of Infectious Diseases and under its auspices, the focus of US biological defenses since the Nixon administration has been on the development of countermeasures such as detection capabilities, protective equipment, vaccines, diagnostics, and therapies to protect US military personnel.[74]

The destruction of existing US biological weapons agents was a similarly extensive undertaking. Anticrop BW agents stored at Rocky Mountain Arsenal, Colorado, were destroyed by the army. This included almost 160,000 pounds of wheat rust fungi and over 1,800 pounds of rice blast fungi. Additionally, Pine Bluff Arsenal was essentially dismantled as its stockpiles of BW agents were destroyed. This included 220 pounds of anthrax, 800 pounds of dried tularemia bacteria, 330 pounds of dried VEE virus, almost 5,000 gallons of VEE viral suspension, approximately 5,000 gallons of Q fever rickettsia suspension, and tens of thousands of munitions filled with various BW and toxin agents.[75]

Incidentally, the Soviets were invited to witness each BW demilitarization or conversion to peaceful or defensive purposes. Yet these gestures of transparency were perceived by the Soviets as guises for deception. As Leitenberg and Zilinskas reveal in their seminal work on the Soviet biological weapons program, "Soviet authors writing in military publications in 1987 referred to the 1969 US decision to end its offensive BW program, the conversion of US BW facilities, and the US signature and ratification of the BWC as 'pure deception' and 'a complete lie.'"[76]

Nevertheless, the BWC, despite its flaws, has stood the test of time. The number of signatories nears universality with 180 nations despite some significant holdouts, most notably Israel, North Korea, and Syria. Gerard Smith's fears of chemical or biological weapons becoming "the poor man's bomb" were realized despite the BWC (and later the CWC). North Korea and Syria are certainly considered "rogue" nation-states sponsoring illicit BW programs. Unlike signatories to the CWC, members of the BWC do not have to disclose past biological weapons programs. In other words, the treaty has persisted but the flaws have never been adequately addressed.[77]

The fate of the Geneva Protocol remained in the balance well after Nixon was reelected but then resigned ignominiously over the Watergate scandal. Nixon had submitted the Geneva Protocol to the Senate on 19 August 1970, nine months after his public declaration in November 1969 that he would do so. The Senate Foreign Relations Committee opted not to take action on the 1925 treaty on the grounds of a crowded docket in the final weeks of the 91st Congress. The real reason was the continued controversy over whether US use of tear gas and herbicides in Vietnam constituted violations. In December 1969, the UN General Assembly had adopted a resolution (only the United States, Australia, and Portugal voted in opposition) stating that the Geneva Protocol prohibited all chemical agents, which was directly aimed at US uses of herbicides and riot control agents in Vietnam. It fell to Nixon's successor, President Gerald Ford, to take action; in 1974, he submitted both the Geneva Protocol and the BWC to the US Senate for ratification, which occurred on 16 December 1974. Yet like his predecessor, Ford left open uses of riot control agents in war by issuing Executive Order 11850, which permitted them "in defensive military modes to save lives."[78]

Many of the ironies of the administration's CBW arms control decisions may in fact be paradoxes. Nixon's thinly disguised disinterest, and Kissinger's tepid involvement may have allowed the limited success that was achieved in the realm of CBW arms control. Especially with the White House's focus on SALT, other elements within the administration were able to enact this departure from past policies. Yet before condemning the White House for disinterest, one must remember Nixon's political astuteness. One of his earliest biographers, Roger Morris, who was a former NSC staff member, explains that the president's decisions stemmed "less from any visible doubts about chemical-biological warfare than from his accurate instinct and experience that it was a policy in which the bureaucrats governed essentially without the President."[79]

And about Kissinger's motives, Morris writes that the national security adviser "saw in a review the prospect of a relatively painless unilateral arms control initiative valuable in setting the stage for later diplomacy with the Soviet Union."[80]

Michael Guhin, the NSC staffer tasked by Kissinger to coordinate the interagency responses from the NSSM process, recalls quite vividly that "at Defense, Laird was the first one that wrote in and said, 'we've got to do something about our chemical and biological weapons policy. You know, we've got a nightmare growing here, and we've got differences between State and ourselves.'"[81] The policy change trajectory was lumbering. Laird and NSC staffers were not so much the originators, as the real impetus came from Congress and was catalyzed by CW accidents, revelations in the media, and pressure from the scientific community. In an effort to deflect adverse public attention, Laird quickly pushed the BW offensive renunciation through but partly to preserve the more contentious CW program. By splitting BW from CW, Laird preserved use of the latter in the Vietnam War as a likely concession to the Joint Chiefs and the services to obtain their acquiescence in the realm of BW.

Yet minimal White House involvement except at key moments quite possibly led to several lost opportunities in terms not only of arms control but of strategic linkages. During the Nixon presidency, the term "WMD" was used with ever greater frequency in the United Nations, but the administration continued to deal with the categories separately. And it is rather odd that a president and national security adviser who emphasized "linkage" made no attempt to apply that concept to biological weapons arms control, especially when the Soviets at times seemed willing to do so. In other words, Nixon showed no inclination to include BW nonproliferation or arms control measures in his formula for linkage to political settlements, whether Vietnam, the Middle East, or Berlin—let alone SALT or nuclear nonproliferation.

There is also a certain paradox to Nixon's downplaying the strategic significance of BW. It may well be because the specter of nuclear war outweighed the ancillary threats posed by other forms of weapons of mass destruction. The great mystery of biological warfare is that in modern times it has never been used by nation-states beyond small sabotage attempts or covert actions against individuals. One BW specialist has offered that "the reason was that biological weapons lacked the single most important ingredient of any effective weapon, an immediate visual display of overwhelming power and brute strength."[82] Nixon may have understood this. He allegedly commented in 1970, "We'll never use the damn germs, so what good is biological warfare as a deterrent? If somebody uses germs on us, we'll nuke 'em."[83] And in April 1972 following the ceremony for the signing of the BWC, Nixon expressed frustration to Treasury Secretary John Connally about "that jackass treaty on biological warfare." Nixon declared, "We've had the Non-Proliferation Treaty, the biological warfare, that Seabeds—but with all the arms limitation in the world there's still enough arms left to blow up the world many times over. What we need is restraint on the part of the great powers."[84] In Nixon's world, the nuclear arsenals of the superpowers loomed as the greatest threat to global peace and security. Not surprisingly, then, the White House continued to focus on nuclear arms control. Within a month of Nixon's 1969 renouncement of offensive BW capabilities, the US and Soviet delegations began SALT in Helsinki.

4

Nixon's Crown Jewel of Arms Control

SALT AND ABM

> On the SALT part: the pathetic idealism on arms control in this country means it would be best to speak on it often. We know that the cosmetics have a lot to do with how people see this, regardless of substance.
>
> —President Nixon, February 1971

WHEN RICHARD Nixon assumed office, the United States faced a Soviet nuclear arsenal of approximately one thousand ICBMs. His predecessor had faced only about two hundred ICBMs in 1964. For all practical purposes, strategic nuclear parity now existed between the superpowers. Faced with what they regarded as that grim reality, Nixon and his national security adviser could not discount the willingness articulated by a spokesman for the Soviet foreign ministry that his government was open to discussing "mutual limitation and subsequent reduction of offensive and defensive nuclear weapons." A few weeks later during a meeting with Secretary of State William P. Rogers, Soviet ambassador to the United States Anatoly Dobrynin reiterated the Kremlin's interest in such negotiations. Within the United States, there was widespread expectation that strategic arms talks would soon begin, since a decent interval had passed since the 1968 Soviet invasion of Czechoslovakia. Political pressures for negotiations were growing. A Council on Foreign Relations study group chaired by Carl Kaysen, a senior national security official in the Kennedy administration, sent the President-elect a report in January 1969, which concluded that an early strategic arms limitation agreement was "imperative." The report called for a unilateral moratorium on American deployment of ABMs and MIRVs.[1]

Despite domestic pressures, formal SALT negotiations did not open until November 1969, and it took approximately two and a half years, almost to the end of Nixon's first term, before the first major agreements—the ABM Treaty and the Interim Agreement on the Limitation of Strategic Offensive Arms—would be reached. The unexpected intrusion of dealing with CBW controls was only one small factor. Far more pressing foreign policy matters, namely the never-ending Vietnam War, dominated the first six to nine months of the new administration. The delay reflected too the extraordinary complexity of strategic arms negotiations and the need to reconcile the differing objectives of the two sides, not to mention placating respective allies who were uneasy about the implications for a nuclear umbrella they were accustomed to having. Both superpowers believed that they had put on the table the crown jewels of their security. The Nixon White House also faced the imperative of building a workable domestic political and bureaucratic consensus for its approach to strategic arms control and to its national security policy more generally. This process took as much or more time and effort than the negotiations with the Kremlin itself. But if those hard-won policies succeeded in reshaping world politics toward an era of negotiation—and if credit was given where credit was due—the president believed he would reap not only the benefits of public acclamation and reelection but a place in history.[2]

Beginning of Interagency Studies Ad Nauseam

Despite these external and internal pressures to proceed rapidly, the White House insisted upon a deliberate pace in developing SALT negotiating positions. Nixon and Kissinger were not clear on what that position ought to be but were determined that SALT policy should not be imposed on them either from within their own government or from the Soviets. Their first public move was to explore the possibility that apparent Soviet eagerness to engage in SALT might provide them with diplomatic leverage over other matters—linkage. In identical letters to Secretary of State Rogers and Secretary of Defense Laird, dated 4 February 1969, Nixon sought to make it clear to the bureaucracy that the principle of linkage would explicitly be applied to matters concerning SALT and specifically to the opening of the negotiations. He made the case for linkage in his first meeting with Dobrynin on 17 February and in a letter to Soviet premier Kosygin on 26 March.[3] And Kissinger would remark on more than one occasion, "I won't use the word linkage, but

I will say the President has consistently taken the position that success and progress in one negotiation is bound to improve prospects in other negotiations."[4]

Rogers and Smith were reluctant to toe the White House line. They worried that linking the opening of SALT with other issues would cause unnecessary delays. Rogers warned in an NSC meeting in mid-February 1969 that pressures for SALT negotiations would build after two or three months and argued that the United States was obliged by the terms of the Nonproliferation Treaty to enter into such arms limitation negotiations in good faith. "If Soviets say let's talk, we have to. We're under the gun," the secretary of state declared. His view fell on deaf ears, as the president was careful in his early communications with Soviet leaders to keep his options open and not make linkage categorical.[5]

Nixon and Kissinger closely controlled the SALT decision-making process. Early resistance from Rogers and Smith to linkage coupled with leaks from the bureaucracy reinforced their existing determination to run matters from the White House. Kissinger expressed early on his dissatisfaction with the quality of SALT option studies, which initially were conducted by an interagency steering group chaired by Smith and which the national security advisor believed reflected the views of bureaucratic holdovers from the Johnson administration. He took advantage of an interagency fight over US intelligence capabilities to put himself at the head of a verification panel that, despite its apparently limited charter, immediately became the focal point of SALT policy planning. For Kissinger's critics, the entire elaborate NSC/NSSM process of which the verification panel was part became little more than an information funnel and debating society rather than problem-solving machinery.[6]

Kissinger used the verification panel and a broad range of studies conducted under its auspices to develop an understanding of the stated and unstated goals of the key players in the bureaucracy. Nixon was famously uninterested in the details of SALT, though he fully grasped the essentials, which gave Kissinger plenty of running room to set policy through private consultations with Nixon. The rich body of presidential recordings also reveals how heavily the president relied on Kissinger. The tapes capture Nixon on more than one occasion asking Kissinger to "keep talking, I need the background."[7] Through his control of the process, Kissinger did his best to ensure that Nixon would not be blindsided or hemmed in by one or another internal faction, whether the diplomats or the Pentagon. And above all, he sought to ensure that the president would receive full credit for any accomplishments in SALT.[8]

Over time Ambassador Anatoly Dobrynin emerged as a third party to this White House–dominated arrangement. He served as a back-channel conduit for floating ideas and working out principles that would move SALT forward—machinations done without the knowledge of senior American officials, including Rogers and Smith, who became dual-hatted as ACDA director and chief SALT negotiator. Nixon complained repeatedly to Rogers with variants of "You can tell Smith that I don't have confidence in him" or "It can't be Smith that is going to get credit [for arms control]. He's a small player, and I don't trust him."[9]

As part of the process of asserting White House control, Nixon and Kissinger made it clear that strategic arms control policy was to flow from, and not determine, overall US national security policy. In late January, through NSSM 3, the president commissioned a study reviewing "our military posture and the balance of power." This included consideration of what would constitute a credible US nuclear posture in the emerging strategic environment. Government officials concerned with arms control did not miss the fact that the first study concerning arms control, NSSM 28, was not issued until 4 March 1969, clearly down the order of importance to the White House.[10]

On 24 June 1969, through NSDM 16, Nixon established four criteria for the stated goal of "strategic sufficiency." Kissinger had recommended endorsement of the criteria "because it will establish clear guidelines for the SALT talks and for consultations with our allies."[11] Did the concept of strategic sufficiency have any practical relevance? Did military criteria really determine the shape of arms control policy once negotiations were under way, or was this merely rhetorical boilerplate, to be manipulated by the White House according to its political priorities? Deputy Secretary of Defense David Packard, who chaired earlier parts of the NSSM 3 exercise, when later asked about what "sufficiency" meant, reportedly responded: "It means that it's a good word to use in a speech. Beyond that, it doesn't mean a goddamned thing." While Packard clearly considered the term "strategic sufficiency" so much sales jargon, Packard recognized the NSSM 3 effort as a clarion call for strategic forces capable of missions other than those associated with an assured destruction posture. As chairman of the NSSM 3 study effort, and the primary OSD representative to the Defense Program Review Committee and the verification panel, Packard understood—like Kissinger—that superpower parity might decrease stability in a crisis. Packard consistently sought technologies and capabilities for US strategic forces that, in a crisis, would provide the president options short of nuclear holocaust.[12]

The president, too, was clearly bothered by the implications of sufficiency. In NSC meetings that reviewed the work of NSSM 3 and its implications for arms control, he observed that accepting parity or inferiority would place the United States in a difficult diplomatic position during times of crisis and that the four sufficiency criteria "add up to massive retaliation, don't they? 70 million or nothing. This isn't adequate." He was also highly critical of intelligence assessments that did not take into account worst-case projections of future Soviet strategic forces because he thought the CIA had been far too sanguine in its forecasts after the Cuban Missile Crisis.[13]

Early in the administration, at one NSC meeting, Nixon was visibly disturbed when a briefer from the Joint Strategic Target Planning Staff reported that the United States now had "significant vulnerabilities." The briefer explained that "during Cuba we could win under any circumstances. . . . 5–1 in favor of US preemption. We had clear advantage, position of strength. But [the] picture has been changed. Today's megaton exchange. They are now ahead or equal. . . . Parity may not exist, balance may easily be upset. e.g., today our missiles are vulnerable to pin down; theirs aren't. Our bomber force [is] vulnerable to inadequate warning. Our command control is vulnerable." In response to this gloomy depiction of the current strategic landscape, Nixon exclaimed, "Astounding change in six years. When did we become aware of this change? When did SIOP [single integrated operational plan] plans warn of this. . . . What about our projections now? Whack! 5 to 1 and we're now even. Can't use projections. We have tended to underestimate."[14]

Deliberation became the order of the day concerning an antiballistic missile defense. Regarding an ABM as a potential high-level programmatic bargaining chip, Nixon and Kissinger believed that successful negotiations would require a major incentive for the Soviets to restrain their offensive buildup. The only significant US strategic program aside from MIRVs in train was the Sentinel ABM system, which theoretically could be traded in for Soviet offensive force concessions and perhaps the Poseidon SLBM. The administration inherited Sentinel from the Johnson administration but faced stiff resistance in Congress. Nixon

A launch of a Poseidon missile. (National Archives)

and Kissinger feared that Congress might unilaterally cut the legs out from under their SALT negotiating strategy by refusing to fund ABMs, especially as the Johnson administration program seemed to lack convincing strategic logic.[15]

To get ahead of the congressional game, Nixon appointed Packard to lead an ABM review panel, while instructing the NSC to examine alternatives to Sentinel under the FY 1970 budget framework. In February 1969, Packard's study recommended a modified version of Sentinel, basically utilizing the same hardware but reorienting its emphasis. The twelve-site system, renamed Safeguard, was to be built in phases and would focus on the protection of Minuteman ICBM installations, Strategic Air Command bomber bases, and the national capital area, while providing some area defense against the emerging Chinese missile threat and accidental launches. The program could be expanded if arms control failed to contain a future Soviet first-strike threat. The first phase, involving two sites, would focus on Minuteman defense. The White House endorsed the Packard study recommendations in March, even though they entailed a lengthy fight for funding in Congress that some administration insiders were uncertain they could win.[16]

Throughout the spring of 1969, a series of congressional committee hearings examined the strategic and foreign policy implications of an ABM system. Most of the witnesses were hostile to Safeguard, including distinguished scientists with expertise in nuclear matters such as Nobel Prize winner Hans Bethe and former Lawrence Livermore Laboratory director Herbert York. They and others testified that extant ABM technology was too complex to function as intended and could be relatively easily defeated by various Soviet countermeasures. They also argued that the Soviets, who would assume the worst about American intentions, would respond to a US ABM deployment by increasing their offensive forces, which would only fuel another dangerous round of the arms race and make it difficult if not impossible to reach a SALT agreement.[17]

For the next five months, the administration lobbied Congress heavily on behalf of Safeguard, placing primary emphasis on the security rationale for ABMs. In testimony designed to refute the critics of Safeguard, Secretary Laird repeatedly warned about the threat that the Soviet missile buildup posed to the US ICBM force. In early August, the Senate narrowly rejected amendments that would have cut off funding for the initial phase of Safeguard.[18]

Nixon regarded this as one of his most important early political victories. Not only did it save the ABM program in which he had invested so much political capital, but it also reestablished the executive's principal role in setting the direction of defense and arms control policy. And it also marked a defeat for his prospective opponents in the 1972 election, such as Senator Edward M. Kennedy (D-MA). Nixon believed that it reassured the allies that the United States was not in headlong withdrawal and that it would not accept a position of being a second-rate nuclear power. The United States, in his view, now had its essential bargaining chip to play in SALT.[19]

To be sure, this was not a final victory for the ABM program. Many congressional votes lay ahead. But it bought the administration time to try to work out an approach to arms control that would lead to an agreement that would obviate the need either for full deployment of Safeguard or any deployment at all. Or, if the Soviets proved clearly obdurate in SALT, Nixon could make a more persuasive case for the necessity for ABMs.[20]

The NSSM 3 exercise and the Packard study were based on analyses that appeared to be US-centric. Kissinger, perhaps to a fault, worried that the NATO allies would misread SALT in that light, as an effort to abandon extended deterrence and, in the case of Britain and France, to compromise their national deterrent forces. He planned to address this challenge through periodic and detailed consultations with the Western Europeans, and he did not want any perceived urgency over the beginnings of SALT to spook the NATO allies. When Nixon made state visits to many key NATO capitals in February 1969 and then alliance representatives passed through Washington in the spring and summer of 1969, they were briefed on the state of SALT preparations. For the time being, the NATO allies raised no major objections to the approach that the United States was following. Their key interest lay more at this juncture in the Nixon administration's stance on NPT ratification (see chapter 5). Nixon and Kissinger stressed the need to keep the two agreements separate.[21]

The issue of China and SALT came up in an unexpected way. Efforts by Washington to develop meaningful contacts with Beijing were bound to take time in the best of circumstances. Matters were complicated when border skirmishes between the Soviet Union and China seemed to have the potential to erupt into full-scale war. The administration considered how to respond to that possibility and how the proposed US-Soviet bilateral strategic arms control negotiations should fit into that response. Nixon told the NSC that he did not think it in America's interest to see the Chinese "smashed" in a Sino-Soviet war. Neither Nixon nor Kissinger wanted to give the impression that they would be indifferent to, much less support, a preemptive Soviet strike against Chinese nuclear facilities, an idea that some Soviet officials and media outlets had circulated.[22]

In August 1969, eight months into the administration, the interagency principals continued to deliberate on its specific policy toward not only a SALT position but also the implications of a Sino-Soviet crisis or a major war. NSC staff member William Hyland posed the question to Kissinger, "Would we start or continue SALT? If we did the Soviets and most of informed opinion in the world (and in China) would see it as

favorable to the USSR; if we refused to talk this would be a clear retaliation, not impartiality." Hyland also asked, "Would we continue negotiations on a seabeds disarmament treaty?" (see chapter 5). Another NSC
staff member, Helmut Sonnenfeldt, questioned the argument "that the
Soviets might be more reluctant to go into SALT in the event of major
hostilities." He thought this would be true in the event of protracted war,
but, on the other hand, the Soviets might want to use SALT as a safety
valve and to manipulate the Chinese into a bad position. These questions remained unanswered, as the immediate Sino-Soviet crisis abated
and the two communist rivals opened border talks in October.[23]

That same month, Dobrynin conveyed to Nixon the Soviet willingness to open SALT negotiations. The ambassador issued a warning from
the Soviet leadership against any attempt by the United States to profit
from Sino-Soviet tensions. Nixon told Dobrynin that US policy toward
China was not directed against the Soviet Union. Secretary Rogers later
told Nixon that the border talks got the United States off the horns of
this particular dilemma: "This conjunction of Soviet agreement to negotiations both with China and with us, on SALT, enables us to maintain
our posture of non-involvement in the Sino-Soviet dispute. Moves by
us at this time in the direction of opening the door towards China a
little more can hardly be the object of plausible objections by the Soviet
Government when it itself is talking with the Chinese."[24] In a broader
sense, by 1972 the United States hoped that its diplomatic efforts to open
contacts with Beijing would suffice to ease somewhat any Chinese concerns over the upcoming SALT proceedings. Kissinger believed that this
could be done. Though not in the first eighteen months of the administration, in time it became clear that SALT would be intimately if not
explicitly involved with the evolution of triangular diplomacy.

The Slow Development of US SALT Policy

According to its critics, the Nixon administration should have acted
faster and differently on SALT by giving priority to the logic of arms
control as it formulated its overall defense posture. That was not the
course that the administration chose. Missed opportunity or not, the
administration's deliberations would finally have to give way to formulating a specific policy for SALT. What exactly did the White House hope
to achieve through strategic arms control? Nixon and Kissinger hoped

to structure SALT into a broader strategy of détente. The Nixon/Kissinger early conception of détente meant negotiating spheres of stability separately with the Soviets and the Chinese. The White House viewed SALT as an ingredient in a tactical strategy of détente. By negotiating an agreement on strategic nuclear forces, they intended to use SALT as leverage to coerce the Soviets into refraining from global adventurism and controlling nationalist movements.

A more immediate practical goal was to slow or stop the buildup of Soviet land-based missile forces. While the United States had capped the number of its strategic nuclear launchers in the mid-1960s, the USSR had been adding two hundred or more ICBMs per year to its arsenal, with substantially larger warheads than their US equivalents. By 1969 the Soviets had achieved numerical parity in ICBMs with the United States and seemed determined to press ahead. The Soviets also showed signs of accelerating their SLBM program, an area in which the United States had enjoyed a significant superiority. The United States still possessed more total weapons, due to its programs to deploy multiple warheads on its missiles, but the Soviets were in a position to match or exceed this over time.[25]

Slowing or stopping the US ABM program was the obvious quid pro quo to offer in exchange for Soviet offensive restraint. Yet the devil proved to be in the details. Although Nixon and Kissinger planned to run SALT from the White House, they had to develop some sort of intergovernmental policy consensus to keep the major players from sabotaging their efforts. Kissinger decided to avoid constructing a single negotiating position for as long as possible and to instead to devise a variety of options to ascertain what the bureaucratic traffic would bear and then when the formal negotiations began, to draw out the Soviet position without committing the United States.[26]

After almost four months of discussions, the ACDA steering group chartered to implement NSSM 28 circulated its report at the end of May 1969. The group offered four illustrative packages of arms restrictions with suboptions for developing a negotiating proposal:

- Package I froze ICBM launchers to the number then operational and under construction and also banned land-mobile missiles.
- Package II added limits on SLBMs, with land-mobiles permitted within total number of ICBMs.

- Package III froze numbers of all offensive missile launchers, banned land-mobile offensive missiles, prohibited enlarging silos or changing launcher configuration or location, and banned land-mobile and sea-based ABMs.
- Package IV was identical to package III but added a MIRV ban.

Each package contemplated some limit on numbers of ABM launchers without designating a specific level. None restricted bombers, air defense, or missile throw weight (the lifting power of a ballistic missile, which governs the maximum size and number of nuclear warheads) and accuracy improvements, and none of them called for force reductions. The testing and deployment of MIRVs was permitted in all but package IV, which was otherwise the same as package III.[27]

The relationship between the ABM Treaty and SALT as well as MIRVs became sticking points in administration deliberations throughout 1969. Smith did not think that US ABM programs represented the decisive bargaining chip on which the White House counted. And, he contended, if they did provide negotiating leverage over Soviet offensive forces, they could do so just as well if kept at the R&D stage; once metal was bent in earnest, it was bureaucratically and politically difficult to turn such programs off. The ACDA director and his colleagues strongly favored a zero ABM solution because it would greatly ease verification concerns. If each side retained a few ABM sites and associated infrastructure, they would have the material and programmatic incentive to keep improving that system, and they might be tempted at some point to reexamine the possibility of deploying a thick nationwide defense. Smith and his allies sought to constrain the deployment of MIRVs, such as through prohibitions of MIRV testing, which they believed could be verified by national technical means. If both superpowers forswore ABM deployments, there would be much less incentive to proceed with MIRVs, thus reassuring each side that the other was not intent on developing a first-strike capability. There seemed to be a fleeting window to keep this technological genie in the bottle. For Smith, promises to restrict the US MIRV program offered much greater negotiating leverage with the Soviets than limits on ABMs. During the spring and summer of 1969, he broached a number of proposals in the interagency process that would have this effect.[28]

On the military side of the bureaucracy, DoD was hardly an eager participant in arms control. Yet the rapid growth in Soviet offensive

Airmen work on a Minuteman III's MIRV system. (US Air Force)

forces compelled both OSD and the Joint Chiefs to support a missile freeze and to accept some limits on ABMs. Given the current US advantage in SLBM launchers and long-range bombers as well as its advanced MIRV program, Laird favored a quick agreement that would preserve current US advantages and retard the Soviet's missile buildup. He was concerned, however, that the Soviets might use the talks to seize "any opportunity for strategic superiority or advantage." Laird and his key advisors in OSD, including Paul Nitze, focused on the need for strategic arms control to address the growing threat to the US land-based deterrent forces. Laird's main concern was with a Soviet first strike against US ICBMs, but the full threat would also involve attacks against US bomber bases and strategic submarines in port.[29]

The Joint Chiefs, supported by Packard, were also concerned about the vulnerability of US deterrent forces, but they placed the greatest emphasis on opposing any limitations on MIRVs. They insisted that MIRVs and penetration aids were needed to maintain high confidence in US ability to penetrate any future Soviet defenses. Joint Chiefs chairman Earle Wheeler warned that moratoria and similar understandings would be treated as de facto treaties by Washington but not by Moscow, which would leave the United States politically and technically vulnerable to an ABM breakout. There was no guarantee that the Soviets would accept meaningful ABM limits in SALT, and even if they did, they would retain a massive air defense network that could provide the foundations for an ABM breakout. By MIRVing US strategic systems, the Joint Chiefs believed it could deter cheating and provide a hedge against it. For targeting purposes MIRVs provided the warheads needed to cover three hundred new ICBM launchers that the Soviets were building. The operational testing of the Polaris A-3 MIRV SLBM, a program essential to maintaining the US sea-based deterrent, would be halted. Further, effective MIRV controls required the OSI of Soviet missiles, and the Soviets had always rejected such controls.[30]

Balancing the Options

Where did these deep agency differences leave Kissinger and Nixon? On balance, they were sympathetic to the Office of the Secretary of Defense and Joint Chiefs of Staff position and were strongly inclined to reject a MIRV test ban and a zero ABM solution. Nixon believed that technology had been America's strong suit in the competition with the Soviets as well as in international economics, and he felt it was imperative to regain that advantage. Kissinger later famously expressed the wish that more thought had been given to the MIRV issue, but in fact it had been debated extensively in public and through the interagency process. Kissinger, through his staff and participation in an internal MIRV study cochaired by Packard, was well informed on the subject. MIRVs represented a potential bargaining chip, as the United States currently held the lead in this field. He also undoubtedly sensed that MIRVs were the one issue in SALT on which the Joint Chiefs might publicly rebel if they did not get their way. Neither he nor Nixon was prepared to risk an open fight with the military on that issue. In any case, Kissinger's instinct was to pursue technology limitations indirectly, through numerical limits or reductions in weapons systems.[31]

As to strategic defenses, Nixon and Kissinger were reluctant to pursue a zero ABM agreement for reasons beyond the Joint Chiefs' opposition. Nixon was sensitive to the possibility that prodefense senators who went out of their way to support Safeguard might feel betrayed politically if the administration traded ABMs away altogether. Kissinger suspected strongly that the Soviets would at least insist on retaining their Moscow Galosh system to protect themselves against a decapitating attack by China and that American efforts to negotiate a zero ABM solution would be misinterpreted by the Kremlin as being overtly anti-Soviet in the game of triangular diplomacy.[32] Kissinger's instinct was to deploy some level of ABM capability, which ostensibly reflected his concern about the potential spread of nuclear weapons as well as the need to provide leverage over future Soviet actions. He would later write, "It seemed to me highly irresponsible simply to ignore the possibility of an accidental attack or the prospect of nuclear capabilities in the hands of yet more countries. . . . Even a small nuclear power would be able to blackmail the United States. I did not see the moral or political value of turning our people into hostages by deliberate choice."[33] Yet, incidentally this concern did not translate into a simultaneous push to ratify the NPT.

In contrast, the Smith-State-ACDA approach to arms control, with its emphasis on technological restraint, moratoria, and weapons bans to break the momentum of the arms race, did not sit well with the president and Kissinger. They were increasingly suspicious that Smith and his allies were lobbying Congress behind the scenes to create political pressure on the SALT policy process. In practical terms, they wanted to frustrate any effort by Smith to put forward a comprehensive negotiating package that would include MIRVs and ABMs, but they had to do so without seeming to sabotage the negotiations with what would seem to the public and moderate congressional members to be an obstructionist American position. The White House feared that it might lose control of SALT to an alliance among an antidefense Congress, the arms control bureaucracy, and the liberal media. The president as yet could claim no foreign policy successes that would buy him political capital on Capitol

Hill with key senators such as Charles Percy (R-IL), Edward M. Brooke (R-MA), Clifford Case (R-NJ), and Margaret Chase Smith (R-ME).[34]

The preoccupation of the Nixon White House with these bureaucratic disagreements meant further delays in actual negotiations with the Soviets. On 12 November 1969, through NSDM 33, Nixon instructed the US SALT delegation to "develop a work program for the main talks and to acquire information concerning Soviet views in order to aid us in the formulation of future positions," without committing the United States to any specific position. The delegation should put forward "Illustrative Elements" based on the current version of alternative (package) II. ICBM and SLBM launchers would be limited to those presently operational, allowing each side to vary its land- and sea-based mix within that ceiling. Nixon reminded the delegation that, under Safeguard, he was committed to the concept of area defense. Within that guideline, the delegation could explore ABM limitations. As to the tricky subject of MIRVs, it was neither on nor off the table: "In the interest of exploring Soviet attitudes, the question of MRV/MIRV may be included in a work program."[35]

First (but Lasting) Impressions

With these opaque instructions the first session of SALT held in Helsinki in November–December 1969 was off to an inauspicious start. Nonetheless, the White House succeeded in its basic purpose of determining the level of genuine Soviet interest in negotiations. Although the Kremlin offered no formal proposal, it did not treat SALT merely as a propaganda exercise. Still, the head of the Soviet delegation, Vladimir Semenov, rejected any attempt by the United States to link progress in SALT with other issues. The Soviets made it clear that an agreement to limit ABM systems was at the top of their agenda, apparently confirming a reversal of the position held by Kosygin in 1967 at the Glassboro summit. The Soviets did not respond in detail to the Illustrative Elements, although they complained that there were no proposed limits on long-range bombers, an area in which the Americans held a clear advantage.[36]

The discussions also revealed some unexpected and troublesome Soviet positions. Semenov argued that "strategic" weapons should be defined as any nuclear-capable delivery vehicle that could reach the homeland of the other side. This included so-called forward-based systems (FBSs), such as American land- and carrier-based aircraft deployed within striking distance of the Soviet Union. It might also cover the use of naval bases in NATO Europe to service American strategic nuclear submarines or even the nuclear forces of Britain and France. But it did not include Soviet medium- and intermediate-range missiles targeted on Western Europe. Smith immediately objected. The United States regarded FBSs as "tactical" nuclear weapons not to be included in any strategic arms agreement.[37]

The Soviet delegation also raised what the United States regarded as political rather than "hardware" issues. One issue regarded as tangential to the Nixon administration was Soviet insistence on agreeing on actions to be taken in the event of a "provocative attack" by an unnamed third country designed to precipitate a war between the superpowers. Smith assumed the clear implication was that the third country was China, though perhaps also Germany in the long run. The Soviets also broached the idea of some sort of supplement to the NPT in the form of an agreement not to transfer strategic weapons systems to other countries. They also raised the problem of the accidental or unauthorized use of nuclear weapons. Semenov proposed agreements to limit the areas in which missile submarines and aircraft carriers could operate and to limit the flights of nuclear-armed aircraft to the national airspace. Perhaps most importantly, the Soviets did not formally raise the question of MIRVs. To those on the American side who opposed MIRV constraints, this was something of a relief because it relaxed political and bureaucratic pressures to put MIRVs on the table. Smith, however, thought that the Soviets were simply waiting for an American proposal, which was part of their standard negotiating practice. He felt that they likely calculated that congressional pressures would force the United States eventually to put MIRVs on the table.[38]

On the other hand, the OSD representative, Paul Nitze, was apparently influenced by informal discussions with Soviet delegates to take a darker view of their intentions. He had made the case to them for seeking assured second-strike capabilities on both sides. He felt that this argument had fallen on deaf ears. The Soviets, at some level, despite their eagerness to discuss ABM limits, still had in mind the goal of first-strike strategic superiority even if they did not necessarily have a firm resolve to strike first. But the possibility that they might develop such a resolve, especially if the Americans conceded too much in SALT, would over time weigh increasingly heavily on Nitze's mind.[39]

As the first round of talks drew to a close at the end of 1969, the Nixon White House was confirmed in its belief that Smith would have limited usefulness as chief negotiator. While his reporting from Helsinki gave them confirmation of Soviet areas of concern, the White House developed an almost cavalier disregard for his opinions, believing he gave undue concern to Soviet security anxieties. The president and his national security adviser believed many of the Kremlin's notions about preventing accidental or unauthorized attacks were merely guises to drive a wedge between the United States and its allies as well as to preclude any overtures toward China. What emerged most clearly from the opening volleys at Helsinki was that there was no clear path forward to agreement. The Soviets sought ABMs above offensive limitations, while the United States sought the converse; the Soviets were willing to consider "linkage" among various arms control or nonproliferation matters. The United States sought linkage with foreign policy issues outside the realm of arms control.[40]

Stalemate

Not surprisingly, when the SALT negotiations resumed in Vienna in April 1970, the logical next step for the United States heading into the next round of talks was to develop a formal proposal that went beyond the Illustrative Elements. Yet Kissinger refused to permit the delegation to do so. He convinced the president that the negotiations were not ripe for such a proposal and that he still could not bring about a bureaucratic consensus. The administration also had to fight for another round of congressional funding for Safeguard. Smith and his allies, including ACDA's General Advisory Committee, chaired by the well-respected John J. McCloy, were pushing for a pause in deployment for phase II of the system, as part of their argument for a zero ABM negotiating position. Nixon and Kissinger were convinced that ACDA and its bureaucratic supporters were once more actively encouraging the resistance to ABMs in Congress. At the same time, Kissinger signaled the Soviets that the domestic political campaign to sell Safeguard to Congress did not mean that ABMs were off the SALT negotiating table and that the administration was proceeding slowly with its phased deployment so that there would be an opportunity to reach agreement on ABM limits. Kissinger grew increasingly compelled to break the diplomatic and interagency deadlock by going outside regular channels and devising a new framework to move the negotiations going forward, as part of a broader effort to reinvigorate Nixon's era of negotiations.[41]

MIRVs and Safeguard continued to be major sticking points not only with the Soviets but within the US government. To break a deadlock regarding the latter, another alternative to Safeguard gained bureaucratic momentum. The United States would propose to limit each side to a single ABM site that would defend what was termed the National Command Authority (NCA), essentially Moscow and Washington. Kissinger went along with this bureaucratic compromise, despite what he soon regarded as its lack of strategic coherence and political feasibility. DoD was reluctant to abandon the ABM option altogether, especially given the prospective Soviet threat against the US ICBM force. A single site, if it came to that, would at least preserve the technology base and offer protection against a Soviet decapitation strike. Smith and his staff continued to favor a complete ban, but if accepted by the Soviets, the NCA-only proposal would still preclude the deployment of destabilizing nationwide defenses. The Soviets might well be interested in such a deal, as they had already deployed a defense of Moscow, thus creating a negotiating symmetry. And given that congressional opinion almost certainly would reject deployment of a system designed to protect politicians and generals (as Kissinger put it), Smith and the arms control community believed that the end result of an NCA-only negotiation position would probably be a complete ABM ban.[42]

The MIRV debate within the US government also continued unabated. Smith pressed for a ban, and the Pentagon refused to budge on its insistence that the US program continue unless the Soviets permitted OSIs of its missiles. Nitze and OSD insisted instead on an agreement that would reduce the ICBM and SLBM forces on both sides to a common lower level and otherwise restrict Soviet throw weight.[43]

The emerging US framework reflected a set of political and bureaucratic compromises that satisfied no major faction. The result of interagency deliberations was a menu of four options developed by Kissinger and put forward for the president's consideration. Option A limited ICBMs and SLBMs to the US total of 1,710 and froze the numbers of bombers (527 for the United States and 195 for the Soviets). It permitted a Safeguard level of ABMs (twelve sites). Option B offered the same offensive limitations as option A, but ABMs were limited to NCA or banned altogether. Option C included the same offensive and defensive limitations, but it added a ban on MIRVs provided the Soviets agreed to OSI. Option D proposed major reductions, going down from existing total of 1,710 ICBMs and SLBMs by 100 per year until both sides reached a level of 1,000 by 1978. Under option D, ABMs were limited to NCA or banned; there was no ban on MIRVs. Each option had something for everybody among the competing government factions, but none was completely satisfactory to anyone, and each contained what was presumed to be a nonstarter for the Soviets. Specifically, the Kremlin was most unlikely to agree either to OSIs or significant reductions in its missile forces.[44]

In the end, in NSDM 51, Nixon instructed the SALT delegation to put forward option C, then option D—not as formal proposals but as conceptual packages to be explored with the Soviets. Smith, ACDA, and the State Department largely favored option C, undoubtedly with the hope that political pressures would lead the president to change the American position on MIRV verification, opening the possibility of a MIRV ban. The Joint Chiefs and Packard favored option A, with Nitze and other Pentagon civilians supporting option D. In an NSC meeting, Nixon indicated he too favored Nitze's reduction approach, but the complexity of the matter and the confused bureaucratic wrangling led him to leave the matter to Kissinger, who, although favoring option B, essentially punted for the time being. Kissinger was also beginning to recognize the morass that the NCA-only proposal was about to create. He realized that Congress was highly unlikely to approve funding for the defense of Washington, which meant the Soviets would possess the only operational ABM system.[45]

In Vienna, Semenov immediately expressed interest in the NCA-only ABM concept. The Soviets, however, rejected the offensive force limit proposals as not accounting for FBSs. They also rejected MIRV constraints that required OSI. Based on informal indications, Smith and some others in the US delegation reported to Washington that the Soviets might be responsive to a serious American proposal on MIRVs, such as a compromise in which the Soviets would accept a ban on flight testing, to be verified by national technical means coupled with a Soviet proposal for a production and deployment ban.[46]

Kissinger, however, believed that Smith and his overly eager colleagues were on fishing expeditions, trying to use supposed Soviet coyness to pressure the White House to agree to changes in the US position that would conform to their own policy preferences. Laird also complained to Nixon about what he regarded as Smith's loose negotiating procedure and pursuit of his own agenda. In particular, Laird complained that Smith had not actively pursued option D, the reductions option. Nixon and Kissinger were furious whenever leaks to the press—whether from Vienna or Washington—seemed to reinforce pressure to make what the White House regarded as concessions. They sent repeated warnings to Smith to ensure that the delegates toed the party line.[47]

If progress in SALT was to be made and domestic political pressures alleviated, the United States would eventually have to make changes and come forward with a formal proposal. After predictable bureaucratic wrangling, through NSDM 69, dated 9 July 1971, Nixon authorized Smith to put forward the first formal US proposal, known in various forms—option E, the 4 August proposal, or the Vienna Option. The two sides would limit their strategic missile and bomber forces to nineteen hundred delivery vehicles, which would require some reduction in the Soviet missile arsenal and in the US bomber force, which was scheduled to be cut in any case. There would be a sublimit of 1,710 strategic missile launchers, and a 250 sublimit on heavy ICBMs (aimed at the SS-9s). These figures were characterized as "initial," indicating that there was room for negotiation. There were to be no negotiations involving FBSs, however, or on MIRVs. On the defensive side of the equation, the delegation was to put forward a zero ABM option, without taking NCA level off the table.[48]

Hard Bargaining

As the United States developed and then introduced this formal proposal, the Soviets put forward a starkly different framework for SALT. Semenov in Vienna and Dobrynin in the secret back channel with Kissinger argued as they had during the first round of negotiations for limiting ABMs at the NCA level and to the problem of "reducing the danger of missile-nuclear war between the USSR and the US resulting from accidental or unsanctioned use of nuclear weapons." Limits on offensive forces could wait until later and could not even be discussed until the two sides agreed on the definition of "strategic," which to the Soviets meant that the United States would agree to include FBSs in some fashion. Dobrynin, sensing that Nixon was anxious for a near-term summit and for good news for the November congressional elections, told Kissinger that the Soviets did not believe that there was sufficient time to negotiate an agreement covering offensive as well as defensive forces before the end of the year.[49]

The Soviet initiative promoted by Dobrynin was unacceptable to Nixon and Kissinger. It would break the linkage between ABM limits and Soviet restraint on its missile buildup that the White House had been trying to forge. Kissinger found the political side of the proposed Soviet framework to be especially alarming. Semenov had made a private démarche to the American delegation in Vienna that concentrated almost exclusively on a joint declaration to prevent accidental or unauthorized acts of war.[50]

The accidental war "ploy," as Kissinger later described it, "had the makings of a first-class booby trap." As he later opined, "If it sought to safeguard the superpowers against a technical malfunction of their own weapons, it could be dealt with by establishing rapid communication links and agreed procedures for reacting. But if the 'unsanctioned' use referred to the weapons of other nuclear powers, we faced a major political problem. We would be cooperating with the Soviet Union against two allies, the United Kingdom and France—and against the People's Republic of China, with which even then we were trying to establish contact." Kissinger likewise feared that any limits on FBSs would generally undermine allied confidence in the US security guarantee.[51]

Kissinger also faced increasing concerns from the Department of Defense as Laird and the Joint Chiefs worked through the implications of the "Vienna Option." Laird expressed growing unease with the vulnerability of the Minuteman force, given the proposed ban in SALT on ABMs or NCA-only, and new evidence about technical improvements in the Soviet SS-9 and SS-11 ICBMs. The new Joint Chiefs chairman, Admiral Thomas Moorer, and other senior officers debated whether to withdraw the Joint Chiefs' support for the Vienna Option. Lieutenant General Royal B. Allison, their representative on the US delegation, successfully argued against such a move because it would break up the talks and because it would not preclude options that would protect Minuteman.[52]

Smith believed that the Vienna Option was a decisive turning point for the worse in SALT because it formally abandoned any effort to ban

MIRVs or search for some sort of middle ground on the issue. Nitze also believed that the option was a negative turning point because it made unwarranted concessions to the Soviets. He concluded that the Soviets were bound to pocket its concessions, which he felt they later did, without agreeing to corresponding US advantages. However regrettably, he concluded it would fall to the delegation to make the best of what was bound to be an imperfect deal.[53]

In the December 1970 session in Helsinki, the Soviets formally proposed a separate agreement covering ABMs, with defensive systems limited to the NCA and offensive force limits to come later. To the ire of the White House this proposal was leaked to the American press and predictably generated political pressure on the administration to settle along these lines, especially when it was revealed publicly that construction of new Soviet ICBM sites seemed to have slowed. A *New York Times* editorial on 17 January 1971 urged acceptance of an agreement covering ABM limits only. Although Smith had earlier been on record as opposing an ABM-only agreement, Kissinger was suspicious that Smith would use the supposed Soviet "signal" of restraint to push for such an agreement.[54]

Smith denied responsibility for the press leak but believed that the Soviets were not simply being intransigent. He concluded that their concerns over accidental war and provocative attacks and US FBSs were real and not simply a clever political strategy to stir up trouble with American allies and the Chinese. He thought that the apparent stalemate in negotiations had much to do with a lack of American initiative and imagination to deal with these issues. Smith advised Kissinger that "my personal objection to formal limit on ABMs, while offensive systems remain unchecked, stands; and I think we should in general terms continue to stress interrelation of defensive and offensive systems but not flatly reject the Soviet proposal."[55]

Nixon and Kissinger found Smith's optimistic appraisal of the possibilities in SALT at the end of the Vienna round naïve. Kissinger told the president that

> we should not overlook the negative signs. For example, the Soviets made no attempt to deal seriously with our extensive proposals of August 4. Moreover, they presented a truncated counterproposal and then suddenly shifted to the entirely new concept of ABM only agreements and immediately started applying pressure for favorable

consideration—though it was clearly agreed at the outset of the negotiations that the objective was to limit both offensive and defensive systems. . . . In short, one can argue as Ambassador Smith does, that we
have made some progress, and on some points this is quite true. One
must also recognize, however, that the points which divide us are more
critical to final success than the areas of general and rather ill-defined
agreement.[56]

Back-Channel Machinations

The year 1970 and the early months of 1971 had not been a good time
for the president on the foreign policy front. The apparent stalemate
in SALT was hardly the only or even the main concern in the Nixon
White House. There was no sight to a negotiated end to the war in Vietnam. The invasion of Cambodia in April 1970 followed by the shooting
of unarmed protestors at Kent State in May had galvanized domestic
antiwar opposition. A South Vietnamese ground offensive in Laos supported by American airpower and logistics began in February 1971 triggered major domestic protests. The Soviets had constructed what the
administration interpreted as a nuclear submarine base at Cienfuegos
in Cuba, violating the 1962 understanding that ended the Cuban Missile
Crisis. The Rogers Plan for Middle East peace had stalled, and the Soviets were surreptitiously funneling arms to their Arab allies. Kissinger
and Rogers battled behind the scenes for control of the national security apparatus, with Kissinger frequently threatening to resign. Fruit-
ful contacts with the Chinese had yet proved elusive. The American
economy showed serious signs of inflation, and the dollar was under
pressure overseas. Although the 1970 midterm elections had not proved
disastrous for Republicans, Nixon's reelection chances in 1972 seemed
precarious at best.

The president desperately sought foreign policy wins. Kissinger knew
he would be held responsible by Nixon for achieving them. And a SALT
agreement, despite the apparent stalemate in the formal negotiations,
was one avenue that still offered some prospect of success. The Soviets
had not suspended or broken off SALT during the Cambodian invasion,
even though Kosygin suggested at one point they might, and Semenov
had severely criticized the American action before the American SALT
delegation. Moscow apparently also placed considerable importance on

the negotiations. In the spring of 1970 Nixon had begun pressing Kissinger to arrange a summit meeting with Soviet leaders at which SALT could be signed or, even better, at which Nixon personally could wrap up the final details with all credit going to the president. Kissinger initially tried to deter Nixon from what he regarded as a premature initiative until all the various strands of the administration's policy began to bear fruit so that Nixon would not look like a supplicant.[57]

As of early 1971, Kissinger still had been unable to deliver anything like a bureaucratic consensus on SALT within the government, much less progress in the formal negotiations. The various components of the American negotiating position seemed likely to come unstuck under Soviet intransigence and, the White House believed, because certain elements of the bureaucracy wanted it so. Kissinger concluded that these deadlocks had to be broken by going outside normal channels. The use of back channels is common in diplomacy, between and within governments, but Nixon and Kissinger were determined to use theirs to conduct negotiations directly with the Soviet leadership, bypassing the messiness, resistance, and leaks that in their minds plagued the American bureaucracy.

In the case of SALT, senior officials, including Rogers, Laird, Smith, and Moorer, were to be kept completely out of the back-channel loop—not only its content but also its existence. Kissinger later rationalized that the back channel "sprang into action either when there was a deadlock between the parties in the negotiations or among the American agencies or within the negotiating team. In such circumstances, Nixon would rely on the Channel to break the stalemate by charging me with implementing, with Dobrynin, the option he preferred from what the NSC system had generated." Yet Nixon and Kissinger also felt free to improvise policy when they perceived the opportunity and then confront the interagency with a fait accompli.[58]

Kissinger and Dobrynin had secretly been discussing SALT on and off throughout 1970. In a session at the Soviet embassy on 9 January 1971, Kissinger told the Soviet ambassador (according to the American record) that the United States was "prepared to make an ABM agreement, provided it was coupled with an understanding to continue working on offensive limitations and provided it was coupled with an understanding that there would be a freeze on new starts of offensive land-based missiles until there was a formal agreement in limiting offensive weapons." "Some provision" would have to be made on submarine-based systems, but this could be left to detailed negotiations. If the Soviets were agreeable, the basic issues could be settled in the back channel before the formal SALT negotiations resumed in Vienna in March and codified in an exchange of letters or public statements between President Nixon and the Soviet leadership, presumably Kosygin. The two SALT delegations could then work out the details. (Smith, when he later learned of Kissinger's maneuvers, complained that there was no reason why the US proposal could not have been made directly in the formal SALT negotiations, to much better effect.)[59]

Dobrynin reported the offer somewhat differently to his superiors: "He, the President, agrees that first a separate agreement relating solely to defensive strategic arms should be concluded and signed. At the same time, he proposes that immediately thereafter the sides resume active negotiations to seek an agreement in the area of offensive strategic arms (after recording their intention to do so in the agreement concluded on defensive arms). For the duration of these subsequent negotiations (on offensive weapons), the President proposes imposing a 'freeze' ('standstill') on all offensive land-based types of strategic arms on both sides."[60]

The Soviet-American differences over the sequencing of the offensive and defensive agreements would plague the negotiations over the next year. Until then Kissinger felt that SALT had finally been moved off dead center. Over the next few weeks, he and Dobrynin met several times to define their positions. Both agreed that there would be no limits on "modernization" or "qualitative" limits on offensive forces during a missile freeze, including MIRVs. Kissinger indicated that the United States was willing to be flexible on the kind of ABM limits it would consider; Dobrynin expressed doubt that the Soviets would accept a zero ABM agreement, though he did not rule it out categorically. This probably reinforced Kissinger's conclusion that the Soviets would insist on retaining the Moscow ABM system. The two discussed the possibility that the Soviets would retain their Moscow Galosh system, and the United States could proceed with deploying three or four Safeguard sites, which protected ICBM fields.[61]

Dobrynin was not immediately ready to move the Soviets off their FBS position. Kissinger thought there might be some sort of tacit arrangement to cover this, as long as it limited aircraft carrier deployments. Eventually FBS was dropped as a formal matter, though the Soviets insisted that it be taken up in later negotiations and that supposed American "concessions," namely the number of ballistic missile submarines (nuclear) (SSBNs), reflected reasonable compensation for FBSs.[62]

As the discussions proceeded, Kissinger seemed at best ambivalent on whether the freeze must include sea-based strategic systems (SSBNs and/or SLBMs). Dobrynin declared that the Soviet leadership did not want to include SSBNs at this time, but he held out the carrot of concluding a SALT agreement at a summit. In the meantime, to show progress he suggested that the Vienna talks reach an agreement on dealing with third-party nuclear provocations. Kissinger demurred but thought an accidental war agreement presumably stripped of any political land mines might be handled that way. The discussions progressed to the point where Nixon sent a letter to Kosygin summarizing the American understanding of the outlines of an agreement.[63]

The swift progress on SALT anticipated by Kissinger did not occur. Kosygin's response received in late March reiterated the Soviet insistence on agreeing to ABM limits first and only then discussing the details of an offensive force freeze. Kissinger threatened to go public with the American offer. Dobrynin pleaded understanding for the slowness of the Soviet decision-making process especially as senior leaders were preoccupied with the 24th Soviet Party Congress, which was held from late March to mid-April 1971.[64]

Dobrynin was away in Moscow between February and April, during which time both Nixon and Kissinger showed considerable anxiety as they waited for his return. The White House believed that the Party Congress likely would determine the future composition of the Soviet leadership and its approach to nuclear arms control. Nixon concluded that there was a fight in Moscow between hawks and doves, with the military resisting strategic arms control but the civilians appreciating the need for détente because of Soviet economic difficulties and the Chinese problem. After the completion of the Congress, Nixon and Kissinger noted some positive developments: the emergence of Leonid Brezhnev as the leading figure in the Soviet leadership and Brezhnev's apparently conciliatory tone at the Party Congress toward the West and arms control.[65]

For his part, Kissinger continued to express confidence to Nixon that a SALT agreement would eventually be reached. The president adopted a more skeptical tone, perhaps as a psychological defense mechanism in case the talks failed or as a device to allow him to rein in Kissinger.

At times he pressed Kissinger to "play a firmer game" with Dobrynin. "Hit it hard. I want you to leave the threat I will have to make a public statement on arms control if we don't work out the letter thing." The Soviets in Kissinger's judgment needed to make a deal because their leadership had a domestic situation as complex as Nixon's and perhaps more intractable.[66]

Aspirations of Linkage

The nascent US opening with the Chinese had also given Nixon maneuvering room with the Kremlin. Indeed, on the front with China, portents of a possible "thaw" or even "opening" emerged. In early April 1971, the Chinese government invited the American national table tennis team to visit the PRC, and the United States announced it was relaxing certain trade restrictions on the mainland. Later that month, the White House received a secret communication through the Pakistani government that Beijing would welcome an American envoy.[67]

Kissinger also believed that if the Soviets tried to stall on SALT he had a diplomatic card to play. The Berlin Four Power talks designed to clarify the status of Berlin and the rights and responsibilities of the nations that assumed control of the city after World War II (the United States, the Soviet Union, Great Britain, and France) were critical negotiations for the Kremlin. Kissinger's working assumption was that Moscow's anxiety to reach an agreement over Berlin provided the Nixon administration with leverage over the Kremlin in SALT. Kissinger told the president that he was prepared to hold up the Berlin talks even though US stalling tactics might bring down the government of West German chancellor Willy Brandt or at the very least make Brandt's domestic political situation more difficult. Kissinger had a rare bureaucratic ally in executing this strategy: Kenneth Rush, the US ambassador to West Germany, who was the American representative at the talks. Kissinger and Nixon trusted Rush—unlike Smith—and made him privy to their attempts at linkage and to back-channel discussions with Dobrynin on Berlin.[68]

Nixon and Kissinger also considered various other aspects of linkage involving SALT. "If we get SALT, we'll get the summit," Nixon told Kissinger. Kissinger did not see why the Soviets would want to have the summit without resolving the substantive negotiations because if the Soviets did not "give" on SALT, he could just stall on the rest of the superpower agenda. Nixon still held out hope that a SALT agreement might indirectly provide incentives for the North Vietnamese to negotiate seriously: "The only possibility of something happening here is tied to their concern about the Chinese and Russians, for example, if something develops in a breakthrough in SALT, which is possible." Kissinger remarked that a SALT breakthrough announcement was bound to jolt the North Vietnamese: "No matter what the Russians tell them, they can't be sure what side deals are being made."[69]

Despite these points of leverage in SALT, Nixon and Kissinger felt compelled to consider what might happen if back-channel efforts to reach a basic SALT framework failed. Kissinger argued that if the Soviets did not make a major move in the direction of the American position, the United States would "have to go hard on them," because the Soviet offensive and defensive deployments were "scary." Nixon said he expected that public opinion would probably turn hard right if the Soviets appeared to be gaining strategic superiority and that it would be necessary politically as well as strategically to respond with an American counterbuildup.[70]

With the results of the back channel in doubt, Nixon instructed the US SALT delegation that it was to hold its ground when the formal negotiations resumed in Vienna on 15 March. The only major move was to introduce the idea of an ABM agreement in which the United States would be allowed four ABM sites to protect its ICBMs, while the Soviets could retain their Moscow Galosh system. (Zero ABM and NCA-only also remained on the table.) Smith reported that this option was unacceptable to the Soviets but suggested that they might be interested if the United States was prepared to attenuate or break the offense-defense linkage.[71]

Toward a Breakthrough

In late April 1971 Kissinger informed Nixon that the Soviets had finally accepted, through the back channel, the basic parameters of a joint commitment to move forward on SALT. The United States and the Soviet Union would reach an interim agreement to halt the deployment of strategic offensive weapons. This agreement would be coupled with a treaty of indefinite duration limiting ABM systems. Yet there were still many details to be worked out, such as the dates that the offensive freeze would begin and end, pending a more permanent agreement; what types of strategic offensive weapons would be covered; and the number and location of ABM systems permitted on both sides. The technical details could be resolved later through the formal SALT negotiations, but an announcement of the breakthrough could be made in the next few weeks, perhaps along with a commitment to a US-Soviet summit that autumn.[72]

For the next several weeks, Kissinger and Dobrynin continued to discuss the remaining loose ends of the joint public announcement tentatively scheduled for release on 20 May, and the text of formal letters that would be exchanged privately between Soviet and American leaders. Nixon and Kissinger became suspicious that the Soviets were still trying to reach an agreement on defensive systems first. Kissinger and Dobrynin sparred on language that would support the American position of offense-defense linkage. Kissinger was also concerned that the Soviets were using the front-channel negotiations in Vienna to float informal proposals to Smith that would undercut the offense-defense linkage that he had reached in the back channel or rob Nixon of the credit for progress in SALT.[73]

Behind the scenes Nixon now faced the tricky problem of informing key national security officials, especially Rogers, Smith, and Laird, of the impending SALT announcement. In the months leading up to the 20 May announcement, Nixon and Kissinger had numerous discussions in the Oval Office about how to explain this sudden and unexpected development to these senior officials. The president was concerned that one or more of these men or their key subordinates might resign in protest over this apparent lack of confidence—or that they might leak their own version of events to the press and thereby spoil the public effect of the announcement and alert the Soviets to the degree of dissension within US ranks. Nixon and Kissinger calculated that Rogers, Smith, and Laird could be made to see that success in SALT transcended the less-than-transparent means by which it was achieved. But the White House could not be sure on this point, and there was much anxiety over when and how the news should be broken to the principals.[74]

Kissinger and Smith met early on the morning of 19 May, before Nixon's planned meeting with Rogers. Nixon timed this sequence so that Smith would not have the opportunity to tip off Rogers. Kissinger immediately reported to Nixon that Smith had reacted very positively to the news and that the ACDA director had taken the position that it was the substance, not the means, of progress in the negotiations that mattered.[75]

Smith had a somewhat different recollection: "There was no need for me to tell Kissinger what I thought of this procedure in negotiating behind the back of all responsible Administration officials save the President. But I tried to make the best of it by saying that the product and not the process counted, and I thought the product looked positive. I got the impression that Kissinger was more interested in the major political thrust that the accord would give the negotiation than in its specific provisions." Smith said that he pointed out to Kissinger ambiguities and problems in the public announcement and in the back-channel negotiating records, such as the absence of a freeze on SLBM construction (only ICBMs seemed to be covered). Smith also objected to Kissinger's characterization of the announcement to the press as a "a major step forward in breaking the SALT deadlock by Soviet acceptance of the principle of linking offensive and defensive limitations." In Smith's opinion, the Soviets had agreed with this linkage from the beginning and had only partially broken away from it in late 1970. Smith was convinced that all this could have been done, and done better, through the formal SALT negotiating process. Kissinger's diplomatic style meant that careful deliberation had given way to a one-man show in which he was pitted against the entire Soviet national security establishment. To characterize the announcement as a "breakthrough" was really a matter of public relations, not diplomacy. Smith considered resigning in protest but decided to soldier on.[76]

Nixon's session with Rogers shortly thereafter went less smoothly. Haldeman had called Rogers in London on 15 May to indicate that the president wanted to see him on a sensitive matter when he returned to Washington after his overseas trip. After Rogers briefed the president on the situation in the Middle East, Nixon, clearly embarrassed, haltingly described the impending SALT announcement. The president indicated that events had developed very quickly while Rogers was out of the country and that the breakthrough had been confirmed only that week. Rogers said little but was clearly upset. Haldeman spent much of the rest of the day trying to calm the waters. Nixon instructed Haldeman to remind Rogers of an earlier discussion between the two in January in which the president had however vaguely referred to the idea of high-level contacts on SALT. Nixon closed the loop with Rogers in a telephone conversation on the afternoon of 19 May. Haldeman thought that Rogers had been mollified by the president's explanation of events and particularly by Haldeman's assurances to the secretary of state that he would not be embarrassed publicly by his lack of knowledge about the SALT back channel.[77]

Kissinger briefed Laird early on the afternoon of 19 May. Kissinger reported to Nixon that he had no difficulties with the secretary of defense, although Laird had warned that the prospect of an impending arms control agreement would make it difficult to obtain congressional support for strategic programs, especially for ABMs. Laird made the same point in a subsequent Oval Office meeting with Nixon. The secretary of defense warned: "But I'll have to hard-line it, Mr. President, as far as my position is concerned. I've got to take a little harder position in order to sell our program up there." Kissinger also reported that Moorer had responded enthusiastically to the news that the president had not given in to pressures to accept an ABM-only agreement.[78]

Nixon, Kissinger, and Haldeman spent a great deal of time working on the president's prepared comments to the nation, to be delivered in a nationally televised address at noon on 20 May, together with the text of the joint US-Soviet statement on SALT. The text would be released simultaneously in Moscow: "The governments agreed to concentrate this year on working out an agreement for the limitation of the development of anti-ballistic missile systems. They have also agreed that, together with concluding an agreement to limit ABMs, they will agree on certain measures with respect to the limitation of offensive strategic weapons." Nixon finally had his "Big Play" on arms control and US-Soviet relations, and he was determined to maximize the impact through brief remarks that dramatized the impact. Throughout the editing of the speech, Kissinger also argued that the administration's policy of linkage had been applied successfully to the SALT negotiations.[79]

Framework for an Agreement

The 20 May back-channel "breakthrough" had allowed Kissinger at long last to impose some order on what he regarded as the unruly diplomatic and military bureaucracies and to gain Nixon a breathing space in Congress and with public critics. The announcement was generally well received by the media and the public. In the opinion of both major factions in the government, however, Kissinger had achieved this break-through at the expense of the original goal of SALT—a single, compre-hensive agreement that would cover both offensive and defense forces. For the arms control community, this lack of a linkage between the two elements meant that the arms race would not be constrained but would likely be channeled into unpredictable qualitative dimensions, especially due to the lack of control on MIRVs. The saving grace would be strict limitations on ABM systems, which Smith and his colleagues thought vital and were determined to see made as strict as possible. For defense conservatives, the 20 May arms control framework based on a freeze of offensive forces rather than an agreed mutual ceiling essentially conceded the Soviets a numerical lead in ICBM launchers. It did not solve the critical problem of Minuteman vulnerability and quite pos-sibly made the problem insoluble if the final agreements closed off cost-effective remedies. Laird and the Joint Chiefs were determined to see that those avenues remained open.[80]

The Kissinger-Dobrynin back channel had left many key issues unresolved. Smith could not be sure exactly what positions Kissinger had privately taken with the Soviets of which Smith and the US del-egation remained uninformed. The 20 May public announcement left the sequencing of negotiations on ABMs and offensive forces unclear. It was also uncertain whether the freeze would include submarine-based systems or strategic bombers, or ICBMs, and if so, at what level. To complicate matters, in July 1971, *New York Times* correspondent Wil-liam Beecher published details about the American negotiating position much to the anger of Nixon and Kissinger, who were then in the midst of trying to discredit the leaker of the Pentagon Papers, Daniel Ellsburg.[81]

The devil really was in the details. When would a freeze take effect? How long would the interim agreement last? Would an ABM Treaty be perpetual or tied to a future permanent offensive agreement, and how many and what kind of ABM sites would be allowed? Some of these issues might be deferred to follow-on negotiations, specifically, the American desire to limit future Soviet first-strike capabilities. Kissinger was clearly prepared to kick that difficult can down the road. Over time it was decided that the final version of SALT would take two forms: a treaty covering ABMs (which would require Senate approval) and an executive agreement codifying the temporary freeze in offensive forces (which Nixon decided he would submit for majority approval by both houses in the form of a legislative resolution).

Certainly in the public mind, SALT had become a pillar of détente. Nixon, despite his occasional private protestations to the contrary, believed that he needed SALT as the capstone of a successful summit. SALT finalized during a summit would help assure the president's reelection. Presumably with Vietnam also finally settled he would be in a much stronger position to pursue his framework of peace and address the problematic asymmetries in SALT.

The Nixon White House spent the next year "operationalizing" the 20 May framework agreement, for it was no more than a framework. Kissinger originally hoped this could be done relatively quickly in Helsinki when the formal negotiations resumed in July, perhaps leading to agreements to be signed at a Soviet-American summit in Moscow in the fall of 1971. This timetable was preempted by another Nixon "big play" in the offing. Kissinger secretly visited Beijing in July 1971, following up on the April invitation, leading to Nixon's dramatic public announcement in July that he would travel to China early the following year. As the White House was preparing the 20 May SALT announcement, Kissinger had already sought to send assurances privately to Beijing that the pending agreements would not adversely affect Chinese interests.[82]

During his time in Beijing in July 1971, Kissinger told Chinese premier Chou:

> We [will] attempt to discuss with you, if we can find the means, any proposal made by any other large country which could affect your interests, and that we would take your views very seriously. Specifically, I am prepared to give you any information you may wish to know regarding any bilateral negotiations we are having with the Soviet Union on such issues as SALT, so as to alleviate any concerns you might have in this regard. So while these negotiations will continue, we will attempt to conduct them in such a way that they do not increase the opportunity for military pressures against you.

Kissinger also told the Chinese that recent remarks reportedly made by Laird—to the effect that Japan should look to its own nuclear weapons for protection—was contrary to White House policy.[83]

Nixon's China trip meant that the Soviet summit would come later, in the spring of 1972. The president announced planning for this other "Big Play" in October 1971, which effectively set a deadline for the completion of any major SALT agreements because Nixon was determined to take full and personal credit for success in strategic arms control. But it also meant that the talks could not come to an agreement too rapidly; a few outstanding items would be left for the summit so that Nixon could personally seal the deal. Nixon and Kissinger worried constantly that Smith might take liberties and reach an agreement on his own and thus steal the president's political thunder.[84]

To keep up the appearance of momentum in the talks, the two sides agreed to sign a hotline modernization agreement and an accidents measures agreement. Both agreements, which were negotiated by the SALT delegations, were signed in October 1971 by Rogers and Soviet foreign minister Gromyko during his visit to the United Nations. As these were considered by Nixon to be minor accomplishments, he was happy to give Rogers some public appearance of involvement in SALT. Kissinger also checked off another diplomatic box in the policy of détente with the culmination in October 1971 of the Four Power Agreement on Berlin.

As formal SALT negotiations continued, the two delegations struggled for months to resolve the proper sequence for negotiating the defensive and offensive agreements. The Soviets wanted to give preference to reaching agreement on an ABM Treaty, while the Americans feared that Moscow would try to pocket that agreement without any corresponding effort to address offensive forces. The Department of Defense was particularly concerned. Laird and the Joint Chiefs expressed increasing dissatisfaction with the 20 May framework. They believed that an offensive freeze would now come too late to assure anything like quantitative equity in number or size in ICBMs and possibly in SLBMs if they were included. Laird continued to argue that with missile modernization the Soviets could achieve strategic superiority in the mid-1970s. The American delegation struggled to find some way to limit the size and number of the next generation of Soviet ICBMs by making a distinction between "light" and "heavy" ICBMs.[85]

Laird, Nitze, and the Chiefs made occasional noises about the need to reject the 20 May framework in favor of more comprehensive offensive limitations. Yet, their frustrations aside, they sought to make the final agreements as favorable as possible from a defense perspective. They had long sought a tight relationship in SALT between offensive and defensive forces; the larger the Soviet offensive force, the greater the permitted US ABM capability (and the opposite if the Soviets agreed to limit or reduce their offensive forces substantially). Although the United States had abandoned this offensive/defensive linkage in the SALT negotiations, elements in DoD still felt that ABM had a role to play. There was no consensus within the department about a minimum level of ABMs, but four sites (with a total of four hundred interceptors) to defend ICBM fields, plus NCA defense, was often cited as the Joint Chiefs preference.[86]

The Pentagon also sought to keep other technology options open in an ABM Treaty. This would be achieved by permitting the deployment of what was known as a hard-site ABM system—defensive technologies designed specifically to protect ICBMs in their silos but not soft targets like cities and industrial facilities. The Joint Chiefs in keeping with their prejudice against technology limits were also reluctant to categorically prohibit "futuristic" ABM systems, such as lasers, whose qualities and capabilities were unknown by definition. Finally, DoD wanted a qualifier in the ABM Treaty that its duration would depend on reaching a follow-on agreement to significantly control offensive forces within a specified time. A viable US ABM program would provide essential negotiating leverage to obtain such controls in the future.[87]

Smith, meanwhile, continued to try to drive a killer stake through the heart of an ABM Treaty. Under instructions, he submitted a variety of proposals that would give the United States a 3:1 or 2:1 advantage in ABM sites. But Smith never quite gave up on his goal of zero ABMs; he believed that an allowance for even a small ABM capability, while meaningless militarily, would become the springboard for a breakout if an ABM Treaty was ever annulled. But if zero was off the table, he would do his best to hem in strategic defenses through diplomatic art. He pressed successfully for significant and detailed controls on ABM-related radars to address fears that the Soviets would develop a nationwide radar infrastructure that would support an ABM breakout. This certainly had the support of DoD. Nitze made himself something of an expert on the subject and played a key role in working out the details.[88]

Smith and his ACDA colleagues also wanted binding language against "futuristic" ABM systems, such as lasers, or any other technical workarounds that might undermine the essential goal of permanently prohibiting any nationwide strategic defense. They thought themselves largely successful in doing so, with Kissinger's support, although the issue would reemerge forcefully during the Reagan administration and its "broad interpretation" of the ABM Treaty. Smith also wanted no allowance for hard-site defense. He pressed for language in the preamble of the ABM Treaty that would set the goal of zero ABM. This Nixon and Kissinger would not have, but they agreed that the duration of the ABM Treaty would not be formally contingent on the success of future offensive negotiations. Rather, the treaty would include a standard provision allowing either side to withdraw on six months' notice if supreme national interests were in jeopardy.[89]

Much of the interagency deliberation was taken up with the issue of whether to include SSBNs and SLBMs. Kissinger had been at best lukewarm on the question during those deliberations and in the back channel with Dobrynin. Kissinger's thinking on this matter is not perfectly clear. He was probably concerned that the proposal for such limits, like zero ABM, would be a nonstarter with the Soviets. Dobrynin had given him that impression, and Kissinger did not want to hold up SALT on this matter. Submarine-launched missiles were more stabilizing than ICBMs because they did not pose a first-strike threat, and this was an area in which the United States held both technical and geographic advantages. The United States also had plans to modernize or increase its own SLBM

White House cabinet discussion before issuing US negotiating position on limiting offensive and defensive missiles, 1 May 1972. Left to right: Alexander Haig, Henry Kissinger, Admiral Thomas Moorer, Lt. Gen. Royal Allison, Richard Helms, Gerard Smith, William Rogers, President Nixon, and Melvin Laird. (Nixon Presidential Library)

force; in early 1972, DoD had recommended that the navy proceed with the development of a new ballistic missile submarine, which would not come on line until the late 1970s at the earliest. This submarine was one strategic modernization program that Kissinger thought would be acceptable to Congress.

Both the arms control community and DoD, however, had wanted SSBN/SLBM controls, and in January 1972, Laird had suggested a plan in which the Soviets could trade in old ICBMs and SSBNs/SLBMs to reach an agreed-upon ceiling of modern submarine-based systems. Kissinger floated that idea in the back channel with Dobrynin. Laird, however, had not suggested any specific number of SSBNs/SLBMs to Kissinger, who felt free to explore exactly what might satisfy the Soviets.[90]

Second "Breakthrough"

Much of the remaining SALT logjam was apparently broken during a secret meeting between Kissinger and Soviet leaders in Moscow in April 1972. Kissinger had been dispatched to settle the details of Nixon's visit the following month, but his visit came during the outset of an offensive against South Vietnam by Hanoi. Nixon planned to respond forcefully with a massive bombing campaign and a blockade of the North's ports, among other actions. In Nixon's mind, this put the summit in jeopardy, and he was determined not to suffer the political embarrassment of having the Soviets cancel his visit as Eisenhower had been embarrassed when Khrushchev canceled the planned Paris summit after an American U-2 plane had been shot down over Soviet territory. Kissinger was strictly enjoined by Nixon to stick to Vietnam and discuss nothing else, including summit preparations and SALT, unless he received satisfaction on the Soviet response to Vietnam, for example, by a commitment by the Kremlin to cut off arms supplies to Hanoi. Even then the president, shifting to his role as the solitary statesman above politics, told Kissinger that he was sorely tempted to cancel the summit preemptively, even though it would mean that he would lose the opportunity to sign SALT, at least for the moment.[91]

To Kissinger's surprise, the Soviets did not seem overly concerned with the American response to Hanoi's offensive. The Soviets came forward with two proposals on SALT that moved substantially in the American direction, as far as Kissinger was concerned. Brezhnev proposed a

2:2 ABM site arrangement, in which each side could protect its national capital and one ICBM site with no more than one hundred interceptors and launchers allowed at each site. Kissinger would have preferred to allow each side to choose its ABM deployment site or sites, given the unlikelihood that the Washington ABM defense would ever be approved by Congress, but he thought this a reasonable compromise, and Nixon had previously approved accepting a 2:2 arrangement of some sort. Brezhnev also put forward, as his own idea, the SLBM trade-in notion, under a final ceiling of 62 SSBNs and 950 SLBMs allotted to the Soviets. The interim offense agreement would last for five years, rather than the shorter duration preferred by the United States but given that the United States could not field any new strategic systems of its own during this period, Kissinger thought it acceptable.[92]

Nixon was furious when he learned that Kissinger had violated his instructions in Moscow to focus on Vietnam. Simultaneous reports from Smith in Vienna—that Semenov had suggested that the Soviets might be willing to move on the SSBN/SLBM issue—also triggered familiar presidential anxieties that the diplomatic establishment was trying to steal his credit. Deputy National Security Advisor Alexander Haig worked to calm the waters while Kissinger was away, and in the end, Nixon grudgingly accepted the progress on the summit and SALT that Kissinger reported.[93]

When Smith learned of the tentative points of settlement that Kissinger had made in Moscow, he once again felt blindsided and uncertain of what else had been agreed to under the table. As with the 20 May framework, Smith believed that Kissinger's deal would have been achieved just as easily through regular channels while ensuring that the fine points in the US interest were adequately addressed. Smith and Rogers were especially alarmed at the proposed SSBN/SLBM ceiling for the Soviets, which they regarded as excessive. The previous working assumption had been that any such ceiling would be based on something like the current level of US submarine systems (41 SSBNs, 656 missiles). In justifying his deal to permit the Soviets 62 submarines and 950 missiles (in the final agreement, the United States would be allowed 44 SSBNs and 710 SLBMs), Kissinger had gone to and even beyond the high end of the estimates of the intelligence community about the planned Soviet submarine program. Admiral Moorer and the navy supported these estimates, supposedly because they could be used to justify the US Trident submarine program to Congress.[94]

Smith was generally not one to think that such disparities were strategically significant, especially given American advantages in other dimensions of the nuclear competition and his assumption that SLBMs were not a first-strike weapon. But it offended his sense of professionalism not to have done better, when better was to be had. Smith and Rogers were concerned that this disparity allowed to the Soviets in SLBMs, together with that permitted in ICBMs (the Soviets were to be capped at an estimated 1,618 land-based missiles, compared to 1,054 for the United States) was bound to lead to political criticism that the Americans had gotten the worst of the agreement. In the final stages of the negotiations, Smith even proposed dropping SLBMs out of the agreement altogether, to avoid such political criticism. Nixon overruled such objections, following Kissinger's claim (backed by Moorer) that the Soviets could otherwise have as many as eighty-five submarines in service by 1977.[95]

Moscow Summit and Implications for Future Strategic Arms Control

Most of the major SALT issues were seemingly resolved as Nixon arrived in Moscow for his long-desired summit with Soviet leaders, but the climax of nearly three years of negotiations was hardly calm. Throughout the spring the two SALT delegations in Helsinki continued to work on the texts of the agreements and associated statements. Smith and Nitze were summoned to Moscow with the final documents only at the last minute and were excluded from the last-second bargaining. The leaders finally agreed on baseline numbers for the Soviet submarine force, including the trade-in provision, and the minimum distance allowed between the two permitted ABM sites. On 26 May 1972, Nixon and Brezhnev signed the ABM Treaty and the Interim Agreement on Offensive Forces. The limits for the latter were codified in a separate understanding, as Kissinger sought to mitigate the political impact of the concession of substantial numerical advantages in missile launchers to the Soviets. The Americans made one final effort to restrict the heavy Soviet ICBM program through an agreement or understanding on limiting increases in silo size. The best they could achieve were unilateral statements that set out the American position.[96]

The Moscow summit as the capstone of the administration's tactical détente contained several items critical to the future of strategic arms

President Richard Nixon and General Secretary Leonid Brezhnev signing the ABM Treaty and Interim SALT Agreement, 26 May 1972. (National Archives)

control. Kissinger and his Soviet interlocutors crafted a statement of principles designed to govern future conduct between the two superpowers, calling on both to exercise restraint in their competition and to avoid seeking unilateral advantages at the other's expense. Kissinger clearly hoped that this spirit of cooperation would extend to the next round of SALT. The two sides also came to a number of scientific and economic agreements, and the United States would shortly thereafter offer other commercial inducements, such as investment in the Kama River truck plant. This could be construed as a sweetener to encourage the Soviets to be accommodating in the arms control arena, applying linkage, broadly understood.[97]

Behind the scenes while still in Moscow, Nixon and Kissinger struggled to obtain final endorsement on SALT from Laird and the Joint Chiefs. The proximate cause of the disagreement had to do with the counting rules that would allow the Soviets to reach their ceiling of 62 SSBNs and 950 SLBMs, but it amounted to a general protest against what the uniformed military regarded as excessive concessions by Kissinger. Nixon and Kissinger, through Haig in Washington, pressed the

Joint Chiefs to concur with the SALT package. The Joint Chiefs finally reached an agreed-upon statement of conditional support, in expectation that the flaws in SALT I would be addressed in future negotiations. "The Joint Chiefs of Staff are in accord—provided that we take action necessary to insure the acceleration of our ongoing offensive programs as well as improvements in existing systems."[98]

On 2 June 1972, the Joint Chiefs sent Laird what amounted to conditions for endorsing the outcome of SALT. They asked for three "assurances" in the shape of "a formalized national program" that would undergo annual review, reminiscent of the LTBT safeguards. First, there must be a broad range of intelligence capabilities and operations to verify Soviet compliance. Second, DoD must be permitted to undertake an aggressive improvement and modernization program. Third, the administration should commit to a vigorous R&D program. Otherwise, they warned that further negotiations on offensive systems could not be concluded without jeopardizing national security. The United States must retain the ability to rapidly augment its strategic capability should the treaty and/or interim agreement be abrogated or future offensive force talks be unsuccessful.[99]

While Nixon returned from Moscow in public triumph, he and Kissinger were well aware of the discontent over SALT behind the scenes. They would have to submit the agreements for congressional approval, which provided their political opponents across the political spectrum the opportunity to pick apart any perceived weak parts of the agreements. They felt confident that Rogers, Smith, and the diplomatic establishment would be in their corner, especially to defend the ABM Treaty. But the White House faced potential embarrassment by revelations about their Machiavellian maneuvering throughout the entire SALT process. Laird and the Joint Chiefs might not rebel openly but their uneasiness about the outcome of SALT would hardly be a secret among Nixon's conservative critics. And although Nixon and Kissinger might promise to meet the military's conditions for being in "accord" with SALT, there was no guarantee they could do so. But all in good time. The White House strategy focused on obtaining favorable congressional votes for the agreements, winning reelection for the president, then seeing what the future of strategic arms control might bring and what the Soviets might be willing to allow. SALT I was just a beginning.

Conclusion

Because Nixon's secret recordings did not begin in 1969 when foreign policy goals and priorities were initially articulated, the tapes provide a rather skewed perspective on White House motivations for the initial SALT agreement. The written record suggests that a larger complex of considerations drove negotiations in the first year: preserving crisis stability largely through limiting Soviet heavy ICBMs, and linking an offensive agreement to a defensive one (what became the ABM Treaty) was an exceptionally important means to an end. Throughout SALT, Nixon and Kissinger juggled diplomatic, strategic, and domestic political goals, with priorities shifting according to circumstances and audience. Yet by February 1971, when the White House tape recordings began, that calculus of motivations had shifted to an extent, and both Nixon and Kissinger spoke increasingly about the political importance of SALT. In one NSC meeting, the president stated that "on the SALT part: the pathetic idealism on arms control in this country means it would be best to speak on it often. We know that the cosmetics have a lot to do with how people see this, regardless of substance."[100] And privately, he repeatedly argued that what was important was the public's recognition that a US-Soviet accord had been achieved as well as the political clout such agreements would provide him. Numerous scholars have pointed out that "Nixon wanted and needed identification with an advocacy of peace for his political success and for his place in history."[101] Many of the more than two hundred hours of recorded conversations after February 1971 broaching SALT substantiate that motivation. Whenever Nixon and Haldeman discussed the administration's being down in polls over Vietnam, they spoke about SALT as a tactic to bolster the president's image with the "liberal" press or "liberals" in Congress. In short, SALT represented a peace policy on a front other than Vietnam.[102]

Nixon stated most bluntly and cynically his belief that SALT was mere détente window dressing when he told Haldeman just a few weeks before the treaty was signed that "I don't think people give much of a shit about SALT. Do you?"[103] Yet their emphasis on *appearing* successful partially explains how SALT became inextricably connected to a superpower summit. Nixon and Kissinger could not allow SALT to be negotiated before a summit lest they be denied credit for securing a treaty. The summit represented the climax of their strategy of détente.

Nixon and Kissinger's preoccupation with the appearance of success as they pursued SALT provides a way to evaluate their broader strategy of détente. Apart from any political considerations, SALT was designed to halt further deterioration of the US strategic position that the Nixon White House believed could not be addressed in the current domestic political climate. Nixon frequently lamented the loss of US nuclear superiority, and they both believed that neither that superiority nor global dominance were any longer possible. In their view, the United States could, however, play a pivotal role in stabilizing an increasingly multipolar world—as they saw the nuclear ambitions of many countries representing. They further believed that SALT was the best they could do under their current circumstances and hoped that a broader framework of détente might compel Soviet restraint across the board and allow them to finesse various problems (perceived and real) in the nuclear realm. More recent scholars are less charitable and argue that under the guise of relaxing tensions, SALT attempted to maintain US nuclear superiority and global dominance while only temporarily slowing the arms race. The more recent view too starkly conflates the Nixon and Ford years in which the latter administration more actively pushed to preserve and expand US nuclear capability and options, which would enhance the credibility of extended deterrence. Regardless of their motivations, SALT as a tool of containment and linkage represented the attempt by the Nixon White House to negotiate spheres of stability with the Soviet Union. Yet SALT neither alleviated mutual suspicions nor resolved other international conflicts. Superpower proxy wars in the Third World continued, and expectations about improved relations with the Soviet Union were left largely unfulfilled.[104]

5

Nuclear Nonproliferation and a Strategy of Ambivalence

[SALT] has not a goddamn thing to do with the Nonproliferation Treaty, and the Test Ban Treaty and all the rest. This is nuts. I wasn't for those things, not really.

—President Nixon, June 1972

IF A SALT agreement represented the crown jewel of the Nixon White House, the Nonproliferation Treaty was a nagging and persistent distraction. With the NPT signed under President Richard Nixon's predecessor on 1 July 1968, it remained for the new administration to urge or discourage US Senate ratification. It also fell to the Nixon administration to encourage other nations to become parties to the treaty by not only signing but eventually ratifying it. Without US Senate ratification, for instance, the NPT would shortly become null and void. As noted above (see chapter 1), the NPT would not go into effect until the United States, the UK, the Soviet Union and forty other countries deposited the instruments of ratification. And a number of the key nonsignatories were awaiting US ratification before they signed; many of those that had signed wanted to see US action before they ratified. In essence, there was both political and diplomatic significance to the sequential steps of nations' signing and ratifying for the NPT to go into practical effect.

Given the criticism voiced by then candidate Nixon, it was not surprising that the Senate opted not to approve the NPT right away. Nixon's repeated refrain following the Soviet invasion of Czechoslovakia in August 1968 was that the United States should not ratify the NPT "while Soviet troops held an iron grip on the Czechoslovakian people."[1] The Senate took the cue, waiting until after the US presidential election brought Nixon into office. At that time, the NPT had been signed by eighty-five countries; however, it had been ratified by only seven, including the UK. Fourteen months would pass before the NPT entered into force, with the necessary ratification by the United States and Soviet Union and the major signatories depositing the treaty ceremoniously at the White House on 5 March 1970.[2]

Nixon's tepid interest in NPT ratification specifically and nonproliferation policies generally have led many scholars to characterize this period as the "lost years" for the international nonproliferation regime. This chapter does not take general exception to that characterization but presents a fuller, more nuanced account of nonproliferation measures of the Nixon era, showing that numerous factors influenced the administration's position on NPT ratification and implementation. During the first nine months of Nixon's presidency, the treaty competed not only with White House focus on establishing a SALT negotiating stance but also with review of CBW policies. Additionally, Nixon and Kissinger never regarded the treaty as their initiative and gave it measured support at best. The NPT ran counter to their *realpolitik* foreign policy outlook; as a treaty premised on universal membership, it did not permit the nuanced approach to nonproliferation that Nixon favored.[3]

As the ratification hung in the balance at the outset of the Nixon presidency, broad disagreement existed within the administration over how to handle nuclear proliferation. Nixon, like many of his predecessors, approached nonproliferation with inconsistency and pursued measures that were often counterproductive. The president's crafted confusion and penchant for secrecy left many within his administration uncertain of how to pursue nonproliferation vis-à-vis other nations. The administration's position on the treaty's ratification and its policies toward nuclear nonproliferation generally became marred by equivocation. Elements of the administration grappled with the tension between nuclear sharing with allies and the nonproliferation norms set by the treaty. The Nixon White House took a purposely ambiguous stance on the timing of NPT ratification so it could tread that tight rope. For allies and neutral countries, it leaned toward varying degrees of nuclear sharing within the boundaries set by the treaty or equivocation toward nuclear ambitions. For foes it sought to thwart nuclear weapons program development through political means. As a result, the Nixon administration pursued a strategy of nuclear ambiguity, which was theoretically at odds with the tenets of universality underpinning the NPT.[4]

Establishing a Position on the NPT

Given Nixon's public opposition to NPT ratification in the wake of the Czechoslovakian invasion by the Soviets, the Kremlin anticipated luke-warm support of the NPT from the new presidential administration. Perhaps portending the future back channel that would develop between Kissinger and Anatoly Dobrynin, the Soviet ambassador reached out twice between the election and the end of 1968 to President Johnson through his national security advisor Walt Rostow. In relaying the thrust of Dobrynin's message regarding Soviet intentions to link strategic missile talks to the NPT, Rostow summarized: "Moscow is clearly ready to go—and eager—if you can work it out. Their reasons are quite similar to our own: to cre-ate a good backdrop for the NPT in January; to keep the momentum of the work on missiles going into the next Administration; and, therefore, to avoid a long delay in both the NPT and the missile affairs."[5] Outgoing Johnson tried to persuade his successor to get on board with the NPT. The two met on 12 December 1968 at the White House. While no minutes of the meeting have been found, Johnson went into the meeting intending to stress that "a world of nonproliferation where Europe, Latin America, and Free Asia rely explicitly or implicitly on US nuclear strength, would tend to be a unified world in which the reservation of the right to fire nuclear weapons would remain in the hands of the US President. A world where NPT fails—and small nuclear capabilities develop—will tend to be frag-mented, vulnerable, and dangerous."[6] Nixon no doubt agreed with John-son in principle but was likely noncommittal.

The Soviets approached the new administration before the inau-guration through Boris Sedov, counselor at the Soviet embassy and a Soviet intelligence officer. Sedov shared with Kissinger a message that "the Soviet leadership would do their utmost . . . to ensure ratification by states of the non-proliferation treaty." Kissinger asked whether the Kremlin's message meant that "the USSR would try to create an atmo-sphere in which ratification of the treaty would be possible in the United States, or was it proposing joint action with the US to secure ratification by third parties." Sedov indicated that both meanings were intended. Kissinger reported to Nixon that he gave Sedov no reply other than that they were studying the problem.[7]

In the early months of his presidency, "studying the problem" became the Nixon White House mantra. Despite clear signals from Moscow that the Kremlin wanted not only the United States but other nations to ratify the NPT, the president's early feelings on ratification had as much to do with how to deal with the various US allies and other countries as it did with the Soviet Union. At the first NSC meeting held during week two of the new administration, Nixon firmly stated his position on how officials should approach NPT ratification. According to minutes from the meeting the president emphasized that he "wanted it understood that there was to be no arm twisting of other states on the NPT issue, that it is completely up to them as to whether or not they follow U.S. lead." When Secretary of State William Rogers cautioned that "we must be careful not to give the impression that we don't care whether they follow suit," the president cut him off, declaring, "This may be so but we will just state that we are hopeful that they will follow suit, without adopting heavy-handed tactics."[8]

Six days later, through NSSM 13, the president followed up with an instruction to the interagency principals to study the position of key countries on the NPT. On 1 March, the interagency group put forward three courses of action: "passive"; "low-key diplomatic approaches"; and "uniquely tailored approaches for particular countries which we believe require and warrant more intensive treatment." The interagency group also recognized a domino effect—US ratification would induce Soviet ratification, both of which in turn would likely facilitate NPT signature by West Germany and Japan; those signatures would then influence countries in Europe, the Middle East, and Asia to sign. Unfortunately, only the executive summary of the twenty-eight-page NSSM study is declassified. Yet the administration's primarily country-specific approach toward nonproliferation and NPT ratification can be gleaned from the larger body of documents that have been released. The large number of countries collectively reviewed in the NSSM study represented too many anomalies to the NPT's tenets for universality; therefore, the Nixon administration approached nonproliferation with nations either individually or regionally.[9]

US Senate Action

Although Nixon wanted to keep US ratification of the NPT independent of whether other countries signed or ratified the agreement, he was aware that most nations did not share that view and looked to the

United States for leadership. Largely for public consumption, in early February 1969, Nixon requested the Senate to "act promptly" and ratify the NPT even though the interagency was in the midst of formulating the NSSM recommendations. The Senate Foreign Relations and Armed Services Committees held hearings in late February 1969 to review the political and military implications of the treaty. In closed sessions both the chairman of the Joint Chiefs of Staff and the Department of Defense director of research and engineering endorsed the NPT, declaring unequivocally that the treaty would not change US security commitments. On 13 March, the Senate provided its consent to NPT ratification by a vote of 83–15. Even though the president issued a statement that he was "delighted" to see Senate action, the administration made no noises about depositing instruments of ratification anytime soon.[10]

West Germany as a Central Problem

The Federal Republic of Germany (FRG) was central to the Nixon administration's approach to NPT ratification. It represented the single country of most concern, warranting "a tailored approach" and "intensive treatment" as set forth by the NSSM study group. On 5 February, the same day that Nixon asked for Senate consideration of ratification, Kissinger issued NSDM 6, stating, "The President directed that, associated with the decision to proceed with U.S. ratification of the Non-Proliferation Treaty, there should be no efforts by the U.S. Government to pressure other nations, in particular the Federal Republic of Germany, to follow suit."[11]

The White House was acutely aware that "fear and resentment of the NPT as a Soviet instrument (promoted with U.S. collaboration) of constraint upon Germany" was foremost in the minds of many FRG leaders. West German government domestic politics complicated its own NPT stance. FRG opposition to the NPT was primarily rooted among the conservatives, the Christian Democratic Union (CDU), who had shared power with the Social Democratic Party (SPD) from December 1966 to October 1969, forming what was called the Grand Coalition. Kurt Georg Kiesinger of the CDU was appointed chancellor; Willy Brandt (SPD), the governing mayor of Berlin, became vice chancellor and minister of foreign affairs. Kiesinger and his CDU sought to distance West Germany from the treaty when it was signed in 1968. The conservative party feared that signing the NPT would leave them at the mercy of the Soviet threat; the Soviets continued to inform them that it retained a special right under the United Nations enemy state clauses and Potsdam accords to intervene in Germany if necessary. Opponents argued that the NPT safeguards would interfere with the civilian use of nuclear power and also denounced the treaty as a "nuclear Versailles." The German elections of October 1969, however, ended the Grand Coalition and left power to the opposition SPD under Brandt, who saw to it that West Germany signed the NPT in November 1969.[12]

While the Grand Coalition remained in power during the first eleven months of Nixon's presidency, his administration and his national security advisor firmly believed the primary Soviet motivation behind the NPT in the first place had been to foreclose West German nuclear weapons acquisition and to weaken NATO by preventing closer nuclear partnership among its members. It is often forgotten that throughout the Cold War the double containment of both Germany and the Soviet Union framed US national security policies, especially in the realm of nuclear weapons policy. Nixon, like his predecessors, sought to curb West German military developments while keeping it firmly tied to the Western alliance and safe from Soviet invasion. The second component of double containment, the management of West German nuclear weapons expectations, had never been a simple task; Bonn's pursuit of *Ostpolitik* (opening of relations with the Eastern bloc) complicated the Nixon administration's policies by adding an unanticipated second political trajectory to take into consideration.[13]

Of all the arms control initiatives under consideration by the Nixon administration, NPT ratification was initially a top candidate for "linkage" to the political settlement of other outstanding superpower issues. During his first call on the new president, Dobrynin had mentioned the "desirability of making progress on some issues, even if settlement of other issues should not be feasible. The Non-proliferation Treaty is just such an issue. If we can move ahead on this it would be helpful in our efforts on other issues." Nixon responded that the "only cloud on the horizon is Berlin" and stated unequivocally: "If the Berlin situation should deteriorate, Senate approval of the Nonproliferation Treaty would be much more difficult. . . . We should bear in mind that just as the situation in Czechoslovakia had influenced the outlook for the treaty last fall, so would the situation in Berlin now have an important bearing on the Senate's attitude."[14] On 13 March, following Senate ratification of the NPT, Dobrynin reported back to the Kremlin that it seemed unlikely the Nixon administration would exert pressure on Bonn to sign the treaty. And the administration did not, largely because of CDU resistance within the Grand Coalition.[15]

The White House lived up to the Soviet ambassador's predictions, turning its focus to an agreement over Berlin and not linking it to the NPT. Nixon, like his two Democratic predecessors, found that the building of the Berlin Wall in 1961 had not eased the problem of Western access to the German capital located hundreds of miles into East Germany. The Nixon administration accepted the division of Berlin as inevitable but not the renunciation of Western control over its sectors of Berlin. In March 1970 the four former World War II powers (Britain, France, the United States, and the Soviets) undertook to end disagreement about the status of Berlin. The Four Power talks on Berlin continued for almost eighteen months and for the longest time made no progress due to conflicting legal arguments, administrative practices, and political and economic interests. To break the logjam, Kissinger used his back-channel communications with Dobrynin to persuade him of the efficacy of having secret talks with the West Germans. Brandt, who became the new chancellor in October 1969, was very much in favor of any approach that would bring about an agreement, since *Ostpolitik* depended on securing a Berlin agreement. The White House practiced back-channel diplomacy with Moscow and Bonn to negotiate terms of a Berlin agreement. The secret communications allowed the White House to discuss Berlin and link progress on a quadripartite agreement to movement on a host of issues of mutual interest between the superpowers—all without interference from the State Department. The NPT was not part of that mix, as the administration continued to soft-pedal its importance, given how bitterly contested it was in West German internal politics. Ultimately the Four Power talks eventuated in the Quadripartite Agreement of September 1971.[16]

Japan and US Nuclear Indifference

Japan was the other World War II vanquished power-turned-ally that the Nixon administration grappled with regarding the NPT. When Nixon took office, Japan had not signed. Yet unlike West Germany, the administration consistently regarded Japan as neither a significant factor in the NPT ratification nor a significant proliferation risk (which at least until Brandt became chancellor remained a lingering concern with the FRG). The NIE on Japan issued at the outset of Nixon's presidency and a special NIE released three months before the president's ignominious resignation offered essentially the same assessments. The intelligence community conjectured that the Japanese government was unlikely to produce nuclear weapons in the near future even though the country had the capacity to do so within a few years. An additional caveat in the 1974 special NIE stated, "At minimum, Japan will keep open the possibility of developing nuclear weapons—whether or not it ratifies the NPT."[17]

This estimation resonated with a White House that put little stock in the NPT's ability to impede proliferation. Given the perceived "low risk" of Japan "going nuclear," proliferation fears rarely intruded into the administration's deliberations of Japanese policy during Nixon's tenure. Instead the US focus was squarely on economic policy, particularly trade, and the strategic implications surrounding the reversion of Okinawa. Nixon's presidency coincided with a transition in relations with this key Asian ally, which by 1969 had experienced phenomenal recovery, with unprecedented economic growth. This led the president to expect Japan to assume a larger share of responsibility for military expenditures, assistance to developing countries, and international economic adjustment vis-à-vis balance of payments and trade. The Japanese government in turn viewed the US base structure and military privileges in Okinawa as concessions granted in a bygone era. Many Japanese leaders therefore wanted to see an immediate removal of those bases as well as the immediate and unconditional reversion of Okinawa to Japan. The island, however, was home to a vast complex of American logistics and air bases. The US force deployment issue, which required extensive internal discussions and bilateral negotiations, dominated much of the administration's strategic thinking about Japan—not nuclear nonproliferation and the NPT. The WMD issue that affected US-Japanese relations was not a nuclear problem but rather the July 1969 revelation of a sarin nerve gas accident on Okinawa (see chapter 3), which triggered a storm of protest on that island and in Japan generally.[18]

Although from the White House perspective the NPT was peripheral to US-Japanese relations, the government of Prime Minister Sato Eisaku and the Japanese press were not quiet on the issue. Japan had several objections to immediate signature and ratification of the NPT. One paramount concern focused on nuclear safeguards and insistence that Japan not be discriminated against in its pursuit of peaceful uses of atomic energy. By the late 1960s and early 1970s, Japan already possessed an extensive and technologically advanced civil nuclear energy program, with seven nuclear power reactors in operation. Additionally, Japan chafed at the hypocrisy of the United States and other nuclear weapons states whom they believed had no intention of eliminating their own nuclear arsenals as prescribed by the NPT. And lastly, the Japanese increasingly questioned the US nuclear umbrella as a sufficient deterrent.[19]

Despite reservations about the utility of the NPT for Japan, its governments during the Nixon period abided by the doctrine crafted by the Japanese in the first years after the end of World War II. This triad was called *Hikaku san-gensoku*, or the three principles of nonnuclearism: "no possession; no manufacture; no introduction."[20] Yet Japan's possession of nuclear weapons per se was not prohibited by the Japanese constitution; only offensive nuclear weapons were constitutionally proscribed. Yet the general Japanese abhorrence of the weapons that had been unleashed over Nagasaki and Hiroshima trumped the theoretical legality of Japan's possible possession of defensive or tactical nuclear weapons in the immediate post–World War II period. By the early 1970s, however, some within Japanese defense circles began talking about the "nuclear option." The Japan Defense Agency's 1970 White Paper on Defense reaffirmed the belief that "it would be possible to say that in a legal and theoretical sense, possession of small nuclear weapons, falling within the minimum requirement for capacity necessary for self-defense and not posing a threat of aggression to other countries, would be permissible."[21]

The Nixon administration's stance on Japan rarely deviated from the recommendation set out by NSSM 13 in March 1969, which was "low key diplomacy, neither overtly pressuring Japan to sign NPT nor actively supporting an independent nuclear force." US indifference was often perceived by the Japanese as equivocation about its possessing nuclear weapons. The administration did not speak with one voice to the Japanese on nonproliferation matters and certainly did not share one view. As was too often the case in all arms control and nonproliferation matters under consideration by the administration, the State Department found itself at loggerheads with the White House and NSC. At one point Winston Lord of the NSC staff articulated the increasingly shared view with his boss, Kissinger: "Would Japan going nuclear necessarily be against our long-range interests?"[22] And the president and his national security adviser intimated as much in numerous secretly recorded Oval Office conversations when discussing the significance of Japan for the Nixon Doctrine, which asked allies to carry more of the burden of their own defense. As late as June 1972 as Kissinger was preparing for a visit to Tokyo in the wake of the signing of the SALT agreement and ABM Treaty, Under Secretary of State U. Alexis Johnson implored the national security adviser to put to rest "uncertainty on the part of the Japanese Government and general public with respect to how firmly the U.S. Government is committed to the concept that Japan should not acquire nuclear weapons."[23] That clarity was never offered during Kissinger's visit nor throughout the remainder of Nixon's presidency.

The consequences of that US equivocation were fortunately not reaped. Once West Germany signed the treaty in December 1969, Japan capitulated and signed the NPT in February 1970. Sato's government, however, did not hesitate to declare publicly that Japanese ratification should not be expected in the near future. The Japanese government registered numerous reservations aligned with their aforementioned concerns and did not ratify the treaty until 1976. The administration can be criticized for its shortsightedness. Though preoccupied with winding down the Vietnam War, the opening to China, and trade issues with Japan itself, the president could have entrusted the Department of State with pressing for Japanese signature and ratification of the NPT. What did the administration have to lose—except White House control over an aspect of foreign policy and clarification over its own feelings about Japan possibly "going nuclear"? After all, Japan was essentially what was then termed a "threshold" nation, meaning it had the technological, economic, and industrial infrastructure in place to move forward with a nuclear weapons program but had not done so.

Great Britain, France, and the Limits of Nuclear Sharing

Regarding Great Britain and France, Nixon was one in a long line of postwar US presidents plagued by the dilemma of how much to assist or at least turn a blind eye to NATO allies in their development of independent nuclear arsenals. This conundrum was particularly true of Great

Britain, which after all had worked with the United States during World War II to develop the atomic bomb, only to have that collaboration abruptly ended after the war when the US Congress passed the Atomic Energy Act of 1946. The Eisenhower administration had pressured Congress for modifications, however, and the wording of the 1954 and 1958 amendments to that legislation permitted Anglo-American collaboration in weapons development by specifying that only countries that had "made substantial progress in the development of atomic weapons" could receive assistance. At that time, only two countries—Great Britain and the Soviet Union—qualified under those terms. The complete transfer of nuclear weapons was prohibited, but components, materials, and design information (called Restricted Data) were allowed.[24]

Due primarily to US technological know-how, the British nuclear deterrent was based around submarine-launched Polaris missiles. At the time of Nixon's presidency, the British nuclear force consisted of four nuclear submarines, each armed with sixteen Polaris missiles, which in turn carried three warheads. The British government of Prime Minister Harold Wilson was pleased to see the new US president abandon the folly of the NATO multilateral nuclear force, which would have consisted of approximately twenty-five surface ships, each carrying eight A-3 Polaris missiles with a range of twenty-five hundred miles, manned by crews drawn from at least three European nations and with the control system to be left in the hands of the United States. Originating in the last days of the Eisenhower presidency and pursued intensely by the Kennedy and Johnson administrations, the multilateral force was conceived as a way to give NATO allies a voice in nuclear decisions without a finger on the nuclear trigger. The Nixon administration made it clear from the outset that the carrot of quiet US-UK technological nuclear assistance was instead in the offing.[25]

During his first trip abroad in February 1969, Nixon visited London and other major Western allies, intimating in conversations with Prime Minister Wilson that the United States saw strengthening the British deterrent as beneficial to enhancing the overall NATO alliance. Wilson's government was a strong advocate of pursuing SALT and seeing the NPT come into force (as long as the former did not impinge on the British nuclear force). The UK was the first major power to ratify the latter. The British labor government was a bit dismayed at Nixon's seemingly tepid endorsement of the NPT and his insistence on tying the opening of SALT to political settlement of issues with the Soviet Union. Wilson had his own economic and strategic motives: both SALT and NPT could permit economizing to maintain an affordable but sufficient British nuclear deterrent, and Soviet ABM defenses under construction around Moscow threatened to weaken the strike capability of the UK nuclear force.[26]

Nixon was not unsympathetic. Over the next two years, as the British faced the need to harden their nuclear warheads to penetrate the Soviet ABM system, his administration tried to meet British requests for their Polaris Improvement Program, code-named "Super Antelope," designed for missile penetration through decoys of Soviet ABM defenses. In 1971, the White House approved the project definition phase; the following year the US provided space in its facilities for underground testing, permitted flight testing of British warheads at its ranges, and shared simulation facilities for testing the separation of reentry vehicles from its system. The White House felt satisfied that it was getting what it sought in return: the British Polaris SLBMs were fully integrated into the NATO command (even though the British government could take full control of its force if it wanted to for national security reasons).[27]

Throughout Nixon's presidency, the British faced the dilemma of buying US Poseidon missiles equipped with MIRVs or continuing with Super Antelope. Secretary of Defense Melvin Laird and his immediate successors at the Pentagon wanted to decide for the British, opting initially against providing MIRVed Poseidon missiles lest it risk disrupting SALT with the Soviets, who would balk at a MIRV option that could undermine a superpower agreement. When during Nixon's second term the Pentagon proposed giving US technical assistance to a de-MIRVed Poseidon version, the British government in turn rejected this option as too costly. The Nixon administration got nowhere in trying to convince the British that Super Antelope was technically flawed and a de-MIRVed Poseidon was what they should pursue. Wilson's successor Edward Heath, who was having to deal with the economic fallout following the 1973 Middle East War, rebuffed US advice. Relations were already tense between the two allies—neither Britain nor France endorsed US military aid to Israel during the Middle East War, much to the White House's irritation. Britain moved forward with Polaris modernization, renaming Super Antelope as "Chevaline" (a fast South African animal), to mark planned modification to technical designs. Less than a decade later, in 1982, Britain's first improved Polaris missiles entered service at sea, largely without US assistance.[28]

More starkly than with Great Britain, the administration's path toward nuclear cooperation with France met with considerable roadblocks. Unlike Great Britain, which was a primary signatory of the NPT and the first major power to ratify it, Charles de Gaulle's French government had been disdainful of the Johnson administration's vaunted pursuit of the NPT. The imperious French president viewed the treaty as yet another attempt, coupled with the Johnson administration's pursuit of a NATO multilateral nuclear force, to thwart an independent *force de frappe*. As the NPT was being signed in the summer of 1968, France was rapidly ascending to thermonuclear status, detonating two devices in the Pacific with yields of 2.6 and 1.2 megatons respectively.[29]

The French president was pleased to bid au revoir to the Johnson administration and deal with the *realists* in the Nixon White House. The two presidents had enjoyed a personal rapport dating to Nixon's tenure as vice president under Eisenhower and in the years afterward. Even though it was in 1958 that amendments to the 1954 Atomic Energy Act permitting some US sharing of Restricted Data with Britain were not extended to the French government, neither Eisenhower nor then vice president Nixon were publicly critical of de Gaulle. By the time Nixon was president, however, Gaullist France had withdrawn from NATO's military command. Nixon and Kissinger realized that the French government would continue on the course toward further developing its independent nuclear arsenal with or without US consent or assistance. The incentive inherent in even a small nuclear force of national prestige and political leverage was simply too great for the French to abandon its program. The Nixon White House believed that the enticement of nuclear technical assistance (which would save them time and money and improve operability), might lure the French into accepting US policy goals and perhaps even back into the command and control structure of the NATO military alliance. At minimum it might reduce the chance of independent French action vis-à-vis the Soviets. One senior French defense official recalls Kissinger saying, "We're at a point where we want to turn a page with the French; we want to get better relations, and this is one way to do it."[30]

As part of his campaign to usher in better relations with the Western European allies, Nixon included Paris in his early March 1969 European tour itinerary. In uncharacteristic de Gaulle fashion, the French president personally greeted Air Force One at Orly airport and spoke in English. The two old friends then held a series of private discussions at Élysée Palace. Nixon did not bother to raise the subject of the NPT, as de Gaulle had made it clear that France would not be a signatory. During one meeting, Nixon was quite explicit in suggesting a change in US policy toward the *force de frappe*, telling de Gaulle that "he took a different view of the French nuclear deterrent. He thought it was good for the U.S. to have another power like France with a nuclear capability. Looking down the road to the future in nuclear matters and as European cooperation develops the French nuclear capability might well provide a base."[31]

Given the domestic and alliance political sensitivities any form of nuclear aid posed, the ensuing US under-the-radar forms of limited assistance to the French government were kept secret for decades. Princeton University political scientist Richard Ullman first exposed the broad parameters of the US nuclear sharing with France in an article published in 1989 that was based on a series of interviews with French officials. The National Security Archive has since published a small batch of documents released under the Freedom of Information Act, and the Department of State's *Foreign Relations of the United States* documentary series has released other relevant official material. Nixon's explicit but private conversation with de Gaulle just a month into his administration shows that the fundamental decision to chart a new course toward France was made earlier than previously thought—less than a month into the administration.[32]

Almost immediately Nixon faced limits to the extent of nuclear cooperation that he and de Gaulle thought could be handled exclusively between the White House and the Élysée. Nixon had come into the presidency with a deep suspicion of the American bureaucracy. His diatribes about the impediments posed by the Departments of State and Defense bureaucracies rang ever true in this new area of cooperation, handcuffing what he had determined was sound policy to bring France "back into the fold." Implementation of any type of nuclear aid required cooperation by parts of the US bureaucracy, primarily the Pentagon. Secretary of Defense Laird never completely endorsed nuclear sharing with the French for a variety of reasons, ranging from its secretive nature to his own fears of appearing to circumvent the intent of the NPT. Perhaps most importantly, he did not want to assist France without a quid pro quo in the form of its help on US monetary claims for relocating those American forces that had been ousted from France when Paris withdrew from the command structure of NATO in 1966. One US official confided, "Things went much more slowly than we had promised. That was very tough, because NSC could not beat up on the Pentagon. I don't think that Defense was ever really on board the program intellectually."[33]

The Pentagon indeed delayed the start of cooperation. After a head of state meeting between Nixon and the new French president Georges Pompidou, who visited Washington in the February 1970, Kissinger instructed Laird essentially to get into line and define "courses of action and difficulties associated with them." The national security adviser directed him that "you should be guided by the President's decision to be forthcoming." Laird dutifully sent Assistant Secretary of Defense for Research and Engineering John Foster to meet with his French counterpart in June 1970 to explore their "wish list." But the Pentagon dragged its feet in reviewing those courses of action deemed possible.[34]

It was another year, March 1971, before Nixon issued NSDM 103 on "Military Cooperation with France." With limited distribution to only the secretaries of state and defense, Kissinger conveyed the president's directive. Rogers was to redefine "advanced computers" for compliance with export restrictions but in a way that could be useful in French nuclear laboratories; Laird was instructed to continue discussions with his French counterpart on France's ballistic missile program. On the same day, the president issued NSDM 104, "Cooperation with France on Nuclear Safety," with limited distribution State and Defense (courtesy copies went to the DCI, AEC chairman, and Joint Chiefs chairman), which established grounds for implementation.[35]

Showing a natural propensity for secrecy, Nixon and Kissinger had good reason to keep exploratory talks and initial overtures of assistance closely held, as revelations would prove to be political dynamite both domestically and internationally. The White House wound up seeking areas of "safe" cooperation and avoided actual designs of nuclear weapons prohibited by the Atomic Energy Act. Cooperation proceeded through carefully controlled steps, a process that became known as "negative guidance," or what was jokingly termed "twenty questions" by US Defense officials involved. French physicists and technicians would describe their processes and design ideas, and their US counterparts would inform them in general terms whether they were pursuing the right course. French scientists and defense officials hosted Pentagon counterparts, for instance in June 1971, and showed them their missile production facilities at Bordeaux. The State Department became essentially a bystander to the shift toward nuclear cooperation, and ACDA was kept entirely in the dark. In the end, nuclear assistance did not go as far under Nixon as the White House wanted. Like his predecessor at the Pentagon, Secretary of Defense James Schlesinger questioned the efficacy and utility of cooperation with the French. Ultimately France was given only modest technical consultations during Nixon's tenure. By the time Nixon left office, French technicians remarked to their government that nuclear cooperation had "yet but scratched the surface"—a double entendre in the sense the French hoped for more than they seemed to receive.[36]

Italy and the "Hedging" of Middling Powers

With the refusal of France to sign the NPT, "middling" Western European countries like Italy exploited the opportunity to delay reaching a final decision on whether to ratify and become part of the NPT. Italy's attitude toward the treaty was emblematic of the increasing global trend toward some form of "nuclearization," both for peaceful uses and weapons, especially among middling nations caught between and seeking leverage over the two superpowers. Among Western European allies, Italy had long harbored nuclear aspirations. Beginning in 1955, Rome had put those ambitions on hold through a bilateral agreement with the United States regarding weapons stockpiling that only served to fuel Italian domestic political debate over the extent the country should have some type of nuclear parity with the other major Western European powers. Italian scholar Leopoldo Nuti has written extensively on Italian nuclear matters and uncovered documents from the disarmament bureau of the foreign ministry that reveal numerous Italian contacts with potential opponents of the NPT, including Japan and India, during the period of negotiation in the late 1960s.[37]

Italy signed the NPT in late January 1969, a few days after Nixon entered office. But a protracted Italian domestic debate meant that the nation did not ratify the treaty until 1975. The Italian government likewise wanted the United States to drag its feet on ratifying the NPT. While the Nixon White House took a hands-off approach toward Italy's

NPT position (omitting discussion during Nixon's visit to Rome in February 1969), the State Department through its embassy tried to persuade Italian leaders to get on board, which resulted in cross-purpose messages. Italian leaders questioned the impact of the safeguards agreements of the NPT on the Euratom community, and the White House considered finding a way around the controversial article of the NPT dealing with the establishment of safeguards procedures to ensure that nonnuclear weapons states did not divert nuclear energy from peaceful uses to the manufacture of nuclear weapons. Euratom, established in 1957 by the European Economic Community (EEC), or Common Market, maintained its own safeguards system. Italy, like other members of the Common Market, feared that a total replacement of Euratom's control and verification procedures could deal a severe blow to European economic integration. Like other EEC members, Italy sought an agreement between Euratom and the International Atomic Energy Agency (IAEA) over inspecting of nuclear facilities in member states. And Italy, like other Western European countries, regarded uranium enrichment as critical for the fuel supply in the growing European nuclear sector. (Enrichment is the process whereby the amount of the U-235 isotope in a quantity of uranium is increased from the level in which it is found in natural uranium. The complicated and costly process of enrichment, then done by gaseous diffusion methods, could produce uranium in which U-235 comprises about 3 to 5 percent of the total. That constitutes a low-enriched uranium, used to fuel nuclear energy reactors.)[38]

It took well into Nixon's second term in April 1973 before an agreement was reached between the IAEA and Euratom for inspections. The conclusion of a safeguards agreement, however, only removed technical reasons for Italian NPT ratification delays. Political objections remained, and Nuti builds on the theory of "hedging" conceived by political scientist Ariel Levite. Italy wanted to retain the technological capacity to weaponize without actually doing so—"a national strategy lying somewhere in between nuclear pursuit and nuclear rollback."[39]

As the case of Italy illustrates, even with NATO allies, Nixon and Kissinger did not apply a blanket approach toward NPT ratification. As the disparate approaches to key Western European nations show, the Nixon administration tried to balance nuclear sharing with nonproliferation norms embodied in the treaty—not an easy task. And NATO allies were the easiest countries with which to deal.

Regional Rivalries as Proliferation Concern

In the late 1960s, the Middle East and South Asia were rife with seemingly perpetual political and military turmoil. Nixon's presidency coincided with a critical turning point in power struggles in both regions, which carried nuclear ramifications that still grip those areas today. Decisions made, agreements reached, and actions not taken by his administration inexorably altered the nuclear landscape of both parts of the world.

Signs of "nuclear metastasis" in those regions existed at the time of Nixon's inauguration, but so did hopes of containment. Israel and Saudi Arabia were the only two countries in the Middle East that were NPT holdouts. All other nations, including Turkey, Iran, Iraq, and the United Arab Republic, had signed the treaty.[40] In South Asia, India was a major nuclear threshold country that had not yet signed the NPT when Nixon took office. Pakistan had not yet made the decision to "go nuclear" and declared it would sign the NPT only if India did likewise. Indian prime minister Indira Gandhi faced strong public opposition to signing the NPT because of the widespread view that the treaty was discriminatory and that the country needed to reserve the option of developing nuclear weapons. Gandhi had made the decision to proceed with a nuclear weapons program long before Nixon came to office. Beginning with the Sino-India border wars of the early 1960s followed by China's successful thermonuclear weapons detonation in 1964, Gandhi's government harbored nuclear aspirations to counter this perceived existential threat. India appeared to find little comfort in the US, British, and Soviet declarations guaranteeing nonnuclear weapons states against nuclear threats. Primarily because the Chinese had refused to sign the treaty, Indian officials feared that their adherence to the treaty might subject their country to nuclear blackmail by Beijing.[41]

From its earliest days in office, then, the Nixon administration recognized the strong possibility that India was actively pursuing nuclear weapons. During an early Kissinger secret back-channel conversation with Dobrynin on 21 February 1969, the two men broached the subject of nuclear proliferation and the status of the NPT. The national security adviser intimated that "concerning individual countries, cooperation in this area would be required primarily with regard to India. It would evidently be necessary to return to this issue somewhat later."[42] Kissinger and Dobrynin never returned to the issue of India signing the NPT.

In March 1971, a political crisis that began in Pakistan with the government's efforts to suppress Bengali demands for virtual autonomy in East Pakistan and concluded with the establishment of the state of Bangladesh at the end of the year precluded any further US-Soviet discussion of India and the NPT. Instead, the region became mired in a web of Cold War conflict. The bloody Pakistani civil war witnessed India intervening on behalf of the East Pakistani rebels. Initially, Nixon was reluctant to take sides in the civil war, but as the conflict broadened, his decisions were influenced in part by his desire to protect the emerging opening to China, which had been facilitated by Pakistani president Yahya Khan. Nixon and Kissinger managed the US response to the conflict out of the White House with the support of the NSC staff. The nuclear proliferation implications of the India-Pakistani conflict could have been left to the State Department and ACDA, but this would have meant openly sharing their often secret machinations with two institutions they deeply distrusted.[43]

The administration's tilt toward Pakistan was highlighted by the dispatch in December 1971 of the aircraft carrier USS *Enterprise* to the Bay of Bengal to restrain India in the war that had developed between India and Pakistan as a result of the crisis. India's response to the Washington-Beijing-Islamabad axis was to deviate from its traditional Cold War policy of "non-alignment." Fearing possible Chinese intervention, Indira Gandhi found the Soviet leadership receptive to signing a treaty of friendship and cooperation. With assurances offered in this bilateral accord of August 1971, India was able to send a clear signal to Washington and Beijing.[44]

The 1971 South Asian crisis, including the reactions of the superpowers, hastened both India's and Pakistan's decisions to become nuclear powers. For the government of Gandhi, the primary lessons drawn from the war were twofold: India could not permit itself to be either a pawn or a victim of superpower machinations, and India must have a nuclear weapon to deter its archrival, Pakistan. Regarding the latter, Indira Gandhi evidently received intelligence that Pakistan was planning to develop the bomb. In June 1972, she made the closely held decision to accelerate the development of a nuclear device already under way. Indian fears of China, which initially prompted India's pursuit of a nuclear weapon, were now compounded by the threat posed by Pakistan. And the lessons taken by Pakistan were similar. The Pakistani government of Ali Bhutto came into power in December 1971 after the surrender of Pakistan's army and the independence of East Pakistan, which became Bangladesh. A little over a month later, in January 1972, learning of India's nuclear aspirations, Bhutto also decided to pursue a nuclear weapons program. He convened a secret meeting of over four dozen leading Pakistani scientists to review the nuclear option. They promised a weapon within five years. In actuality, it would take decades. For India, it took less than two years, and on 18 May 1974, in an ironically named test, "Smiling Buddha," a plutonium-based nuclear device, was tested underground in the Rajasthani desert.[45]

The Nixon administration has been sharply criticized for missing the intelligence signals about India's path toward nuclear weapons and for its muted response to the May 1974 "peaceful" nuclear test. Intelligence community estimates had varied on the likelihood of India detonating a nuclear device, and when the "Smiling Buddha" test took place, Nixon was in the throes of Watergate. The larger point, however, is not simply that the administration missed the warning signs or that the White House and NSC were distracted. The real tragedy lies in their shortsightedness toward Pakistan's quest for nuclear weapons unleashed by the 1971 South Asian crisis. That conflict left US-India relations lukewarm at best and certainly denied the administration much influence over Indira Gandhi, whom Kissinger and Nixon derisively called a "witch" and a "bitch" in secretly recorded Oval Office conversations.[46] Yet the administration's tilt toward Pakistan could have translated into newfound sway over Bhutto. In the wake of India's nuclear detonation, the new Pakistani leader abandoned his predecessors' position that it would sign the NPT only if India did so first. In an effort to avert a regional arms race and realizing how nascent Pakistan's nuclear capacity was, Bhutto did float a proposal in 1974 for establishing a nuclear-weapons-free zone in South Asia. The proposal, however, was rejected by India and ignored by the international community. These authors have found no evidence in the documentary record of the Nixon administration entertaining the idea of a nuclear-free zone for South Asia.[47]

Yet the president could have offered to play honest broker or at least encouraged the start of talks about a nuclear-weapons-free zone. After all, the Latin American nuclear-weapons-free zone (see section below) was one nonproliferation mechanism both Nixon and Kissinger truly endorsed—unlike the NPT. They remained, however, caught in a

Cold War prism in which the pursuit of détente with the Soviet Union and opening of relations with China caused a gross underestimation and foolish disregard of the nuclear ambitions of the two South Asian archrivals. In other words, Nixon ultimately subordinated nonproliferation concerns to other foreign policy issues at a critical juncture when nuclear ambitions were at the core of these regional rivals' strategic identity.

Similar misjudgments marred the administration's approach toward nonproliferation in the Middle East. Early in his presidency, Nixon pursued a major policy shift, a "tilt" toward Iran and Israel that carried severe nuclear proliferation consequences for the entire region. Nixon understood that the United States had important economic interests in oil-rich Saudi Arabia, but he had strong political and personal objections to many Arab countries and their leaders. And personal affinities mattered to him. If Nixon and Kissinger privately considered Indira Gandhi at times a shrew, they considered Israeli prime minister Golda Meir the apotheosis of a stateswoman. Nixon recalls his impressions in his memoir: "Indira Gandhi of India acted like a man, with the ruthlessness of a man, but wanted always to be treated like a woman. In contrast, Golda Meir acted like a man and wanted to be treated like a man, with no special concessions to her womanhood, and she appreciated that."[48]

As the president drew closer to Israel after a state visit of Prime Minister Meir in late September 1969, he distanced himself from the anti-Zionist King Faisal of Saudi Arabia and "tilted" toward Iran's Mohammed Reza Shah. When questioned about his faith in the shah, Nixon declared emphatically, "I like him; I like him; and I like the country. And some of those other bastards out there I don't like." On another occasion, he remarked that Iran was America's "one friend there" in the Gulf region, and "by God if we can go with them, and we can have them strong, and they're in the center of it, and a friend of the United States, I couldn't agree more—it's something."[49]

The shah quickly became the linchpin for the administration's Persian Gulf policy. What one scholar calls a "policy of Iranian primacy" proved divisive within the administration. The Pentagon objected to providing Iran with an enhanced conventional deterrent capability on the grounds that it could spark a regional arms race. Discounting those concerns, on 7 November 1970 Nixon issued NSDM 92, which "approved a general strategy of promoting cooperation between Iran and Saudi Arabia . . .

while recognizing the preponderance of Iranian power and developing a direct US relationship with the separate political entities of the area."[50]

Nixon and Kissinger paid scant attention to Iran's nuclear ambitions, which admittedly were quite nascent at the beginning of his presidency but intensified during his abbreviated second term. Iran's nuclear program dated to the 1950s when the United States provided assistance through the Atoms for Peace program, which promoted civilian applications of nuclear energy. Not only was the shah spending vast amounts on buying conventional weapons from the United States, but Iran's nuclear materials and facilities were also safeguarded by the IAEA as prescribed by the NPT, which Iran signed in 1968 and ratified in 1970. Yet the shah had intimated that if a country such as India developed a nuclear weapons capability, then Iran would likely follow suit.[51]

In 1974, well into Nixon's second term, the shah announced a departure in Iran's energy program. Flush with more than double the revenue from oil production that resulted from the October 1973 Arab-Israeli War, the shah embarked on an ambitious nuclear energy program. His rationale was twofold: Iran's petroleum reserves were finite and no guarantee for long-term energy needs and the quest for national prestige. He selected a Swiss-trained nuclear physicist to head a new Atomic Energy Organization of Iran and reached agreements with both France and West Germany to build nuclear reactors. The shah insisted both internally and to US interlocutors that he had no intention of sparking a nuclear arms race in the Middle East and that his program was purely commercial. But he quietly pursued dual-use projects such as uranium enrichment that could be useful down the road if Iran sought a nuclear weapons program.[52]

India's May 1974 detonation of a nuclear device put a brake on US assistance to Iran on the commercial nuclear front. As public and congressional outcries that India's test had been conducted with a Canadian-supplied reactor and US materials, Iran's nuclear ambitions were thwarted in the last months of the beleaguered Nixon presidency by congressional resistance to approving sales and would become one of the thorny nonproliferation issues confronting the Ford administration.[53]

Israel's nuclear ambitions had been decades in the making when Nixon took office. Both Johnson and Kennedy before him had tried in vain to curb that perceived Israeli strategic need. The government of Prime Minister Ben Gurion had refrained from signing the NPT largely because of his country's alleged precarious security situation, accentuated by continued outbreaks of violence in the Middle East. From Nixon's perspective, however, Israel had not declared itself a nuclear weapons state and therefore did not challenge the NPT's basic structure. At the outset of the new American administration, Nixon was quietly complacent about Israel's ambitions.[54]

That complacency, like the tilt toward Iran, was not shared throughout the administration. How to react and handle Israel's pursuit of a nuclear weapons program proved most divisive within the administration, with the Pentagon again arguing vociferously against it. Laird and Wheeler believed, as their predecessors had before, that an Israeli nuclear weapons program would be like adding kerosene to an already volatile region.[55] Unlike their predecessors' commanders in chief, however, Nixon stalled by issuing NSSM 40, which called for an interagency assessment of Israel's inchoate nuclear weapons program and what effects it would have on US relations and the Middle East region. As anyone who studies the internal workings of Washington knows, the surest way to delay policy action is to ask for a study. And in the end, Nixon refused to link the NSSM 40 inquiry to the sale of F-4 phantom fighters to Israel, which both the Defense and State Departments insisted should be the leverage used to obtain Israel's adherence to the NPT. Without that carrot, Deputy Secretary of Defense David Packard and Deputy Secretary of State Eliot Richardson had nothing but verbal persuasion to use when they called on Ambassador Yitzhak Rabin in July 1969 to press about Israel's nuclear weapons status. Rabin informed Richardson that his government would defer any decision on the NPT until after the Israeli elections in October 1969.[56]

In the meantime, Meir visited Washington in late September and spent one day at the White House. No record exists of the meeting between Nixon and the Israeli head of state on 26 September. The preeminent Israeli scholar on this topic, Avner Cohen, has culled the official archives of both the US and Israel, and the specifics of their meeting are shrouded in secrecy. Cohen's and others' analyses are far from mere speculation and instead based on key principal's recollections. Their conclusions are grounded in comprehensive multinational archival research. The Meir-Nixon agreement solidified Israel's nuclear policy going forward; for the remainder of Nixon's tenure, no one, with the likely exception of Kissinger, knew all or even part of the agreement reached between Nixon and Meir. US-Israeli dialogue about its weapons program created lasting regional and global consequences. From the perspective of most Arab nations, Israel's refusal to sign the NPT undermined the legitimacy of the treaty as a meaningful nonproliferation measure.[57]

The Latin American Nuclear-Weapons-Free Zone and the Non-NPT Approach

The Middle East and South Asia were not the only regions riddled with potential nuclear rivalries. Nuclear technologies with all the attendant military implications were accelerating in South America. Proponents within the Nixon administration—primarily within ACDA and the State Department—worried that as long as Argentina and Chile refused to sign the NPT, it would be easier for Brazil to be a holdout. Smith and Rogers argued that the best strategy for containing Brazilian nuclear ambitions lay in the long term by influencing Argentina and Chile to sign the NPT. The White House, however, apparently put more stock in the Treaty of Tlatelolco, named for the Mexican city in which it was signed in February 1967, as a mechanism to prevent the introduction of nuclear weapons into a region hitherto free of them. Nuclear-free zone agreements differ from the NPT by prohibiting both the acquisition and stationing of nuclear weapons within a specific geographic area; however, they complement the NPT at the same time. Yet another agreement inherited from Nixon's predecessor, the treaty established the Latin American nuclear-weapons-free zone (LANWFZ), which prohibited countries in that region from acquiring, possessing, developing, testing, or using nuclear weapons. Additionally it prohibited other countries from storing or deploying nuclear weapons in Latin American countries. The treaty zone covered the entire Latin American and Caribbean region as well as large sectors of the Pacific and Atlantic Oceans.[58]

Nixon preferred this regional approach to handling the nuclear ambitions of certain parts of the world. In his view, it showed real viability for effectiveness in Central and South America. The president left mechanics of the treaty's entry into force, which came on 25 April 1969, to the State Department and ACDA. From the White House perspective, the LANWFZ had more practical effect than the NPT: verification of treaty compliance was accomplished by concluding multilateral or bilateral agreements with the IAEA, and the treaty carried with it the Agency for the Prohibition of Nuclear Weapons in Latin America and the Caribbean, an intergovernmental agency created by the Treaty of Tlatelolco to ensure that the obligations of the treaty were met.[59]

Although the LANWFZ was hailed as establishing an equitable balance of obligations between the nuclear and nonnuclear states, its effectiveness was initially quite limited. Three key countries in the region with nuclear power capabilities signed the treaty but refused to ratify it despite unofficial commitments to abide by its prohibitions. Argentina signed but did not ratify; Brazil and Chile signed and ratified but opted not to accept three requirements in one article of the treaty that had to be met before the agreement would be binding. One of those requirements was ratification of additional protocols by non–Latin American countries. Protocol I required that outside powers with territories in Latin America agree to place their territories under the same pledges as the parties to the treaty. The United States was a key holdout on ratifying Additional Protocol I, while the Soviet Union refused to endorse Additional Protocol II. That second protocol applied to the nuclear weapon states and required them not to "undertake [and] not to use or threaten to use nuclear weapons against the Contracting Parties of the Treaty." For the LANWFZ to become a completely effective arms control mechanism, which took decades, it was essential for at least some degree of accordance among the states within the zone and significant nonzonal states as to the intent and meaning of the important provisions of the agreement. Such coordination did not occur during the Nixon administration.[60]

The Seabed Treaty and Nonproliferation beyond Nation-States

The Seabed Treaty—officially bearing the unwieldly name of the Treaty on the Prohibition of the Emplacement of Nuclear Weapons and Other Weapons of Mass Destruction on the Sea-Bed and the Ocean Floor and in the Subsoil Thereof—invited Nixon's derision as part of that cornucopia of arms control agreements signed or ratified on his watch that he blithely dismissed as "all the rest." The Seabed Treaty was entirely separate from the administration's policies toward NPT ratification. Yet it is included here because it became part of the international nonproliferation regime in the sense that the treaty transcended nation-state boundaries and was the third international agreement designed to prevent the spread of nuclear weapons to new, unpopulated environments. Nuclear weapons had been excluded from Antarctica by the Antarctic Treaty of 1959 and from outer space, the moon, and celestial bodies by the Outer Space Treaty of 1967. Like so many arms control and nonproliferation agreements of Nixon's presidency, the Seabed Treaty origins predated his tenure with a proposal initially put forth in the United Nations in November 1967 by Malta's ambassador to the UN.[61]

There was no official position on a possible seabed agreement at the outset of Nixon's presidency. In early February 1969, Kissinger informed Nixon that the Seabed Treaty was part of an agenda of "complex arms control issues on which the Administration does not now have a position."[62] Like nonproliferation and arms control policies generally, deliberations to formulate a negotiating position quickly revealed somewhat predictable bureaucratic fault lines within the administration. In one of the first NSC meetings covering the issue, Rogers and Smith were most favorable, arguing that the United States should not rebuff the Soviet proposal to begin negotiations. The ACDA director argued that if the administration rejected the Soviet proposal to begin negotiations in earnest for a treaty banning deployment of nuclear weapons on the seabed where the United States had no such plan to do so anyway, then "how could we expect to go ahead with SALT?" The secretary of state agreed but also suggested a possible compromise of tabling the Soviet draft put forth in the ENCD and then postponing discussion until SALT began.[63]

The Joint Chiefs, almost on cue given their typical skepticism toward arms control, argued against a premature start to negotiations. Their generalized concerns centered on the possible detriment to their strategic nuclear posture of giving up use of the ocean floors before study of those implications as well as their uncertainty about adequate verification measures. The Joint Chiefs would ultimately back down from opposition because there were no immediate plans to nuclearize the seabed. Laird's position on whether to accept the Soviet draft proposal was more fluid. Initially he, like his military colleagues, opposed accepting the Soviet position as the launching point for negotiations. He also stressed the importance of not wanting "to trade away any political advantage." By that, he suggested linking a possible seabed treaty to "a part of a package deal that included SALT and proceed only on that basis."[64]

The president relied upon Kissinger for his counsel about whether and how to proceed with seabed negotiations. In the April NSC meeting devoted to seabed proposal discussion, the president told his national security adviser that he was "most interested in [his] technical judgment and not [his] political judgment." Kissinger replied that separating the political considerations from the technical was difficult but that he "thought the seabed treaty was to our national advantage." The national security adviser went on to say, "It would not affect in any way our development of nuclear weapons. We already have so many ways of emplacing and delivering them, including, under the treaty, thousands of square miles of underwater emplacement possibilities along our shorelines for experimental purposes, that the treaty would not be to our disadvantage from this point of view either."[65]

A seabed agreement may not have met squarely with the NPT, but in the president's view it met with the goals of the treaty, which called for curbing the spread of nuclear weapons to new environments. He stressed to his cabinet that it met "our general posture against proliferation," and that "it is important that we not present a picture of dragging our feet."[66] The path to formulating a US government position followed the typical NSC process of study, review group, and culmination of decision following the full body discussion among NSC principals. Yet primarily because the president did not equivocate on his general desire to reach an agreement, the process was not tortuous as it was for SALT and even CBW.[67]

The ensuing negotiations, which took place in the Geneva-based ENCD and then in its successor organization, the Conference of the Committee on Disarmament, encompassed three central questions. First, What should form the geographic boundaries of an agreement? What should constitute seabed militarization? And how should verification of compliance be assured? The negotiations went in several predictable phases: Soviet proposal followed by US counterproposal; joint submission to the United Nations; continued talks in Geneva; and ultimately final negotiation in 1970 to resolve what today seems like minutiae of details over scope, geography, and verification means.[68]

On 3 July 1969, midway through the tedium of back-and-forth and in an effort to break a logjam, Nixon expressed his hope that common ground could be found between the two superpower draft treaties. In the president's view, their positions were not irreconcilable. While the Soviet Union sought complete demilitarization of the seabed, the United States wanted to limit it to prohibition to nuclear warheads. The Department of Defense was most concerned about countering Soviet submarine capability and the retention of its elaborate sonar detection arrays in both the Pacific and Atlantic Oceans. This concern also governed the US insistence on a three-mile versus the Soviet twelve-mile offshore boundary. Ironically, given perennial Soviet concerns about the intrusiveness of verification means in most arms control talks, the USSR position here called for stringent verification of potential seabed installations. The United States was content with a more minimalist approach. In the end, the Soviets relented and agreed to verification by "observation and open consultations." The United States consented to the Soviet insistence on a geographic boundary beyond twelve miles from coastlines but held its ground on a more limited scope of seabed demilitarization. At first the US interlocutors counterproposed with denuclearization (winning the concession of excluding antisubmarine devices from the final treaty) but ultimately included all categories of WMD in the scope of the treaty.[69]

The agreed-upon treaty became the sole arms control effort that compelled Nixon to evoke the term "weapons of mass destruction." In other words, it was one of the few times that the president viewed an arms control agreement across the WMD spectrum of nuclear, chemical, and biological weapons. He declared that "the United States has supported the efforts of the Conference of the Committee on Disarmament at Geneva to reach an international agreement prohibiting the emplacement of weapons of mass destruction on the bed of the sea. . . . The spread of weapons of mass destruction to this new realm would complicate the security problems of all nations, and would be to no nation's advantage."[70] One likely motivation for a more all-encompassing prohibition was to deny the Soviets propaganda material because at the time the US Army was making preparations to dump a quantity of obsolete nerve gas in the Atlantic, and the Soviets probably saw a clear chance for making substantial propaganda gains by playing up the USSR's peaceful position on the seabed.

The Treaty on the Prohibition of the Emplacement of Nuclear Weapons and Other Weapons of Mass Destruction on the Sea-Bed and the Ocean Floor and in the Subsoil Thereof was opened for signature in Washington, London, and Moscow on 11 February 1971. Nixon transmitted the treaty to the US Senate for ratification on 21 July 1971, which unanimously provided its consent on 15 February 1972. Ultimately eighty-nine nations signed and sixty-six ratified the treaty. The lasting significance of the treaty, like so many arms control agreements of the Nixon era, is mixed. As one scholar has noted, "This achievement of sealing off the ocean floors from nuclear weapons shows Nixon at his wisest and most prescient."[71] This characterization, however, is perhaps too generous. Certainly the treaty created an additional demilitarized area under an arms control treaty regime, but the Polaris and other ballistic missile submarines obviated the strategic need for stationary nuclear weapons embedded in the seabed. And the administration's failure to provide any linkage of the treaty negotiations to either SALT or any other agreement casts doubts that the Seabed Treaty made any real contribution to détente.[72]

Legacies of Nixon's Strategy of Ambivalence

Aside from the Seabed Treaty, this snapshot of the Nixon administration's largely country- and region-specific approach to nonproliferation illustrates that between 1968 and 1974 it was far from clear whether the signatories to the NPT would actually ratify it. What could the superpowers do to persuade countries to accede to the treaty? Nixon and Kissinger believed they should focus on superpower arms limitations because controlling the nuclear ambitions of other nations was a risky, ineffectual business. In the end, the president and his national security adviser let their tunnel vision regarding SALT, especially the fact that it was "their" agreement, affect their approach to NPT ratification and concomitant nonproliferation policies. An Oval Office conversation in June 1972 between Nixon and Kissinger is emblematic of their views about the NPT. In griping about Gerard Smith after the successful Moscow summit that eventuated in the SALT I agreement and ABM Treaty, Nixon and Kissinger had the following mocking exchange:

> NIXON: [Smith] tries to say—his whole line has been, Henry, that this [SALT agreement] is the outgrowth of the Nonproliferation Treaty. It has not a goddamn thing to do with the Nonproliferation Treaty, and the Test Ban treaty and all the rest. This is nuts. I wasn't for those things, not really.

KISSINGER: I wasn't either.

NIXON: I supported nonproliferation because we had to. But you see Smith is always trying to put it as if—you know why that is? The son-of-a-bitch is trying to give credit to the Democrats. Do you agree?

KISSINGER: Of course. If it is an obligation entered into as a result of the Nonproliferation Treaty it's a—we didn't support—since we didn't negotiate the Nonproliferation Treaty. It isn't our record.[73]

This conversation underlines their characteristic approach to arms control and nonproliferation; politics coated everything in Nixon's estimation. Even if one discounts the visceral comments of Nixon and Kissinger minimizing the significance and their support of the NPT, the administration certainly compiled a mixed record in pursuing nuclear nonproliferation. In the end, many of the administration's actions toward allies, whether Israel or France, all but undermined the legitimacy of the NPT. The goals of nuclear cooperation and nonproliferation existed on a spectrum but were difficult to pursue in a comprehensive, coordinated, and consistent manner. Those twin goals also highlighted the tension between the nuclear "haves" and "have nots" sanctioned by the treaty. Cooperation with the British proved mutually advantageous to the United States because London agreed to integrate national strategic planning into NATO planning. France, which refused to sign the NPT, was unwilling to accept restraints on its national sovereignty, thereby putting strict limits on nuclear sharing with France. Japan agreed to forswear nuclear aspirations because Washington provided assurances of a nuclear shield. Pakistan was offered no such assurances and, perceiving India as a mortal threat, Islamabad would not embrace nonproliferation. Israel offered a unique case. A staunch yet stubborn ally, it relied upon the United States for military assistance. Yet it refused to sign the NPT or acknowledge or deny the existence of a nuclear program. As the Nixon White House knew all too well, the most dangerous international problems proved to be the least soluble by a blanket policy. The administration ultimately helped those allies who already possessed nuclear weapons or were receiving assistance from other nations to enhance their programs. And they discouraged, through a variety of means (regional nuclear-free zones or threats of curtailing military assistance), all others from joining the nuclear club. And like so many of its arms control decisions, the NPT and nonproliferation reflected an administration with too many bureaucratic oarsmen rowing in different directions.

The Nixonian approach to nonproliferation did not necessarily take the "long view," meaning it discounted the adage "Friend today; foe tomorrow." The 1979 overthrow of the Shah in Iran illustrates that short sightedness. And the Nixon approach did not account for the action of its own allies, whether it was French assistance to certain nations or indirect Canadian assistance to India. Once technical knowledge was given to a country, it could not be taken back. Therefore, one drawback was that it was time contingent, whereas a universal approach as embodied by the NPT set normative standards.[74] The Nixonian country- and region-specific approach carried other pitfalls. Clandestine support to France, for instance, was risky and carried potentially more problems than opportunities. The disclosure of expanded nuclear cooperation could have jeopardized SALT with the Soviets or harmed relations with West Germany. Given that meaningful quid pro quos were not forthcoming with the French government, one can question the wisdom and the efficacy of the White House actions.[75]

Despite the Nixon White House's tepid pursuit of NPT ratification, the agreement remains today as the centerpiece of the international nonproliferation treaty regime. After Nixon left office, ignominiously resigning after the Watergate scandal, the international NPT regime as it is called today, started to take shape. Kissinger, who stayed on with an accretion of influence that came by being dual hatted as both secretary of state and national security adviser, would have a hand in developing those mechanisms as he succumbed to domestic and international pressures to curb the spread of nuclear weapons. Between 1974 and 1976, a series of measures were taken. Kissinger helped craft the Nuclear Suppliers Group, a voluntary association of about fifty industrial nations who agreed to work together to limit the international transfer of dual-purpose, nuclear-useful materials. The IAEA began to release a "trigger list" that identified nuclear items that required safeguards as a condition of export. And the signatory nations to the NPT held the treaty's first review conference and decided to hold such conferences to review the implementation of the treaty every five years.[76]

Yet both the Nuclear Suppliers Group and IAEA published trigger lists that could have been pursued much earlier and were admittedly spurred by India's nuclear test, since the fissionable material came from a Canadian-supplied Atoms for Peace Canada Deuterium Uranium reactor. (This type of nuclear reactor permits the use of unenriched uranium as a fuel by using heavy water as a moderator, thereby lowering the entry barrier for nuclear production.) Nixon and Kissinger were not antagonistic toward the NPT, but their complacency came at a critical juncture when across the globe, there was greater demand for nuclear energy and weapons. Emboldened by the belief that there would be no consequences imposed by the United States, many nations could and did question the treaty's value and moved forward with pursuing nuclear weapons programs or delayed signing or ratifying the NPT.[77]

6

Unfinished Business of SALT II

What in the name of God is strategic superiority? What is the significance of it, politically, militarily, operationally, at these levels of numbers? What do you do with it?

—Henry Kissinger, 1974

ON 1 June 1972, President Richard Nixon delivered an address to a joint
session of Congress that hailed the results of his recent summit meeting
with Soviet leaders in Moscow. He included an exposition of the two
major SALT agreements—the ABM Treaty and the Interim Agreement
on Offensive Forces. "Three-fifths of all the people alive in the world
today have spent their whole lifetimes under the shadow of a nuclear
war which could be touched off by the arms race among the great powers," he intoned. "Last Friday in Moscow we witnessed the beginning of
the end of that era which began in 1945. We took the first step toward
a new era of mutually agreed restraint and arms limitation between the
two principal nuclear powers."[1] What Nixon never acknowledged publicly or even privately was the rather tortuous path by which those strategic arms control agreements were reached. Although such challenges
are common in policy development and diplomacy, the SALT process,
especially within the US government, was characterized by an uncom-
mon degree of what some would criticize as unnecessary concessions
and unhappy compromises. Yet Nixon and Kissinger maintained that
they had laid an essential cornerstone for a new generation of peace and
détente with the Soviet Union—while, not incidentally, buttressing the
president's case for reelection.

Political Landscape of the SALT Agreements

The White House was determined to demonstrate strong support for
SALT and therefore détente through overwhelmingly positive congressional votes on the ABM Treaty and the Interim Offensive Agreement.

Nixon believed this endorsement would resonate with voters in November 1972 and help persuade Soviet leaders in the next round of negotiations that the administration's domestic political position was strong. The pro-SALT campaign mounted by the White House later raised accusations that Nixon and Kissinger had deliberately oversold the SALT I package for short-term political purposes, which created excessive expectations that it and future arms control agreements could not meet. There is certainly truth in this line of argument, but Nixon and Kissinger themselves held out hope at this time that SALT would become the central pillar of an expanding détente—even if détente was a tactic to achieve a host of political objectives both at home and abroad.[2]

Given the widespread public support for Nixon's handling of foreign policy after his return from Moscow as measured by opinion polls, it was virtually certain that prospective SALT opponents could not come close to defeating the ABM Treaty in the Senate or rejecting congressional resolutions of support for the interim agreement. Although liberals and moderates were dissatisfied with the failure of SALT to rein in strategic offensive forces, especially MIRVs, few if any were likely to oppose an arms control agreement package that included the holy grail of strategic stability, meaningful limits on nationwide ABM systems, which presumably precluded the possibility of a successful first strike and thus dampened the offensive arms race. Over the past three years, the White House felt that it had successfully defeated efforts by chief SALT negotiator Gerard Smith and his pro-arms control colleagues in the State Department and ACDA to ally with their supporters in Congress. Now that an agreement had been reached, even one falling short of what the arms controllers had wished, Smith and Secretary of State William Rogers dutifully testified to Congress on behalf of the SALT package, particularly emphasizing the value of the ABM Treaty.[3]

Nixon did not want to risk any politically significant "no" votes from defense conservatives or the emergence of articulate opposition from the Republican right that might be used against him during the coming election campaign. The White House planned to convince prodefense congressmen, prominent conservative journalists, and pundits of the merits of SALT, as it had done after the May 1971 "breakthrough" announcement—as well as mainstream media types, who were thought to be inherently suspicious of Nixon and who might highlight weaknesses in SALT just to spite the president.[4]

Nixon in the Oval Office with Smith, Rogers, and Kissinger. (National Archives)

Nixon's 1 June address therefore provided strong assurances that if Congress provided the approval of SALT and the ABM Treaty, his administration would "take all necessary steps to maintain in our future defense programs." In subsequent congressional testimony, Secretary of Defense Melvin Laird and Joint Chiefs chairman Admiral Thomas Moorer made clear that their support for SALT was contingent on proceeding with essential strategic force modernization programs and success in the next round of talks in reducing the Soviet offensive threat to acceptable levels.[5]

The most obvious shortcoming in the SALT interim agreement from the standpoint of defense conservatives was the concession to the Soviets of a numerical superiority in both ICBM and SLBM launchers and particularly the size of Soviet ICBMs (throw weight) while the United States was prohibited from deploying an effective strategic defense. Administration officials, particularly Kissinger, argued that the Soviet superiority in launchers and missile size resulted from a unilateral US decision in the mid-1960s to stop building additional missile launchers. This "gap" would have emerged with or without arms control, he further argued. SALT I limited the Soviets' future plans and bought time for the United States to address this issue. In the meantime, the United

States retained offsetting advantages that SALT I did not capture. These included its MIRV program, which would provide the United States with a substantial lead in warheads for the time being; forward-based nuclear systems; and geographical asymmetries, which, for example, allowed the US Navy to keep more SSBN stations proportionately than could its Soviet counterpart.[6]

The most serious potential opponent of the SALT I package was actually a Democrat—Washington senator Henry "Scoop" Jackson. The senator, who had been Nixon's initial choice for secretary of defense, was a charter member of the now-fading prodefense, anti-Communist foreign policy wing of the party, but he was politically popular among many traditional Democrats, especially labor unions. Jackson had extensive experience in defense matters, including long-standing service on the Senate's Committee on Atomic Energy. He had constantly raised alarms about the Soviet military threat, going back to the 1950s, and had reliably supported Safeguard and other defense programs. Nixon personally thought well of him. But Jackson had also expressed public concern about "concessions" that the president had made in SALT, especially during the summit meeting in Moscow. Jackson was thought to be a likely candidate for the Democratic presidential nomination in 1976. That would not directly affect Nixon, who was limited to two terms, but the White House thought that Jackson's political calculations as a presidential candidate might incline the senator to become a center of opposition to the incumbent's policies, including arms control. Jackson had already criticized the president's general policy of détente toward the Soviet Union because he believed it was based on a false premise that the Kremlin was willing to abandon its pursuit of global hegemony under communist rule.[7]

Jackson believed that the administration's approach to SALT had been wrongheaded. The ABM Treaty prohibited the United States from deploying enough ABM launchers to protect its ICBMs in the short run and from deploying a more comprehensive, cost-effective defense in the future. He contended that the Soviets had sought limits on ABMs not because they had accepted the reality of assured destruction but because they wanted to constrain a technologically superior US program that interfered with their plans to develop an effective nuclear-war-fighting capability. The Soviets would undoubtedly now secretly try to develop an ABM defense of their own while the American program languished. Jackson objected strenuously to an agreement that allowed the

Soviets substantial numerical advantages in ballistic missile launchers and throw weight. As far as he could tell, the interim agreement merely codified what the Soviets had already planned to do without extracting any significant concessions and gave the Soviets a blank check to modernize their forces in the future.[8]

Despite these severe misgivings, Jackson concluded that a direct assault on the SALT agreements was politically unwise. The liberal George McGovern's nomination as the Democratic candidate for president demonstrated clearly the current sentiments of his own party. Republicans would be loath to do anything to undermine Nixon's chances for reelection. Jackson voted for the ABM Treaty, which passed the Senate overwhelmingly 88–2, and for the joint resolution supporting the interim agreement, which passed by the same vote. The House passed the resolution by a vote of 329–7.

Jackson instead registered his displeasure for the record by grilling administration witnesses during the congressional hearings over what he regarded as weaknesses in the SALT I package. Most significantly, he introduced a Senate amendment to the interim agreement resolution, which called for a permanent agreement that "would not limit the United States to levels of intercontinental strategic forces inferior to the limits provided for the Soviet Union." Such an agreement should reflect "equal numbers of intercontinental strategic launchers taking account of throw weight." The amendment was worded to attract the largest possible support. After all, how could a senator vote implicitly to permit a president to negotiate a treaty that would leave the United States in an inferior position? What metrics would be used to measure the relative status of the two superpowers' nuclear forces? Jackson tried to put his interpretation on the legislative record: there had to be "equal aggregates" in numbers of ICBMs, SLBMs, and strategic bombers, or, in some phrasings, "essential equivalence." The Jackson amendment, as it became known, passed the Senate by a vote of 55–36. It was clearly intended to provide a standard by which any future agreement would be measured by Congress and thus constituted a political redline for the White House as it moved into follow-on negotiations.[9]

The White House engaged Jackson to avoid any major rift over SALT. His affirmative vote on the ABM Treaty was effectively a quid pro quo for the administration's 7 August 1972 public endorsement of the Jackson amendment. The senator in turn dropped a stipulation that any Soviet action or deployment that threatened US deterrent capability would be grounds for repudiating the interim agreement. Jackson and the White House also agreed on a statement that failure to negotiate an offensive arms treaty by 1977 would be grounds for withdrawal from the ABM Treaty. Nixon and Kissinger were also perfectly willing to play the right-wing card with the Soviets by suggesting that they might have to give in to pressure from men like Jackson if the Kremlin was not forthcoming in the next round of SALT.[10]

Bureaucratic Jockeying for a SALT II Position

Despite the carping by Jackson and some Republican conservatives, Nixon and Kissinger were pleased to bask in what they perceived as the general popularity of détente and SALT I as demonstrated by Congress's decisive support for the agreements and by the president's overwhelming reelection victory. They undoubtedly hoped that they could ride the momentum of Nixon's 1972 foreign policy triumphs, capped off by the Vietnam peace agreement in 1973, to have the political clout to overcome any residual opposition by defense conservatives like Jackson. They also hoped they could overcome the antidefense sentiments by demonstrating the effectiveness of what the White House regarded as a realistic approach to peace and national security.

Follow-on strategic arms negotiations took on somewhat less importance to the Nixon White House. The administration struggled to formulate an approach that would address the major issues left over from SALT I, particularly the disparity in the number of strategic missiles and the potential first-strike threat against the US ICBM force. Nixon became increasingly distracted by the growing Watergate scandal that eventually toppled his presidency. Kissinger as usual had many other items on his agenda, especially after he assumed the post of secretary of state in September 1973 while retaining his position as national security advisor. And as noted below, there were major changes in key personnel and agency responsibility that substantially affected the policy process.

The opening Soviet position in the next round of SALT negotiations that began in November 1972 was to American eyes surprisingly intransigent. Moscow insisted that a permanent agreement on strategic offensive arms should reflect the structure and logic of the interim agreement, which would lock in Soviet numerical superiority in ballistic missile launchers. Soviet negotiators returned to the need to address US FBSs, for example, by counting them under the aggregate ceiling for offensive strategic forces and by requiring that US missile submarines be withdrawn from forward bases in Scotland and Spain. They also argued that the new agreement must prohibit the deployment of new systems but allow for modernization. Under the Soviet definition of these terms, the USSR would be permitted to deploy follow-on ballistic missile systems such as the much larger and more capable SS-18 for the SS-9, while the United States would be prohibited from deploying the Trident-class submarine and the B-1 bomber.[11]

For nearly a year after the conclusion of SALT I, the American arms control policy process followed well-worn bureaucratic grooves. The Soviet approach was clearly unacceptable to Washington, but Kissinger did not feel compelled or have the ability to generate an authoritative American response. The US delegation was again ordered to fall back on exploratory discussions and the development of a work plan.[12]

The State Department initially favored some sort of indirect controls on MIRVs such as a two-year freeze on the flight testing of MIRVs. OSD and the Joint Chiefs opposed a MIRV freeze or any direct limits on MIRVs on the grounds that they could not be adequately verified, that they would effectively eliminate the new Trident MIRV missile program, and that they would work against American technological superiority. Dictatorships like the Soviet Union could use freezes to prepare a breakout, while democratic politics would cause American programs to atrophy in anticipation that the freeze would be permanent. The Joint Chiefs maintained its long-standing position that the United States should seek quantitative ceilings alone and avoid those qualitative constraints, which would restrict flexibility to conduct research and development or modernization and replacement of systems. The Joint Chiefs promoted force modernization through the new Trident submarine and associated long-range sea-launched missiles, the B-1 bomber, and an advanced ICBM (generally known as M-X).[13]

The Joint Chiefs consistently argued for equal aggregates. The two sides would be permitted equal totals of strategic weapons systems (ICBM and SLBM launchers and heavy bombers), with complete freedom to mix between land- and sea-based systems. Freedom to mix is the principle that each superpower was free to determine the specific composition of its strategic forces (in this case, among ICBMs and SLBMs), as long as the final vehicle count stayed under an agreed ceiling. Variations of the freedom-to-mix principle appeared in several SALT options because it showcased US attempts to leverage technological superiority. The preferred Joint Chiefs aggregates could be between twenty-two hundred (roughly the size of current American forces) and twenty-five hundred (roughly the size of Soviet forces). There would also be equal limits if subceilings were established—for example, on the number of heavy or MIRV missiles. If there were to be controls on MIRVs, those controls should be on heavy MIRV ICBMs, of which the United States had none.[14]

Paul Nitze, a holdover on the SALT negotiating delegation with considerable influence among defense conservatives inside and outside government, continued his long-standing push for equal limits on throw weight. He argued for the importance of negotiated significant reductions in the total number of launch vehicles, particularly those with heavy payloads such as the Soviet SS-9 (later SS-18) ICBM and the US B-52 bomber (there would be a substantial discount for the bomber payload, because such relatively slow systems did not represent a first-strike threat).[15]

Like the State Department, Kissinger wanted to prevent an unlimited competition in MIRVs. He was reluctant, however, to confront directly the long-standing military insistence that the US MIRV program not be constrained by arms control. He thought that it was shortsighted to fixate on the single and remote danger of a Soviet first strike. The Soviets would face immense technical difficulties in coordinating the launch and successful execution of an attack of hundreds or thousands of missiles, an attack that could not be practiced in advance. Even then, he noted, the United States would retain the ability to retaliate with its surviving submarine and bomber forces. In this regard Kissinger agreed with the arms control community. For him the more realistic threat was one in which an emerging strategic nuclear stalemate might tempt the Soviet Union into exploiting its superiority in conventional weapons for geopolitical encroachment or blackmail. He argued that SALT should be viewed within this broader concern. On the other hand, Kissinger understood that the failure to address a theoretical first-strike threat would have important political consequences, as evidenced by Jackson's criticism of SALT I.[16]

For Kissinger, the problem with the Joint Chiefs approach of equal aggregates was that it did not address the MIRV conundrum and precluded a realistic arms control solution. The Soviets, in Kissinger's opinion, would not agree to bring their own forces down substantially to levels that fully addressed American first-strike concerns. His NSC staff also concluded that significant reductions were likely to make matters worse, not better, at least in an interim period, until very low levels of MIRV vehicles were achieved. He assumed that building up to Soviet levels was politically impossible, and in any case, this too did not address the first-strike problem. And even if Congress could somehow be persuaded to fund major new strategic systems, this would undoubtedly drain money away from general purpose forces for strengthening regional defense, which Kissinger argued was the most urgent military priority.[17]

Kissinger concluded that the American position in SALT II should be based on the principle of offsetting or counterbalancing asymmetries rather than equal aggregates or deep reductions. "The real choice we face is between two broad paths," he told an NSC meeting in March 1973. "We can continue pressing for real equivalence with the Soviets or we can come up with a trade where we maintain our technological advantage and let the Soviets keep a numerical advantage." Kissinger toyed around with various formulas to apply offsetting asymmetries. At this point the Soviets had not yet fully tested a MIRV system, and so it was still possible to contemplate a deal in which Soviet MIRVs would be prohibited in exchange for allowing the Soviets advantages in the number of launchers and throw weight or at least allow the United States a distinct numerical advantage in MIRVs. Kissinger also broached the idea of limiting the Soviets from deploying MIRV warheads in return for the United States not developing long-range air-launched cruise missiles, a program that seemed to alarm the Soviets but was not yet high on the Pentagon's list of priorities.[18]

Despite his high public profile and new position as secretary of state, Kissinger recognized that his bureaucratic position had been weakened from the heady days of arranging back-channel deals on SALT. Kissinger's opponents previously had to account for his privileged position with Nixon and his ruthlessness in using that privilege. The drumbeat of revelations over Watergate steadily weakened the president politically and made him even less attentive to the small matters of SALT. He even told Kissinger to make basic decisions about SALT policy on his own. Kissinger reports that he did not do so, but his bureaucratic rivals were emboldened to challenge his authority to speak for an increasingly detached chief executive. More importantly, many defense conservatives—who generally had given Nixon the benefit of the doubt in dealings with the Soviets, given his staunch anticommunist credentials—now suspected that he might be willing to make major concessions to the Kremlin to save his presidency.[19]

Kissinger's own views about national security were also under closer and critical scrutiny. From the right, stories circulated that he believed the West was in terminal decline and the best that could be done was to appease the rising powers in the East—thus explaining his supposedly weak approach to strategic arms control. The left concluded that he was complicit in the criminal domestic behavior of the Nixon administration if not Watergate itself and in immoral and illegal foreign policy activities, such as the overthrow of Chilean leader Salvador Allende.[20]

Kissinger himself felt that he had lost the critical bureaucratic leverage on arms control that had marked the first term. After the election, the White House initiated or acquiesced in a series of personnel decisions that in Kissinger's mind soon left him isolated by tilting the balance inside the administration in favor of the arms control skeptics. Senator Jackson insisted the Joint Chiefs replace General Royal Allison, the Joint Chiefs' representative in SALT I, because he supposedly had not represented the military position adequately. Jackson also effectively designated Allison's replacement, army general Edward Rowny, although he was not Chairman Moorer's first choice. Smith stepped down as ACDA director and chief SALT negotiator in favor of U. Alexis Johnson, a senior career State Department officer. Kissinger counted Johnson as a bureaucratic ally unlike Smith, but Johnson took a considerably more limited view of his responsibilities as SALT negotiator than had his activist predecessor, and he did not want to be dual hatted as ACDA director.[21]

The ACDA post was assigned to Fred Iklé, another member of Senator Jackson's extended circle. In fact Iklé had first suggested the content of the Jackson amendment to the senator. Meanwhile, ACDA and the SALT delegation underwent what was known in the press as the "purge." The agency's staff was reduced substantially, and it became a research rather than a policy development office. As Philip Odeen, one of Kissinger's NSC staff members, later recalled,

> Kissinger . . . always managed to have a range of options supported by the different agencies. He could always be the guy who comes up with the sensible, compromise position. He would have the JCS over here on the right, and ACDA on the left. And so he could come up with his answer, but it looked like a moderate response. He played that beautifully, and we were always driving to have a wide range of alternatives, so his was reasonable, which is not a new game. That really changed after the '72 elections, when they cleaned out ACDA and suddenly ACDA became to the right of JCS. And then we were often exposed. We were on the left.

Kissinger, in Odeen's opinion, had gone along with these changes because "there was a strong feeling that the front-channel SALT delegation wasn't performing in accordance with its front-channel instructions very enthusiastically."[22]

The result, Kissinger noted, was that "the State Department and the NSC staff became the lone advocates of the arms control process, justifying it on geopolitical grounds, but they did not have a public standing on military strategy. In these circumstances, the military stuck to existing planning. NSC meetings turned into a series of bureaucratic dares to the President." In Kissinger's opinion, this could have been overcome had Nixon, and later Ford, had the support of a strong secretary of defense or at least one as politically savvy as Laird. Unfortunately for Kissinger, Laird's successors, Elliot Richardson, James Schlesinger, and Donald Rumsfeld under Ford aligned themselves firmly with the arms control skeptics. During the first term, Kissinger felt the White House was in constant danger of losing control of SALT policy to an alliance between the diplomats and the antidefense block in Congress. During the second Nixon term, Kissinger believed that he faced the opposite challenge—the loss of control to an alliance between the hard-liners in the government and Jackson and a growing new conservative political alliance that would eventually include Ronald Reagan.[23]

July 1973 Summit

In May 1973, as Nixon prepared for a summit with Soviet general secretary Leonid Brezhnev in Washington, he realized it was best to put forth a proposal even if incomplete. Although Nixon decided to adopt the equal aggregates approach, the US position was a bureaucratic compromise that had something for everyone, rather like the early proposals in SALT I. The SALT II delegation was instructed to suggest a limit of a total of 2,350 ICBMs, SLBMs, and heavy bombers for each side, with "appropriate provisions" to allow freedom to mix. It included a freeze on new deployments of MIRV ICBMs and a ban on further testing that would stay in effect until a permanent agreement reflecting equal aggregates was reached. Kissinger had neither the time nor the energy to fight internally against what he was sure would be rejected out of hand by the Soviets.[24]

After back-channel negotiations with the Dobrynin and a visit to the Soviet Union in May to prepare for the summit, Kissinger decided that it was impossible to reach any concrete agreement on a follow-on SALT agreement. The best that could be done was a general statement of principles along the lines of the May 1971 framework agreement that would guide the negotiations going forward. Kissinger was particularly anxious to deflect continuing Soviet pressure for an Agreement on the Prevention of Nuclear War. He interpreted this as an effort by Moscow to prohibit an American nuclear response to a Soviet attack on China, to place formal limits on US Forward Based Systems and British and French nuclear forces, and to bring about a no first use of nuclear weapons agreement, which would undermine NATO's basic security concept.[25]

Kissinger was concerned that the Soviets would attempt to exploit the deterioration in US-European relations (despite his efforts for a "Year of Europe"), which would soon reach rock bottom with the 1973 Middle East War and the Arab oil embargo, among other difficulties. He worked closely with the senior British Foreign Office expert on Soviet affairs, Sir Thomas Brimelow, "to change the Soviet proposal from a renunciation of nuclear weapons to an agreement to renounce the threat of force in diplomacy. What emerged was like a Russian matryoshka doll that has progressively smaller models nested each inside the other. By a series of carefully hedged conditions, the avoidance of nuclear war became an objective rather than an obligation."[26]

As for the Chinese, Kissinger had taken pains during the SALT I negotiations to find various means, despite limited channels of communication, to reassure Beijing that Soviet-American strategic arms control was not directed at the PRC. During the first direct meetings with Chinese leaders in 1971–72, it appeared that they were not terribly concerned on this front. As Nixon's second term began, Kissinger hoped that normalized relations with China would follow and that triangular diplomacy would proceed smoothly. This hope was dashed by the growing leadership instabilities in Washington and Beijing—Nixon and Watergate as well as Mao's evident incapacity and the impending Chinese succession crisis.

In subsequent travels to Beijing, Kissinger found the Chinese deeply suspicious that American political-military weakness had led Washington to contemplate unwise concessions to Moscow in SALT II. If so, the Americans were signaling their abandonment of a willingness to maintain a balance of power that would preserve Chinese independence from Soviet aggression. Kissinger summarized Mao's views after a visit to Beijing in October 1975: "Mao's theme is our weakness. We are the 'swallow before the storm.' We are ineffectual. What we say is not reliable. He thinks we won't use nuclear weapons in Europe and would suffer another Dunkirk. He says we can no longer stand on Chinese shoulders to reach the Soviet Union. 'China must be self-reliant.' ... He said he likes Schlesinger's view of the Soviet Union better than mine. . . . Our weakness is the problem—they see us in trouble with SALT and détente. That plays into their [Soviet] hands."[27]

As with his dealings with American defense conservatives, Kissinger insisted to his Chinese interlocutors that he was not attempting to appease Moscow through arms control. He would keep them informed of formal American proposals to the Soviets and insisted that "we would never incur an obligation not to use nuclear weapons nor aim at third countries." He would be sure that any Agreement on the Prevention of Nuclear War would have no real effect on American policy or Chinese relations.[28]

On 21 June 1973, in Washington, Nixon and Brezhnev signed a statement on the basic principles of negotiations on the further limitation of strategic arms. The general agreement declared that the aim of the talks would be replacing the interim agreement with a permanent treaty, to be reached by the end of 1974, which would be based on quantitative and qualitative equalities. Limits on MIRVs were to be considered as Kissinger wished. The document enshrined the principle of "equal security," without specifying its definition. The next day, the leaders signed what Kissinger regarded as a banal Agreement on the Prevention of Nuclear War, based on the work he and Brimelow had done.[29]

Kissinger felt compelled to shift gears shortly after the summit, when the Soviets successfully tested their first MIRV system in the summer of 1973. He characterized this as the long-forewarned strategic revolution. It was no longer possible to conceive of a situation in which offsetting asymmetries permitted some American MIRVs in exchange for a larger but MIRV-less Soviet ICBM force. (It was becoming clear that the Soviets were bringing online a new generation of even larger and more capable ICBMs, especially the heavy SS-18.) It was also no longer possible to have a partial freeze on missiles of the same type, as existing national verification means could not distinguish between MIRV and non-MIRV ballistic missiles of the same category.[30]

Over the next year, in the Dobrynin back channel and directly with Soviet leaders, Kissinger put forward various ideas as to how to deal with the MIRV problem under the rubric of offsetting asymmetries. At the same time, he worked to turn aside Soviet demands for FBS compensation and Moscow's distinction between modernized and new systems. This included a ban on heavy ICBMs in return for allowing continued Soviet numerical advantages in missile launchers. Kissinger undoubtedly hoped that, as in SALT I, he could privately reach an agreed formula with the Soviets that would effectively decide the bureaucratic battle in Washington. Although it was impossible completely to deal with the emerging Soviet threat to US ICBMs, Kissinger thought his approach had a chance to slow and limit the emergence of the threat and buy time for compensating US programs and the positive effects of détente to come on line. Kissinger felt that the Soviets could be allowed a formal disparity in the total number of missile launchers in exchange for an American advantage in MIRV systems of about three hundred launchers, which would indirectly limit the size of the Soviet MIRV threat. He believed that such an arrangement was negotiable.[31]

Emerging Conflicts between Kissinger and Schlesinger

Meanwhile Schlesinger, who assumed the post of secretary of defense in July 1973, began to exert his influence on policy in various ways. He and Kissinger quickly became intense bureaucratic rivals. Schlesinger was concerned that the Soviets were using détente as a tactic to achieve their goal of prevailing in the conflict with the United States. He did not oppose strategic arms control per se, but he concluded that the United

States was better off taking a maximalist position in SALT that addressed its strategic needs. If the Soviets could not be brought around immediately to a more reasonable position, Schlesinger insisted that Congress could be persuaded to fund strategic programs necessary to deal with the growing Soviet threat. Once Soviet leaders were convinced of this point, Schlesinger felt that they would become more flexible to avoid an arms race with the United States. Although Schlesinger followed the equal aggregates approach of the Joint Chiefs, he did not object to exploring offsetting asymmetries that would allow the Soviets, for example, somewhat greater throw weight—if the restrictions on Soviet MIRVs were significant enough to make a real difference in the strategic balance, which he felt Kissinger's plans did not do. Kissinger, however, suspected that Schlesinger was not serious about offsetting asymmetries; the secretary of defense merely paid lip service to the idea in order effectively to derail the negotiations.[32]

In January 1974, Schlesinger announced a change in US nuclear policy. The new doctrine, codified in NSDM 242, did not, as was widely reported, shift targeting policy from assured destruction to war fighting. The United States had always held at risk the full range of Soviet assets, even during the late McNamara years. But in the opinion of Schlesinger, US nuclear planning and employment policy lacked the flexibility to deal with less-than-all-out wartime contingencies. For example, Schlesinger wanted to develop limited nuclear options of various sorts that would increase the credibility of NATO's flexible response doctrine. He also cited the need to deal with the US ICBM vulnerability problem—specifically, a scenario involving a so-called surgical Soviet strike during a crisis designed to destroy the Minuteman missile force but minimize American civilian casualties. In that scenario, the United States would retain its bomber and submarine forces, but the Soviets might warn that massive US retaliation would result in an equally devastating response against American cities, thus paralyzing the United States and leaving the Soviets free to dictate the outcome of the crisis. NSDM 242 called for giving the president nuclear response options between suicide and surrender.[33]

Kissinger had long been a critic of massive retaliation, and the concepts behind NSDM 242 had been in development with his and NSC support long before Schlesinger entered the Pentagon. But the Joint Chiefs and the services had long been suspicious of civilian efforts to replace the goal of military victory with notions of intracrisis bargaining and signaling and jealously guarded their war plans from the designs of policy makers. As such, NSC efforts at revision, though loud and persistent, found little purchase against military intransigence. Moreover, Kissinger, as secretary of state, had to deal with the fallout of Schlesinger's announcement at a delicate time in arms control negotiations and his campaign to salvage détente. The Soviets predictably criticized what became known as the Schlesinger doctrine for its alleged aggressive intent and noted that it coincided with another announcement by Schlesinger about an increase in the US defense budget. Supporters of arms control and antidefense forces in Congress accused the administration of adopting a dangerous and destabilizing nuclear war-fighting doctrine.[34]

Meanwhile, conservatives and liberals, for different reasons, supported legislation—most notably the Jackson-Vanik amendment on Jewish emigration from the Soviet Union—that restricted the administration's ability to apply its carrots-and-sticks approach to dealing with the Soviet Union. The Soviets seemed to many to be pushing beyond the boundaries of what détente should allow, especially with their nuclear modernization and activities in the Third World. For Kissinger, SALT increasingly became the most important means to keep open the lines of communication with the Kremlin and demonstrate the viability of the administration's policy toward the Soviets.[35]

In the formal SALT negotiations, the United States essentially treaded water because of internal divisions over the proper course and apparent Soviet intransigence. By the spring of 1974, however, Kissinger believed that he had achieved a rough interagency consensus around his preferred solution, which included at least the tacit concurrence of Schlesinger and the Joint Chiefs. In a meeting with Soviet leaders to prepare for the upcoming Moscow summit, he proposed extending the interim agreement for up to three years provided the Soviets accepted an inferiority in MIRV land-based ICBMs comparable to its advantage in the overall number of launchers. He did not expect the Soviets to accept the numbers as offered, which would limit the Soviets to about 270 MIRV ICBMs. But it would be the basis for further negotiation.[36]

In his discussions with Brezhnev in late March 1974, Kissinger believed that he had achieved a small but significant breakthrough. The general secretary suggested that the United States be permitted eleven hundred MIRVs, while the Soviets would accept a lower level of one thousand. Although this differential was strategically insufficient for Kissinger's purposes, he felt that once the Soviets had conceded the principle of offsetting asymmetries of this sort, he could negotiate a better deal, perhaps limiting the Soviets to eight hundred MIRV systems. In preparations for a meeting with Soviet foreign minister Andrei Gromyko in late April, Kissinger worked up a counterproposal that would limit Soviet MIRVs to 850 (he and his staff calculated that, accounting for Soviet MIRV SLBMs, this would effectively place a ceiling of 600 on the Soviet MIRV ICBM force).[37]

Kissinger now discovered that the interagency opposition to his counterbalancing asymmetries approach was much greater than he had assumed. The Joint Chiefs concluded that any of the proposed MIRV limits under consideration in the interagency process created an unacceptable strategic risk, had only a minimal impact upon Soviet programs, "enhanced and further codified" inequalities of the existing Interim Agreement, and reduced US negotiating leverage in working out a permanent agreement. Schlesinger objected that a ceiling of six hundred on Soviet ICBMs still did not deal with the first-strike threat against the US land-based missile force. Limits above 360–450 Soviet MIRV ICBMs were meaningless. Nitze, according to Kissinger, argued that any agreement that permitted the Soviets more than two to three hundred MIRV ICBMs was strategically intolerable.[38]

Kissinger conceded that there was technical merit to this line of argument. But he rejoined that DoD had put forward no new programs that would address this problem—even assuming Congress would approve them, which he doubted. SALT could not be expected to stabilize the arms race but also solve all of America's strategic dilemmas as well. The United States would clearly be worse off if the Soviet nuclear programs were completely unconstrained. At the very least the United States would have begun to get a handle on long-term Soviet advantages in MIRVs because this would not be a permanent agreement. Although Kissinger was authorized to explore his approach with Gromyko during the April follow-on session, he concluded that the bureaucracy would withdraw or qualify its support if the Soviets actually accepted it. In the event, he made no progress with the Soviet foreign minister.[39]

Meanwhile, Kissinger's growing list of conservative opponents took steps to preempt his preferred approach. In December 1973, Senator Jackson proposed that each side reduce its ICBMs and land- and sea-based launchers to 1,760 and equalize the total payload of the launchers. Jackson made his case to Nixon in a January letter in which he declared that "for the Soviets to peremptorily reject such a program would risk the political gains they associate with the developing détente." With respect to direct MIRV controls or limits, Jackson reiterated an argument long made by the Joint Chiefs: "I seriously doubt that we can expect to control effectively nuclear weapons technology through arms control agreements."[40]

General Rowny, meanwhile, expressed concern that Kissinger would trade off a minor, 10 to 20 percent advantage in MIRV launchers in exchange for an informal commitment to slow the Trident, B-1, and Minuteman improvement programs. He urged the Joint Chiefs of Staff to "make it clear that all MIRV options fail to prevent the Soviets from achieving strategic superiority by 1984" and to "stand firm against any extension of the Interim Agreement." The Joint Chiefs went on record with Schlesinger to reaffirm their opposition to any extension of the interim agreement and to all MIRV constraints currently being considered. The administration must make totally clear, they insisted, upon an equitable permanent agreement and its refusal to be deflected by "excursions which essentially perpetuate the imbalances of the Interim Agreement." On 17 June 1974 chief of naval operations admiral Elmo Zumwalt wrote directly to the president, restating familiar arguments against either perpetuating the interim agreement or limiting MIRV deployments. The admiral also wanted to see SALT placed in a broader framework so that the Soviet failure to negotiate in good faith would jeopardize the benefits they hoped to reap from détente in trade and technology. It was clear that the uniformed military was concerned that Nixon's political weakness brought on by Watergate would cause him to make major concessions in SALT.[41]

Schlesinger in turn found an occasion to register his public opposition to Kissinger's approach to SALT. In April 1974, Jackson had sent a letter to the secretary of defense summarizing his arguments for deep reductions and equal limits on throw weight and inviting Schlesinger to share his views. In June, the secretary of defense, without consulting the president or Kissinger, responded with a public letter that essentially endorsed Jackson's approach: "Your proposal, generally, satisfies most criteria currently being used as guidelines for SALT, and also has other inherently attractive features, as discussed in the enclosed assessment."[42]

Nixon met with Schlesinger on 6 June. Rather than calling the secretary of defense on the carpet, the president, in his weakened political position, tried to persuade Schlesinger to reign in DoD's resisters:

> Let me tell you how I see the players. It is amusing that Defense, State, and everyone now see Communism is bad and you can't trust the Soviet Union, I knew both of those things all along. Nitze's view is that we should stonewall the Soviet Union on everything—SALT, MIRV, TTB, ABM. I understand. There are differences in objectives within the bureaucracy. State would like it to blow up because they didn't dream it up—the same with CIA. In the DOD—not you—they would like to stonewall so we get a bigger budget—more ships, etc. That is not totally selfish. They honestly believe no agreement is to our advantage. It's like in SALT I—although we didn't give anything up. Frankly, as Secretary you have to lead the Department. You must express your views. It has been the practice of recent secretaries to send over letters to get on record—with something that can't be accepted or refused, so it can go either way. I am disappointed to see you go this route.[43]

Later in June, during an NSC meeting chaired by Nixon to decide on a position to be taken at the forthcoming summit in Moscow if the Soviet showed some negotiating flexibility. Schlesinger proposed equal total aggregates of 2,500, with a freedom to mix, with a commitment to reduce these to 2,000 by 1984; a limit on MIRV ICBMs of 550 Minutemen for the United States and 360 MIRV ICBMs for the Soviet Union (with each side permitted 60 heavy MIRV ICBMs); a throw-weight ceiling of 3 million pounds for MIRV ICBMs; no limitation on submarine-based MIRVs; and an extension of the interim agreement to 1979.[44]

Kissinger argued that the Soviets had already rejected such an approach and undoubtedly would do so again. In the NSC meeting, Schlesinger countered by challenging the president to apply his noted forensic skills to persuade Soviet leaders. "Forensic skill could not achieve it; the task would have defeated Demosthenes or Daniel Webster," Kissinger later observed sarcastically. "It would require a downright miracle. Only a conviction that Nixon was finished could have produced so condescending a presentation by a cabinet officer to his President." Nixon recorded in his diary that it was "really an insult to everybody's intelligence and particularly to mine."[45]

At the Moscow summit between Nixon and Brezhnev in late June and early July 1974, Kissinger was not surprised when the Soviets rejected a proposal based on the DoD's preferences. The Soviets also held fast to their position that US FBSs must be accounted for. To salvage what he could in terms of a framework, Kissinger proposed a middle ground between a short-term (two to three years) agreement and a permanent treaty. The result was a goal of a new agreement that would supersede the interim agreement for a period of ten years, through 1985. The two sides could propose either equal aggregates or offsetting asymmetries. Nixon and Brezhnev agreed to meet again during the winter in a minisummit to implement the new approach and give the Soviets time to assess Nixon's political situation. In an effort to maintain a semblance of negotiating momentum, the two sides also agreed to a protocol to the ABM Treaty that would limit each to one ABM site, effectively ratifying the existing plans of each, and to a nuclear threshold test ban (TTB) agreement that would restrict the yield of future tests to 150 kilotons.[46]

Kissinger expressed his frustration with the process with two memorable comments in a press conference at the end of the summit, which were later quoted against him by critics of SALT. First, "Both sides have to convince their military establishments of the benefits of restraint and that is not a thought that comes naturally to military people on either side." Second, when asked what would happen by 1985 if there was no new SALT agreement by 1977, he said, "I believe you will see an explosion of technology and an explosion of numbers at the end of which we will be lucky if we have the present stability, in which it will be impossible to describe what strategic superiority means. And one of the questions which we have to ask ourselves as a country is: What in the name of God is strategic superiority? What is the significance of it, politically, militarily, operationally, at these levels of numbers? What do you do with it?"[47]

SALT II after Nixon

Nixon's resignation in August 1974 raised serious questions about the future direction of SALT under the new president, Gerald Ford, and about how the Soviets would respond to the change in American leadership. Ford made it clear that he would rely on Kissinger as his major aide in national security matters. He quickly developed a frosty personal and professional relationship with Schlesinger, who often displayed his sense of intellectual superiority over the former University of Michigan football player. Ford and Kissinger sent reassurances to Soviet leaders that there would be no major changes in American policy toward the Soviet Union. Ford told Gromyko that he hoped that a permanent SALT agreement could be reached within a year.[48]

Kissinger and Schlesinger continued their internal argument over the proper approach to strategic arms control, especially whether Congress would support a major buildup of US strategic forces if the Soviets failed to accept a reasonable deal in SALT. Kissinger doubted that Congress, in the present political climate, would go along, which in turn would only weaken the US negotiating position. In his view, slowing the arms race by seeking unequal and offsetting aggregates through SALT was the best course. In the end, Ford decided to give preference to the equal aggregates approach advocated by the Joint Chiefs. Kissinger agreed that politically this was the best way to proceed, and it would preserve the only major East-West negotiation still intact. In back-channel negotiations, Kissinger would not take the previous offsetting asymmetries approach off the table but would focus on an equal aggregates agreement of 2,500 strategic launchers and 1,320 MIRV systems (Kissinger would initially propose a 2,200 ceiling). This approach would require a phased reduction in the total number of ICBMs, SLBMs, and heavy bombers. The numerical limits of the interim agreement would remain in effect without change until October 1977. By the end of 1983, both sides would reduce to 2,200 delivery systems, with no more than 250 heavy systems, including both heavy missiles and heavy bombers. The instructions still held out the goal of eventual reductions and limits on MIRVs and throw weight.[49]

After the typical wrangling among the superpower leaders and their aides at the Vladivostok summit in late November 1974, the United States and Soviet Union agreed on what became known as the Vladivostok Accord. The agreement was constituted in the form of confidential memoranda exchanged between Kissinger and Dobrynin on 10 December. As an executive agreement, it required no congressional approval. The interim agreement would remain in force until October 1977, when ostensibly a new agreement running until 31 December 1985 would replace it. Beginning in October 1977, each superpower would be limited to 2,400 central systems and 1,320 MIRV launchers. There was no full freedom to mix along with a right to modernize and replace systems.

Any mobile land-based ICBMs would be counted in the twenty-four hundred aggregate and likewise air-launched missiles with ranges above six hundred kilometers. No additional fixed land-based ICBM launchers would be allowed. Forward-based systems would not formally be included in the new agreement.[50]

President Ford cabled Secretary Schlesinger and the new Joint Chiefs chairman, army general George Brown, who had remained in Washington, that he expected their "full and unqualified support." That expectation went largely unfulfilled from many critics of the agreement.[51]

The Vladivostok Accord was intended to be a framework and placeholder for a more permanent agreement covering offensive forces that Ford and Brezhnev would sign at a summit meeting in the United States in 1975. Political and diplomatic realities soon set in and dimmed those prospects. On the one hand, moderates and liberals supported the accord but without enthusiasm. To them, SALT under Nixon and Ford had become a means to legitimize the continuing buildup and modernization of nuclear forces, fostering rather than slowing or eliminating the superpower arms race. As the accord was in the form of an executive agreement rather than a treaty, the Senate would not formally vote on the matter. But as Jackson had laid down a marker with his 1972 equal aggregates amendment, Senators Edward Kennedy (D-MA), Walter Mondale (D-MN), and Charles Mathias (R-MD) sponsored a resolution supporting Vladivostok but coupled it with a proposal for early negotiated reductions. Kissinger thought this impractical absent the leverage of a major US nuclear buildup beyond that currently planned (and which those senators were bound to oppose). In general, the Ford White House found itself confronted in Congress by powerful antidefense and anti-interventionist forces, who were disillusioned not only by what they regarded as the failure of SALT but by the immoral foreign policies of Nixon and Kissinger.[52]

More importantly, it became clear that the OSD and the Joint Chiefs, despite their formal support of Vladivostok, were hardly enthusiastic about the results and would soon set up bureaucratic roadblocks to Kissinger's plans to move forward. In November 1975, Ford fired Schlesinger on the grounds of general insubordination, including his alleged sabotage of SALT policy. Kissinger, however, was stripped of his position as national security advisor while remaining secretary of state. Schlesinger's replacement, Donald Rumsfeld, a former congressman and White

House aide, was also resistant to exploring a solution beyond Vladivostok, either on substantive grounds or because he was concerned about its adverse political effect on Ford's election campaign.[53]

The Soviets in Kissinger's mind further complicated matters by supporting the successful North Vietnamese offensive in 1975 and by using Cuban troops as proxies in a civil war in Angola. Congress refused to back the countermeasures that Kissinger believed essential to maintaining his carrots-and-sticks formula for détente. Faced by these conflicting political, strategic, and bureaucratic pressures Kissinger was unable to duplicate his virtuoso (or Machiavellian) performance in strategic arms control that prevailed in SALT I.

In the ensuing SALT II negotiations, the major stumbling blocks included the status of the new Soviet Backfire bomber, which had not been considered at Vladivostok. DoD took the position that it was a heavy bomber and thus should be counted as a strategic nuclear delivery vehicle. The anti-SALT coalition outside the government held this position very firmly. The Soviets argued that Backfire was designed as and had the capabilities of intermediate-range system and thus should be excluded from the strategic nuclear delivery vehicle limit. Kissinger and many officials outside of DoD thought that the Soviets had a strong argument.[54]

For their part, the Soviets sought to ban, or count as individual strategic nuclear delivery vehicles, any air-launched missile, cruise or ballistic, with a range greater than six hundred kilometers—which would effectively prohibit the planned US program to deploy air-launched cruise missiles on strategic bombers. Although there was only lukewarm support for the air-launched cruise missile program within DoD as a whole, OSD (particularly Deputy Secretary of Defense William Clements) resisted such restrictions, on the long-standing grounds that the United States should not forgo technologies in which it held an advantage. The State Department and U. Alexis Johnson argued that this was an opportunity to close off a new avenue in the arms race, one in which the Soviets were bound to catch up. Kissinger regarded the air-launched cruise missile as a potential bargaining chip that might be traded for Soviet concessions on such as the Backfire bomber. The two sides also differed on how to verify whether an ICBM was a MIRV or not and how to count MIRV systems, how to define a heavy missile, whether mobile ICBMs should be permitted, and a number of lesser issues. The Soviets resumed their efforts to capture FBSs by making those systems part of any future SALT negotiations and to limit US modernization programs, particularly a new strategic submarine.[55]

Over the following months, through Kissinger's meetings with Soviet leaders and the Geneva negotiations, the two sides worked unsuccessfully to narrow their many differences. Unfortunately a host of issues, notably Backfire and cruise missiles, continued to prove insoluble. Johnson favored signing an agreement that would consolidate that progress, setting those two major issues aside for the next round of SALT. He complained bitterly that DoD, especially hard-liners in OSD, in conjunction with antidétente forces grouped around Senator Jackson, had constantly put roadblocks in the way of further progress. Ford, in the midst of an election campaign, declined to commit the United States, and SALT II was held in stasis.[56]

The critics' position was given particular public credibility and policy coherence through the tireless efforts of Nitze. In the summer of 1974, Nitze had resigned his position on the SALT delegation after becoming increasingly frustrated with his inability to substantially affect the US negotiating position. Although he had supported the ABM Treaty and had played a major role in its development, he believed that the interim agreement contained dangerous flaws and ambiguities that the Soviets would be tempted to exploit. Nitze had publicly supported SALT I, with the reservation that such flaws must be addressed in the follow-on negotiations, or the strategic balance would deteriorate rapidly. In his opinion, the United States should not accept a future SALT agreement based on Vladivostok that would bar technological developments necessary to maintain crisis stability in the face of anticipated Soviet deployments.[57]

Senator Jackson also maintained his drumbeat against Kissinger, détente, and the direction of strategic arms control. He criticized Vladivostok for authorizing an unacceptably high level of MIRVs and up to six times Soviet advantage in throw weight—essentially sanctioning a ten-year arms buildup by the Soviets. If Congress accepted the administration's request to extend unlimited low-cost loans to the Soviet Union, he warned, the United States would essentially be subsidizing that buildup while being forced to pay for new strategic programs in response. He objected to the exclusion of the Soviet Backfire bomber from the aggregate ceilings and warned against Kissinger's reported plans to accept constraints on the range or number of air-launched cruise missiles, an area in which the United States held significant advantages. The proper course, he reaffirmed, was to insist on equal ceilings at sharply reduced levels. Jackson later chaired Senate hearings on SALT that featured prominent figures critical of the Vladivostok approach.[58]

In the end it would be up to Jimmy Carter—narrowly elected in November 1976—to pursue further progress in strategic arms control. After an abortive effort to seek deep reductions, the Carter administration's SALT II Treaty of May 1979 was built on the foundations of SALT I, Vladivostok, and the Ford administration's negotiating work. Initially, it appeared that the Senate would defeat the treaty's ratification (which required a two-thirds majority) or at least attach binding conditions— although the vote could have gone either way, depending on how conservative Democrats and moderate and liberal Republicans decided. After the Soviet invasion of Afghanistan in December 1979, however, Carter withdrew the agreement from consideration. In November 1980, the nation effectively decided the matter, and a new administration with a new approach to strategic arms control would have its chance. The entire SALT process in essence collapsed even though its opponents later felt compelled to continue with strategic arms control under another rubric.[59]

7

Reconciling Nuclear Testing with Arms Control

> I never thought that a test ban was any damn good. I didn't like the first
> one, nor do I like this one. I see the test ban pandering to the view that
> stopping testing will lead to a safer world.
>
> —President Nixon, June 1974

DURING THE first term, Nixon and Kissinger paid little attention to
proposed bilateral or multilateral negotiations to limit or ban nuclear
testing beyond what was restricted by the 1963 LTBT. They were preoccupied with Vietnam, the Middle East, the opening to China, Soviet-
American relations generally, and in the arms control arena with SALT.
The president and his national security adviser privately disparaged
President John F. Kennedy's accomplishment of an LTBT and compared
it unfavorably to what they regarded as their more productive approach
with SALT. Kissinger remarked on one occasion that "the advantage of
a summit, even if it gets a sort of half-baked SALT agreement, whatever
the SALT agreement is, it's a lot better than the nuclear test ban." Nixon
agreed.[1] They had no desire to overcome the continuing opposition of
the DoD and the AEC to further significant test limitations. They were
even willing to use nuclear tests as a means of signaling US resolve to the
Soviets and to domestic conservatives. During the second term, however, the White House proved willing to consider small steps toward
limiting nuclear testing that it believed would not harm US national security and might improve flagging prospects for détente with Moscow.[2]

Background to Nuclear Testing Issues

Despite the White House preoccupation with SALT and other major
foreign policy issues, the Nixon administration nonetheless found itself
addressing the question of further testing limitations especially during

the 1969 session of the ENCD. The Soviet Union had a long-standing proposal for a CTB treaty, but one from which it had the right to withdraw unless the ban were agreed to by the other nuclear powers. The United States regarded this as an exercise in propaganda that allowed the Soviets to posture as being on the side of the angels while knowing fully that China and France would not enter into such an agreement and would resent American pressure to do so. Washington also had to deal with proposals put forward by Japan, Canada, and Sweden for further limitations on nuclear testing.[3]

The Nixon administration inherited the public posture of previous administrations on limiting nuclear testing. That position was plagued by the same preconditions that stymied previous negotiations: the United States would be willing to negotiate a comprehensive ban if such an agreement could be adequately verified, but some degree of OSI would be a necessary supplement to remote technical means, such as seismic detection, to adequately verify a CTB. The Soviets had persistently rejected OSI. The US position provided cover for those in the US government who objected to further testing constraints for military and technical reasons and who also suspected that the Soviets would likely cheat on any agreement. By the time of Nixon's presidency, however, many government and independent experts argued that advances in seismology and satellite sensing technology permitted reliance on remote means for test ban verification. The State Department and ACDA favored actively exploring an agreement for a CTB, especially given US commitments under the NPT and other nuclear agreements but without pressuring other nations to sign. The Joint Chiefs of Staff, however, supported by the AEC, wanted to change US policy and reject a CTB outright. OSD concurred with the Joint Chiefs' technical objections to a test ban but preferred to stick with the current formula for political reasons.[4]

After a cursory review of the long-standing pros and cons during a March 1969 National Security Council meeting, the administration decided to maintain the extant policy on testing. Kissinger and AEC chairman Glenn Seaborg pointed out that two or three years would be needed to develop the ABM and MIRV warheads planned for the stockpile, and Seaborg noted that it was "desirable to be in a position to test our stockpile weapons of all kinds because we have found in the past a number of problems that made this necessary." Nixon concluded that the United States should lay out its former position and "let it rest there," to be followed by a full review of the consequences of maintaining the status quo, with the view of maintaining or modifying that position in the future. According to Seaborg, the president "indicated that if our national security depended in a very serious way on making weapons tests we would have to do so, even under the circumstances of a treaty." Generally, US policy toward possible nuclear testing constraints was subordinated to the massive interagency attention devoted to SALT.[5]

The test ban issue was further complicated by the interests of several nations, including the superpowers, in the possible peaceful nuclear explosions (PNEs). Those applications included stimulating the flow of natural gas from "tight" formation gas fields (impermeable, hard rock underground formations) and digging canals (a study was under way to determine whether a sea-level transisthmian canal in Central America could be built using nuclear explosions). The American Plowshares program would eventually detonate thirty-one nuclear devices in twenty-seven separate tests. The Soviets had an equivalent PNE program. Nixon, with his interest in supporting American development of technology, told Seaborg that he wanted Plowshares to have "a high priority in his administration; in fact, he said he has a special prejudice for this program—the way all people have special quirks and prejudices—and hopes it can go forward expeditiously."[6]

NPT and Environmental Concerns

The question of PNEs also became intertwined with the administration's approach to NPT ratification. Nixon had inherited a request by Australia, a close American ally, involving a PNE project at Keraudren Bay in the northwest part of that country. If the project was approved, the United States would provide nuclear devices and technical support for a series of detonations several hundred feet below the ocean floor in that region. The purpose would be to build a harbor for ships to enter to receive iron ore from the interior for transport to other ports. Brazil, Japan, and Israel had also expressed interest in PNEs. Article V of the NPT held that if practical applications of PNEs were developed by nuclear weapons states, such applications must be made available to all parties on a nondiscriminatory basis. If the United States did not follow up on this commitment, PNE advocates argued that a number of countries might not adhere to the NPT and even develop their own nuclear capabilities for military purposes under the guise of PNEs.[7]

Given the environmental hazards of nuclear explosions of any kind, antitesting critics challenged the dubious economic and scientific benefits of PNEs. From an arms control and security standpoint, such activities arguably provided the superpowers with the means clandestinely to work around restrictions on nuclear testing and would undermine the NPT by giving would-be proliferators an avenue to develop a nuclear capability. There was also the question of whether PNEs would require modification of the LTBT, which prohibited carrying out underground "any nuclear weapon test explosion, or any other explosion . . . if such explosion causes radioactive debris to be present outside the territorial limits of the State under whose jurisdiction or control such explosion is conducted." The United States and the Soviet Union had accused each other of violating the treaty by releasing excessive amounts during their respective underground weapons testing programs, but neither side agreed precisely on how much release would constitute a violation or the technical means by which this would be determined.[8]

Using nuclear explosives for the purposes of excavating close to the surface increased the likelihood of radioactive release. Having third parties involved in PNE programs was bound to complicate matters further. The release of some radioactive debris across national boundaries in Central America was thought likely to occur in the construction of a transisthmian canal, for instance. The Joint Chiefs also expressed concern that efforts to amend the LTBT would open backdoor efforts to negotiate a CTB treaty, with exception made for PNEs.[9]

Interagency Review

In June 1969, Nixon ordered the NSC Under Secretaries Committee to review the annual underground nuclear test program and quarterly requests for authorization of specific scheduled tests, specifically with an eye to whether they might violate the LTBT. The AEC and DoD were enjoined to make every effort to avoid tests that might be regarded as a violation but with a caveat: "If the Atomic Energy Commission or the Secretary of Defense believes after careful study that a particular test should remain in the program despite the possibility that it might give rise to a claimed violation of the [Limited] Nuclear Test Ban Treaty, the sponsoring agency will submit the test for review by the Under Secretaries' Committee." In other words, the president was prepared to allow national security or economic considerations to override arms control treaty restrictions. The Under Secretaries Committee reported in November that amendment of the treaty would probably be the best long-term solution, with technical discussions with the Soviets on PNEs to be resumed at an early date.[10]

As it turned out, declining international interest in PNEs largely removed LTBT modification from the diplomatic table. The Australian government canceled the Keraudren Bay project, and the final report of the Atlantic-Pacific Interoceanic Canal Study Commission recommended against the nuclear excavation option. The United States and the Soviet Union continued their bilateral disputes over radiation release in weapons tests, such as the US Baneberry event (the code name for a nuclear test). AEC chairman Seaborg was of the view that domestic environmental concerns were likely to supplant those of possible LTBT constraints. He noted that the president was under domestic political pressure to cancel any nuclear test, whether weapons related or a PNE, if opponents claimed that environmental damage would result. Nixon, according to Seaborg, had approved a high-yield Milrow weapons test in Alaska only at the last moment, and he was concerned that the Plowshares program would be dealt a great setback if the president felt compelled to cancel the upcoming Sturtevant PNE test in Nevada.[11]

In the summer of 1971, after what ACDA and other arms control advocates thought was a long delay, the president finally ordered a formal policy review through NSSM 128 of nuclear testing and the benefits and costs of testing restrictions, including a comprehensive ban, a moratorium, quotas, and a threshold ban. ACDA director Gerard Smith had recommended the review in light of congressional and international pressures against testing, including growing environmental concerns, especially over the US planned high-yield Cannikin nuclear test in Alaska. Smith contended that progress in SALT had been sufficient to allow an evaluation of the relationship of SALT to various test ban options. The March 1969 NSC decision to maintain current US policy on nuclear testing had suggested that a CTB treaty might be more attractive after 1972, once testing on US MIRVs and ABM warheads had been completed.[12]

The NSSM 128 review focused on the arguments for and against a possible comprehensive ban, assessed the strategic impact of the ban and of the verification issues, and analyzed various policy options. The review offered no specific policy recommendations but, according to an analysis by the NSC staff, concluded that on balance most of the military-technical concerns about the adverse effects of a CTB on the US nuclear posture were not justified: "A CTB is not likely to make any significant difference to ours—or to the Soviet's—strategic deterrent capability, given currently projected forces and threats over the next decade. Whether or not there is further nuclear testing to develop new strategic warheads, both sides will retain substantial and well-hedged assured destruction capabilities." The interagency review further added that "verification of a CTB by national means alone is technically feasible with high confidence." The State Department supported an initiative to move toward an eventual CTB. They contended that a comprehensive ban would buttress SALT by constraining sophisticated Soviet MIRVs and any upgrade of its air defense network to give it an ABM capability. A CTB was also politically desirable in terms of reinforcing US nonproliferation objectives and lessening the tensions and instabilities alleged to arise from the arms race effects of nuclear testing.[13]

The Joint Chiefs of Staff objected vehemently to this line of analysis. Over the past decade, they argued, "the erosion of US technological superiority has been constrained only through the intensive efforts of its nuclear weapon designers and laboratories and through underground test programs." Without such a program, "the US Armed Forces could not confidently exploit advanced nuclear weapons technology which offers many design improvements, such as tailored outputs, selectable yields, reduced size, reduced cost and more efficient use of nuclear material, reduced maintenance, increased safety and reliability, and improved command and control devices. For the foreseeable future, underground nuclear testing will continue to be mandatory, as weapon systems dependability can be confirmed only through such testing. Untested weaponry would erode confidence in US deterrent forces, thereby seriously jeopardizing national survival." The Joint Chiefs also questioned whether a CTB treaty could be adequately verified: "The opportunity exists under a CTBT for potential enemies to gain significant and unpredictable advantages (particularly by clandestine testing) which would be impossible to assess if the United States were not permitted to test."

The Joint Chiefs also argued that continued testing would be necessary to compensate for constraints that the United States might accept in a future SALT agreement: "Any strategic arms limitation agreement will reduce US strategic flexibility and increase the importance of qualitative improvements to weapon systems. Of particular consequence is the Soviet advantage in missile throw-weight, which may permit the Soviets more flexibility than the United States in further improving their systems without requiring nuclear testing. Also, in view of possible Soviet abrogation of proposed strategic arms limitation agreements, ongoing weapons research and development programs, as well as testing, would become increasingly important."[14]

Phillip Odeen of the NSC staff characterized Joint Chiefs' argument to Kissinger as "highly charged" and "emotional." He continued, "It mixes genuine implications and uncertainties concerning a nuclear test ban with unsubstantiated assertions, irrelevancies and debatable assumptions." However, he and Kissinger did not feel that there was any compelling reason to move forward with a CTB treaty at present. He believed it might create a difficult political issue for the president in the upcoming election and complicate the ratification of a SALT agreement by the Senate. Another option—a threshold test ban—would lead inevitably to greater pressures for a CTB but only over a long period of time. "If we really do not want a full test ban now but feel it desirable to make a forward move for political reasons, this could be an attractive option."[15]

Nixon and Kissinger, consumed as they were with SALT on the arms control front, were not inclined to move forward with even a TTB. They also saw the advantages of continued testing in buttressing what they regarded as a shaky political position among defense conservatives.

Cannikin Test Controversy

During the summer and autumn of 1971, President Nixon and his closest advisers devoted numerous Oval Office conversations to issues surrounding an underground nuclear weapons test scheduled to take place beneath the Aleutian island of Amchitka, Alaska, and its implications for nuclear arms control. The test, designated "Cannikin," was a high-yield

The Baneberry underground nuclear test at the Nevada Test Site inadvertently released radioactivity to the atmosphere, 18 December 1970. (Nevada National Security Site, Department of Energy)

event associated with the development of the Spartan warhead for the US Safeguard ABM system. The AEC considered the expected yield too large to be contained by the Nevada test site, so it was moved to a location in the Aleutians, where several nuclear tests had previously occurred.

Opponents filed a lawsuit in federal court (*Committee for Nuclear Responsibility v. Schlesinger*), charging that the test was being conducted without adequate review as mandated by the newly enacted National Environmental Policy Act. Some experts warned that the explosion might trigger earthquakes or tsunamis, but the environmentalists' complaints centered on the long-term aftereffects of radiation leakage. Arms control groups argued that the test would spur the offense-defense arms race and violate the LTBT, which prohibited nuclear testing in the atmosphere, underwater, and in outer space. Other foreign policy experts warned about the adverse political effects of conducting a nuclear weapon test adjacent to Soviet territory, especially at a sensitive juncture in SALT. To support their case, environmental groups sought evidence that six federal agencies, including the Departments of State and Interior and the Environmental Protection Agency, had lodged serious objections to the Cannikin test, ranging from environmental and health concerns to legal and diplomatic problems. The AEC's final environmental impact statement on the Amchitka test, however, concluded that Cannikin represented a vital part of the US weapons development program. The environmental impact statement characterized potential environmental threats as small and inconsequential.[16]

High-ranking Alaska state officials, including Governor William A. Egan and Senator Mike Gravel, both Democrats, objected strongly to the test. Egan sponsored several public hearings that included critical testimony by scientific and environmental experts. In the US Senate, Gravel sought to curtail or cancel entirely funding for Cannikin from the AEC's FY 1972 budget. He attracted the support of nearly forty senators, which was not sufficient to secure passage of the implementing amendment. Rhode Island Democrat John O. Pastore unsuccessfully offered an amendment to delay the test "unless the President gives his direct approval." In the House, Representative Patsy Mink (D-HI) attempted to amend another funding bill by eliminating expenditures for nuclear testing in the vicinity of Amchitka. In the final vote, the proposal was defeated 275 to 108.[17]

Despite these objections, Nixon was eager for the Amchitka test to proceed. The White House recordings about the Amchitka nuclear test reveal much about Nixon's view of the relationship between national security, arms control, and his domestic political situation heading into the 1972 election. In a discussion with Kissinger on 3 August 1971, Nixon sought confirmation that the Pentagon and the AEC were aware that he had directly approved the test. The president also disparaged the environmental concerns. Nixon had been told that the test was necessary to complete development of the Safeguard ABM system and that any delay would set that program back substantially. He believed that the nation's ABM program was one of the few negotiating levers the United States held in SALT. Nixon and Kissinger were prepared to delay the test and its public announcement briefly but only for tactical reasons related to SALT. They discussed putting off the test for a few days if it conflicted with the announcement of a summit meeting with the Soviet Union. Neither man seemed to think that this was a major diplomatic problem, however, certainly not one that justified a delay of weeks.[18]

Nixon's most frequently cited private reason for pushing ahead with the Cannikin test was his determination to reestablish his political credibility with conservatives outside the administration. Throughout 1971 he had prodded Kissinger and other officials to brief key conservative figures such as William F. Buckley and Ronald Reagan about the administration's defense and arms control policies. These briefings had two purposes. First, Nixon wanted to encourage conservatives to support the administration on contentious defense issues. He and Kissinger complained repeatedly that conservatives had deserted their posts instead of making a public case for controversial programs such as ABMs, which they regarded as an essential bargaining chip in the strategic arms control negotiations. Second, in anticipation of diplomatic breakthroughs with Russia and China, and a SALT agreement, Nixon sought to inoculate himself against accusations that he had become soft on national security. Nixon explained to Kissinger, Press Secretary Ronald Ziegler and White House Chief of Staff H. R. Haldeman on 27 October, the day that the AEC announced a date for the Cannikin test: "Yeah, I have made the decision. It'll be announced at two o'clock today. Now incidentally, you [Zeigler] know the significance of that? You don't, you don't realize it, or maybe you do, that helps us . . . on the right. . . . See? Because they've all thought we weren't going to do it."[19]

In the meantime, the matter had reached the US Supreme Court. Attorney General John Mitchell warned Nixon that the decision was likely to be close. The nominations of two Nixon appointees, William Rehnquist and Lewis Powell Jr., were still pending in the Senate. Had those two men been on the Court, Mitchell told Nixon, the issue would not have been a problem, implying his expectation that Rehnquist and Powell would have ruled in favor of the government. To Nixon's relief, on 6 November 1971, the day that the Cannikin nuclear device was scheduled to be detonated, the Court declined in a 4–3 decision to issue an injunction to stop the test while the matter was reviewed by the lower courts.[20]

Several days after the test, on 10 November, Nixon spoke by telephone with Senator Barry Goldwater (R-AZ) to stress his continued toughness on national defense and determination to proceed with programs such as ABM. Nixon used the Cannikin test as an example of his strong position:

PRESIDENT NIXON: Good. Let me say one other thing on the Amchitka thing. You know, going forward and that was essential, because if we hadn't our ABM and everything was down the tube you know for a year.

GOLDWATER: I know it.

PRESIDENT NIXON: So we did it. And it didn't blow up the Arctic and the seals are still swimming.

GOLDWATER: Well, you told me last August you were going to go through with that and I'm damn proud of you for—

PRESIDENT NIXON: I wish you'd tell some of our good . . . because you have stroke with them, you know . . . the conservative friends like [columnist William F. or Senator James] Buckley and others that goddamn it, I'm no disarmer. You know, I'm fighting. As you know, it's the Congress that's trying to disarm, Barry. I'm not.

GOLDWATER: Plus what you inherited: 10 years of no development.

PRESIDENT NIXON: Well, 10 years of [Defense Secretary Robert S.] Mc-Namara for Christ's sakes.

GOLDWATER: Right.

PRESIDENT NIXON: The Russians have caught us now. Now we're just— and listen, if we don't get arms control—Kissinger just walked in— let me tell you, we're going to turn. We're going to start going. I can prove you. I can tell you that.

GOLDWATER: We're going to have to.[21]

On 17 November, Kissinger had breakfast with California governor Ronald Reagan in Washington. Reagan had just returned from a trip to East Asia he had taken at the White House's request. Kissinger reported to Nixon the substance of their discussion. Reagan warned Kissinger about Nixon's political problems with the conservatives and urged Nixon to meet with them in small groups. Kissinger said he had responded to Reagan by pointing out the failure of conservatives to support the administration's foreign policy. "I really let him have it on the international situation," Kissinger told Nixon. "I went through the Jordan crisis, Cienfuegos, Cambodia, Laos. I said, 'How can you say a liberal doesn't make a difference? We wouldn't have MIRV, we wouldn't have ABM, we wouldn't have had Cambodia. . . . We wouldn't have had Amchitka.'"[22]

In White House conversations later that month, Nixon made the startling claim that he had been prepared to defy the Court and order the test to proceed if the injunction had been granted. Nixon reminded Kissinger of a conversation on 6 November, prior to the Court's decision, in which the president had said he would order the test to proceed even if the Court issued an injunction, unless the decision against the government was unanimous:

KISSINGER: You said to me that if—unless—that if the Supreme Court voted against it, you'd go ahead anyway, unless it were unanimous.
PRESIDENT NIXON: That's right. I decided that morning.
KISSINGER: You said that to me that morning.
PRESIDENT NIXON: Of course, because the Supreme Court had no goddamn right to determine this. And I was perfectly prepared to go through, and all hell would've broken loose, and I would have done it.[23]

Throughout November 1971, Nixon continued his rants against the threat that the Supreme Court might have ordered a halt to the test. He brought it up with Reagan and Mitchell when he met with them to hear the California governor's East Asian trip report. At one point, Mitchell mentioned problems that the administration was having with the Supreme Court nominees in the Senate and the need to spur Senate majority leader Mike Mansfield (D-MT) to expedite the process. This prompted Nixon to bring up the Amchitka test:

Well, I put it right to him [apparently referring to Senator Mike Mansfield]. I told him—that is to digress a minute—I said that, "Look, we had that 4-3 decision on Amchitka [unclear word or phrase in audio], you know. For chrissakes, most of the Court had turned around and said we couldn't fire a blast.' . . . The environmentalists—anyway, what has happened here is just nuts. The Supreme Court of the United States comes down 4-3 on that issue. Now, I would have had to exceed the

Constitution—there would have been a hell of a difficult problem if they'd have ruled the other way. That day, I would, in the public mind, have had to follow it. Although on national security grounds I would overrule them. But could you imagine the storm that would have arisen all over this country? The President overruled the Supreme Court of the United States, which I was prepared to do.[24]

And on 22 November, Nixon, Kissinger, and Goldwater met in the Oval Office, at which point Nixon made another assertion about his intention to ignore the Supreme Court had it ruled against the administration:

> And I said, I told Henry that morning, I said, 'I don't give a goddamn what the Court does. We're going to go forward with that test because I found that if we didn't, we'd drop a year behind in the ABM. Also it could ruin our negotiations with the Soviets.' Not one conservative spoke up, saying, 'Thank God that the President went ahead with that test.' I don't mean Barry Goldwater—what I mean—not [*National Review* editor and columnist] Bill Buckley, all these guys, what the hell's the matter with them? Why don't they attack the liberals?[25]

According to Nixon's recollection, he had told Kissinger of his decision just before the Court's decision was issued. There is no evidence that Nixon ordered any staff work to implement such an action. No legal briefs were apparently prepared. The president often gave precipitous orders to the White House staff and government officials that were never acted upon. That said, it is not inconceivable that Nixon might have decided, for political and perceived national security reasons, to take the plunge and issue such an executive order. What would have happened at that point—how the order would have been received by the Pentagon, the Atomic Energy Commission, and the Justice Department, much less by the Congress, the press, and the public—is a fascinating trip down a road not taken.

The controversy over the Cannikin test continued well after the event. Environmental and antinuclear groups became aware of administration documents that warned about the adverse effects of the detonation. Those documents, known as the Cannikin papers, were later cited as evidence for what critics called the continuing pattern of secrecy and cover-up that typified the nation's nuclear testing program. Legal actions concerning the health of local citizens and workers and accusations about long-term environmental damage continued for years to come.[26]

Toward the Threshold Test Ban Treaty

The issue of nuclear testing limits was revived in early 1974, as the Watergate-weakened White House struggled to develop means that would preserve détente and keep the SALT II negotiations moving forward. In February 1974, the Soviets approached Nixon and Kissinger with several proposals in this area: another variant of their long-standing CTB treaty proposal; a moratorium on nuclear testing; or some sort of TTB, which might include placing a quota on the number of permitted tests. During Kissinger's visit to Moscow in March, Brezhnev proposed a bilateral TTB, limiting the yield of tests, which would avoid the complications of dealing with France and China.[27]

Kissinger was interested in exploring a TTB treaty, even though he acknowledged that its arms control utility was limited. One of Kissinger's aides wrote that "the TTB, like the other alternatives, would be relatively meaningless in its contribution to national security. Nor would it receive significant support from domestic political elements pushing for a CTB. It must be understood for what it is—essentially a cosmetic agreement with little real significance." But with the prospects for a comprehensive and permanent SALT agreement on offensive forces waning, Kissinger found it encouraging that the Soviets were not willing to give up on the process entirely and were willing to drop their insistence that other nuclear powers agree. He argued that the Soviets were more dependent on high-yield weapons than the United States and therefore that limiting test yields on balance favored Washington. The Soviets would over time be encouraged to move toward lower-yield warheads, which would limit the technical advantages they held because of their superior throw weight. A bilateral treaty should not cause major difficulties with France or China. There could be a major advance in verification and a precedent for OSI if the Soviet Union revealed its test sites, agreed to test at no other site, and supplied information about the geological formations at each site to permit the United States to calibrate its equipment.[28]

In February 1974 to prepare for future discussions with the Soviets, Nixon directed a broad review of US policy on nuclear testing through NSSM 195, the first assessment since 1971–72. The review was conducted by an ad hoc group composed of representatives from DoD, the Department of State, CIA, ACDA, the AEC, and NSC staff. Meanwhile, Washington and Moscow opened technical talks to work out details for any testing limitation. The initial US idea was to set a limit based on a maximum seismic level, but this was replaced by a ceiling defined in terms of the yield of the weapon. To this point, the US government had never systematically examined what threshold would be acceptable and negotiable; an early guess put it at five to fifty kilotons.[29]

Nixon's directive and the technical talks with Moscow set off interagency debate over what types of testing limits were verifiable and acceptable on national security grounds and how the PNE "loophole" should be addressed. The Soviets initially proposed two thresholds, one below three kilotons and the other at one hundred to two hundred kilotons, with a high quota in the "sandwich" and no restraint below three kilotons. Within the US government, ACDA favored limiting the threshold to 100 kilotons for actual yield and 150 for collateral yield, allowing two tests each year between 100 and 150 kilotons and making the ban effective on 1 January 1975.[30]

Kissinger's sanguine assessment of the low risk of entering a TTB regime was challenged by elements in DoD. Chief of Naval Operations admiral Elmo Zumwalt and the AEC also opposed a threshold ban along the lines being considered. It was no coincidence, the skeptics argued, that the Soviets had made their proposal after completing a series of nuclear tests that would allow them to modernize their high-yield missile warheads, such as those designed for the SS-18 ICBM but before the United States could test its planned new warheads, such as those intended for the Minuteman III ICBM and the Trident II SLBM. A TTB could well represent the next step in a slippery slope that would lead to a CTB treaty, which DoD and the AEC continued to oppose.[31]

In the end, the Joint Chiefs recommended allowing tests that measured up to a design yield of 150 kilotons, which would require a threshold around 195 kilotons, corresponding to 5.8 on the Richter scale; permitting five tests to exceed the threshold annually over five years, providing that any threshold treaty also covered the subject of PNEs and ensuring compliance through "unambiguous monitoring," probably involving at least five collocated seismic stations. They insisted on delaying the start of a ban until July 1976, to give the United States sufficient time to test its new warheads at the full intended yield. Deputy Secretary

William Clements and Dixie Lee Ray, chair of the AEC, endorsed these recommendations.[32]

On 10 June 1974, Nixon approved seeking a threshold of "at least" one hundred kilotons—if the Soviets would supply enough geological information to aid verification and restrict their testing to specific sites. There could be an allowance for "no more than two unintended and slight breaches of the threshold per year"—although not, as the Soviets had proposed, a quota between an upper and a lower threshold. PNEs, with the same threshold limitations, would be permitted only if the Soviets furnished enough information to allow verification. Finally, a ban should take effect no earlier than 1 January 1976. He ordered DoD and AEC to develop a program that would finish essential testing above one hundred kilotons before that time.[33]

The Joint Chiefs objected that they saw "potential to do serious harm to U.S. security interests" and feared impairing the prospects for satisfactory SALT II negotiations. Restraints at or near the levels and date specified by Nixon's directive would affect US more than Soviet weaponry and "significantly restrict if not preclude" efforts to develop a nuclear policy of flexible and limited response. For these reasons, they asked the president to look again at DoD and AEC recommendations. During the NSC meeting on 20 June 1974, Secretary of Defense James Schlesinger summarized this line of argument:

> As a general proposition, if you look only at military considerations, ignoring basic foreign policy considerations, the threshold test ban is more advantageous to the Soviet Union than the U.S. First, the Soviet Union has considerable throw weight to be exploited. We have utilized our technology—accuracies and yield-to-weight ratios—and we have kept down our throw weight. This technology option is closed by a threshold test ban. Second, the Soviet Union has recently concentrated on high yields, and we haven't. Threshold test ban would permit the Soviets to operate in an area we have been exploiting, but prohibit us operating in the area they have been exploiting. Again, these are purely military considerations.[34]

Schlesinger added that "the difference to us in a threshold between 75 and 150 kilotons is not very great. It may be advantageous to the U.S. to have a lower rather than higher threshold. . . . Improvement of weapons technology is no longer the pacing item in weapons development. Even if we stopped testing entirely, we would not be severely damaged. We would have been in the 50s but not now. The important measures are accuracy and RV (reentry vehicle) development."

Nixon was blunt about his own views on any sort of test ban:

> I never thought that a test ban was any damn good. I didn't like the first one, nor do I like this one. I see the test ban pandering to the view that stopping testing will lead to a safer world. But we have to be realistic, and the world and the U.S. public believe the test ban is a great goal worth achieving in itself. In that context, if we can do something with no appearance of any inequality, maybe we can negotiate an agreement. We have to remember that they will do whatever is allowed, but we will not do as much as we are allowed. Restraints which we can negotiate are restraints on them which they would not do themselves. The U.S. will restrain itself, but the Soviet Union has no such restraints built in. From a pragmatic standpoint, we should realize that this is going to take quite a bit of doing.[35]

At the Moscow summit in late June and early July 1974, the Soviets unexpectedly returned to their full CTB treaty proposal, arguing among other things that it would help retard nuclear proliferation. Nixon countered that Congress would not ratify such a test ban agreement. He assured Soviet leaders that he appreciated the value of a comprehensive ban but sought to get to that point by different means, through a step-by-step process. There was some confusion on the American side as to its exact position on the yield threshold. Nixon proposed a 100 kiloton limit but before the Soviets could respond, Kissinger changed the US offer to 150 kilotons (the night before, he had consulted with Washington on this point, and Schlesinger had insisted on not going below that level).[36]

With the president making it clear that a CTB was out of the question, on 3 July 1974, after lengthy discussions between Kissinger and Gromyko, who consulted with diplomatic and technical experts, Nixon and Brezhnev signed a TTB treaty prohibiting underground tests with yields exceeding 150 kilotons, beginning 31 March 1976. A separate protocol provided for exchanges of data about test sites. The two leaders also agreed to seek an agreement on PNEs at "the earliest possible time." Secretary Kissinger informed the Soviets that the US Senate would undoubtedly reject the treaty unless a satisfactory PNE agreement accompanied it.[37]

Upon his return to the United States from the Soviet Union the evening of 3 July, Nixon addressed the nation at 7:45 p.m. from Loring Air Force Base in Limestone, Maine. Putting his personal disdain for the TTB treaty aside, he described agreement in grandiose terms: "It extends significantly the earlier steps toward limiting tests that began with the 1963 test-ban treaty. . . . This is not only another major step toward bringing the arms race under control, it is also a significant additional step toward reducing the number of nuclear and thermonuclear explosions in the world."[38]

The US-Soviet agreement on a partial test ban treaty was contingent on finding some way to accommodate PNEs without leaving a loophole to get around the threshold for military purposes. The matter had been further complicated in May 1974 when India unexpectedly detonated a nuclear device (see chapter 5). The Indian government explained that it did so "in order to keep India abreast of the technology concerning peaceful uses of nuclear energy for such purposes as mining and earth moving," and that "India remains absolutely committed against the use of nuclear energy for military purposes." The Soviets accepted the Indian account but Washington was skeptical. The demonstration of a nuclear capability by India—which Kissinger regarded as a virtual Soviet ally—was bound to have geopolitical repercussions and affect the nonproliferation regime. It would make it easier for other nations to follow suit with a "prestige PNE" of their own or to develop a weapon. Pakistan was the most likely candidate to do so; at the very least, it might demand greater military assistance from the United States. Although the Chinese registered no immediate protest, perhaps concerned with protecting their own right to test, there remained the long-term prospect of a nuclear arms race between the two Asian giants. The administration, however, took a relatively relaxed position toward the Indian nuclear program, which caused considerable political criticism, especially in Congress.[39]

After Nixon: Fate of Further Bans on Nuclear Testing

Washington and Moscow began discussions on a PNE agreement in October 1974, after Nixon's resignation. The Soviets pushed for a threshold for individual PNEs that exceeded the 150 kiloton limit of the TTB treaty, as well as a higher yield allowance for multiple tests. Kissinger was well aware of the pressures within the US government to hold at the 150 kiloton threshold and to insist on a detailed verification regime, including OSIs. As two NSC staffers wrote: "This consensus is reinforced by considerable congressional opposition to the TTB, based in large part on the belief that allowing PNEs above the threshold is a serious verification loophole and contrary to our nonproliferation interests. Unless the PNE agreement has tight verification constraints and either bans or stringently limits PNEs above the threshold, there will be serious difficulty in getting the TTB and the PNE agreement through the Senate. This difficulty will be compounded if the PNE agreement legitimizes PNEs for excavation purposes, since this would require eventual relaxation and amendment of the LTBT." The Joint Chiefs expressed their strong concern that the Soviets were planning to gain military benefits from PNEs; they doubted that verification of peaceful intent was possible, even with prior notification and OSI, although this might prevent "gross" violations.[40]

In April 1976, Soviet and American negotiators reached an agreement that kept the 150-kiloton limit, while allowing for an aggregate yield of 1,500 kilotons for multiple explosions. They committed themselves not to carry out any group explosion having an aggregate yield exceeding 150 kilotons unless the individual explosions in the group could be identified and measured by agreed verification procedures. A detailed protocol specified the advance exchanges of the technical data that would help verify the size of proposed explosions. The Soviets, however, were effectively permitted to veto the presence of observers. The NSC staff, on Kissinger's behalf, had apparently overruled the Joint Chiefs on this last point. In any case, General George Brown endorsed the proposed PNE treaty and protocol. He based his concurrence on assurances by the Energy Research and Development Administration, which had taken over the nuclear weapons functions of the former AEC, that verification procedures were adequate. Ford and Brezhnev signed the treaty documents during their Moscow summit meeting in May 1976.[41]

The Ford administration submitted both the PNE and TTB treaties to the Senate in July 1976, but that body took no action. President Ford chose not to expend political capital to seek their approval. He was in the middle of a bitter primary battle for the Republican presidential nomination with Reagan, who based his campaign in large part on a rejection of the Nixon-Kissinger-Ford policies of détente. Once he gained the nomination, Ford needed to find some way to bring his conservative critics into the fold for the general election. Those critics had no intention of giving the president a political victory in the field of arms control.

There was also no political enthusiasm to ratify the treaties by moderates and liberals. Many arms control advocates had concluded that the approach followed by the Nixon and Ford administrations accommodated and even encouraged the arms race by legitimizing plans that both superpower military establishments intended to follow anyway and by showing tepid support of the NPT. If the United States was serious about arms control, it should have sought in good faith to negotiate a CTB, including a ban on PNEs, rather than a threshold limit that did not effectively constrain either superpower, let alone other nations. Therefore, although the arms control community did not actively oppose the agreements, neither was it prepared to expend political capital on their behalf to ensure ratification, given they fell far short of the CTB treaty they sought.

Efforts to halt nuclear testing had been under way for decades before Nixon took office. The LTBT, disparaged by the Nixon White House, had achieved the first milestone by halting nuclear tests in the air, sea, and outer space. Nixon (and Kissinger) achieved the next steps with partial limits placed on underground testing through the TTB and PNE treaties. Yet the final but elusive goal of a total ban on nuclear testing would fall to subsequent administrations, with some of those actively seeking to dismantle even the initial milestones towards a CTB treaty. The value of the Nixon (and Ford) partial test ban treaties, then, remains nebulous. Were they cosmetic window dressing that even one of Kissinger's own aides admitted—a treaty with no meaningful significance? Or were they a step on a slippery slope that might eventuate in a CTB treaty as the military establishment contended? The tortuous path toward a CTB treaty that remains to this day unratified suggests that the answer remains unclear.

8

Legacies and Implications

> We've had the Non-Proliferation Treaty, the Biological Warfare, that Sea-
> beds, but with all the arms limitation in the world there's still enough
> arms left to blow up the world many times over. What we need is re-
> straint on the part of the great powers.
>
> —President Nixon, April 1972

BY THE time President Nixon left office under the cloud of the Watergate scandal, he left a record of WMD arms control and nonproliferation treaties that surpassed in number all of his predecessors and
would exceed many presidential administrations to come. The Nixon
era was pivotal for US policies to curb the growth and spread of WMD.
In particular, his administration accumulated several enduring layers
of WMD controls, including frameworks for future arms agreements
and the development of behavioral norms: bilateral US-Soviet (Russian)
limits on the number and character of nuclear forces; further constraints
on nuclear testing; selective implementation of an international nuclear
nonproliferation regime; the successful pursuit of an international ban
on a category of WMD, biological weapons, begun as a unilateral US
initiative; and a willingness to address specific transnational environmental WMD concerns such as the Seabed Treaty.

Some of these layers were accumulated because of public pressures,
others in the pursuit of larger diplomatic objectives, and still others
because of initiatives from relatively low levels of the US government.
They did not amount to a comprehensive WMD control policy even
though Nixon and Kissinger insisted on centralized White House control of the policy-making process and an integrated approach to national
security. Despite the impressive number of agreements signed or ratified during his presidency, Nixon left a mixed legacy on WMD controls.
Arms control and nonproliferation as we know it today came to practical maturity during a presidency that prided itself on realism, perhaps

cynicism, especially when it came to the articulation of the purpose and value of those WMD controlling mechanisms.

There is no simple, definitive answer to explain these complexities and seeming paradoxes. Each facet of the Nixonian WMD control patchwork, and their legacies, has a distinctive narrative. That said, none of these non-SALT arms control policies occurred in isolation from the others. To be sure, the White House's attention was directed primarily and at times exclusively toward SALT, but "lesser" agreements were also pursued or implemented during Nixon's tenure. Most of the historiography of either the Nixon administration or of the history of arms control agreements makes only passing reference to a host of initiatives that came to fruition during his presidency. We have attempted to demonstrate that this is unfortunate both for understanding the Nixon-Kissinger approach to arms control and for insight into the trajectory of US government policies toward combatting all categories of WMD.

We offer a perspective that shows their hierarchy of priorities. For example, in one White House recording, Nixon summed up his contempt for what he perceived as his smaller arms control efforts: "We've had the Non-Proliferation Treaty, the Biological Warfare, that Seabeds, but with all the arms limitation in the world there's still enough arms left to blow up the world many times over. What we need is restraint on the part of the great powers."[1] For the president the specter of global nuclear war outweighed the ancillary threats posed by other forms of WMD. But the statement also reflects Nixon's somewhat disingenuous belief that there must be a "generation of peace" based on great power restraint, moving away from an era of Cold War crises and conflicts. Diplomacy was critical to this process, but to be effective and enduring, agreements must accurately reflect a balance of national interests and power. Restraint would lead to arms control, but arms control isolated from restraint would be ephemeral. Treaties and understandings could not be ends in themselves but only a means to that end. Nixon and Kissinger evaluated the efficacy and relative importance of various WMD controls in that light.

For Nixon, a "generation of peace," based on a stable balance of power, also required the continued commitment of the United States to international engagement, a strong military, and a willingness to counter the Soviets and their proxies when they behaved in an unrestrained fashion. Nixon acknowledged that there was an imperative to reorder and reduce commitments abroad. But the president feared that the general public, in the wake of Vietnam, was losing heart for international leadership of any sort and that the Eastern establishment had capitulated to defeatism, at home and abroad. This required in his view a deft political strategy, to reassure the public—and congressional moderates—that "peace was at hand," while also maintaining support for essential defense programs. For the latter, Nixon relied on his conservative base, which required reassurance that he was not "giving away the store" to the Soviets or the United Nations. And Nixon, ever the political animal, felt that the antiwar, antidefense tide could suddenly flow in the opposite direction, outflanking him on the right. Nixon and Kissinger thus evaluated the efficacy and relative importance of various WMD controls in light of this kaleidoscope of domestic public opinion, as well as their international effects.

It was during Nixon's presidency that public awareness of chemical and biological weapons intensified, ending the shroud of secrecy that had enveloped the US CBW programs. It was a series of CW incidents that aroused congressional, scientific, and general public outrage. The administration simply followed with initially limited action to placate that outrage. Nixon's unilateral abnegation in November 1969 of offensive biological and toxin weapons was the first time that a major power unilaterally abandoned an entire category of armament. That eventually led to the negotiation of the BWC. Nixon saw an opportunity to score major political points with his surprise announcement, which he thought still protected US national security, since the United States retained its defensive BW capacity as well as its ability to deter or respond with nuclear weapons.

The focus of Nixon and Kissinger on SALT allowed elements of the bureaucracy room to maneuver to define or change policies with respect to other WMD controls. The decoupling of BW from CW was the result of paradoxically savvy maneuvering by Secretary of Defense Melvin Laird. While Nixon administration policy makers ultimately agreed that the military utility of biological weapons was doubtful, many, especially the Joint Chiefs of Staff, held strong beliefs about the usefulness of tear gas and herbicides, which were used routinely by US forces in Vietnam. Laird's plan, which became the administration's policy, was to decouple chemical and biological weapons, abandon biological weapons, and construct a protocol on chemical weapons that would protect the use of herbicides and riot control agents like tear gas. As a result, the secretary of defense had to relent on pursuing meaningful CW arms control and nonproliferation measures, assuming he would have favored those. Not surprisingly, it took another two decades after the BWC before an international multilateral CW ban was reached. In many respects, it was the administration's review and pursuit of policies related to BW and CW that sets this period off as pivotal across the entire WMD spectrum and laid the foundation for subsequent bifurcated US government policy.

Initially few could question the wisdom of Nixon's decision and follow-on BWC. Yet the decisions were rather hasty. This hastiness was evident in the initial omission of toxins. Moreover, the lack of presidential interest, or at least intimate involvement, may have stymied what was ultimately accomplished. A verification regime was minimal. The means for monitoring and enforcing compliance with its prohibitions or an associated international organization to assist signatories to the treaty in fulfilling their obligations did not exist as they would with the Chemical Weapons Convention's Organization for the Prohibition of Chemical Weapons. Soviet BW cheating began almost immediately.

The other major multilateral effort to control the spread of WMD involved nuclear weapons. The Nixon administration inherited the NPT from the Johnson administration but held the fate of its ratification. Nixon and Kissinger did not share the absolutism of their predecessors when it came to nonproliferation. They were relatively sympathetic to some countries' nuclear ambitions in light of their support for independent but friendly centers of regional power; they occasionally speculated on the value of an independent Japanese nuclear deterrent, for example. Nixon and Kissinger clearly wanted to retain as much flexibility as possible, especially with respect to looking the other way concerning covert or virtual development programs maintained by friendly powers. Critics would contend that this established a double standard that has plagued US nonproliferation policy to the present. Nixon and Kissinger factored in not only Israel and Japan but other key allies (West Germany, Iran, and India) in their nonproliferation calculus. They pursued a contradictory strategy of nuclear ambiguity toward allies by turning a blind eye to many of those countries seeking nuclear weapons programs while officially endorsing ratification of the NPT. Their approach set a troubling precedent for future administrations and ultimately led to the codification of the international nonproliferation regime that persists today but was flawed from the beginning (recognizing that some of course argue it is better than nothing and has served its purpose).

Nixon and Kissinger frequently disparaged the LTBT, the Kennedy administration's signature arms control agreement, in light of their own accomplishments, especially in SALT. The administration continued to place considerable value on nuclear testing to maintain the proficiency of the US nuclear arsenal, as exemplified by the controversial Cannikin test in August 1971. The Cannikin episode reveals Nixon's concern with reassuring his conservative base that his diplomatic initiatives in SALT, and the recently revealed opening to China, were not a sellout. But the administration could not ignore political and international pressures for further testing limitations, especially when it became clear that interest in PNEs among friendly nations had disappeared, in large part because of environmental concerns. Although it rejected proposals to expand the LTBT into a comprehensive ban, the United States in 1976 was willing to accept a TTB treaty (eventually set at 150 kilotons), coupled with a PNE agreement, which were signed after Nixon left office. Although Kissinger did not place much substantive stock in the agreements, it was one of the few areas in which agreement with the Soviet Union was still possible at that time.

The end of the Cold War cleared the way for the United States to stop testing in 1992 despite hesitancy from the nuclear weapons establishment and to sign a multilateral CTB treaty in 1996. Because of conservative opposition, however, the US Senate did not ratify the treaty, and with the deterioration of great-power relations, conservatives have raised questions about Soviet and Chinese compliance, along with the possibility of resuming testing by the United States in response.

That brings us to SALT, the cornerstone of the Nixon administration's WMD control efforts, where all the international and domestic factors came fully into play. The privileged status for strategic nuclear arms control was not a given. The Kennedy and Johnson administrations placed high priority on nonproliferation, which included multilateral nuclear testing restraints. Nixon's approach to SALT was partly by design and partly due to circumstance. But it became one of the main pillars of the administration's national security policy, even more so than Nixon or Kissinger initially envisioned. They were initially pushed in this direction by domestic factors. In the context of increasing public disillusionment with and opposition to the Vietnam War, SALT offered a means to deal with pressures for a reduction in tensions with the Soviet Union and to decrease the perceived chances of nuclear war.

As events evolved, the pursuit of a SALT/ABM agreement became a component of a broader détente with the Soviet Union, symbolizing and codifying mutually agreed superpower restraint. Although they were concerned to limit an alarming buildup of Soviet offensive forces, Nixon and Kissinger did not view SALT/ABM as purely technical agreements that would enhance first-strike stability and dampen the action-reaction phenomenon but rather as part of a stable political framework, along the lines of what the Washington Naval Treaty, in conjunction with the Nine Power Agreement, sought to achieve in the early 1920s. Nixon and Kissinger believed that the Kremlin leadership had incentives to deal seriously across the board, on the basis of national interest, given strains on the Soviet economy, the American opening to China, and a general waning of communist revolutionary enthusiasm.

At the same time, Nixon and Kissinger did not believe that nuclear arms control alone could bear the weight of improved US-Soviet relations and at times privately disparaged the strategic (but not political) value of SALT. Nixon in particular felt that SALT was the best of a bad bargain because of years of neglect of US nuclear forces, which could not be overcome rapidly, especially given congressional resistance to new weapons programs. Some liberals complained that it did nothing to stop the arms race; indeed, SALT merely codified it, which made unilateral US restraint even more important. On the other hand, conservatives—and not a few moderates—wondered at the apparent disparities in offensive forces in favor of the Soviets.

To overcome these conflicting domestic political arguments, Nixon and Kissinger, in the heady days of détente, arguably oversold nuclear arms control, which later led to later disillusionment on the left and, more importantly, a belief among conservatives that American security had been placed in jeopardy by SALT—indeed, by any efforts to reach an agreement with the USSR on nuclear weapons. As détente began to deteriorate and Nixon was forced to resign, Kissinger hung on to strategic arms control as long as he could as a way to keep the superpower relationship from collapsing—even as Kissinger's foreign policy as a whole was being attacked domestically from both the left and the right, albeit for different reasons. Although he was able to cobble together the Vladivostok Accord, Kissinger could not achieve a bureaucratic consensus, or

Soviet support, for a more ambitious effort. That was left to the Carter administration, which also had to backtrack on significant reductions, largely to a hold-in-place SALT II. That in turn dissatisfied conservatives, who were in a position to block Senate ratification, especially after the Soviet invasion of Afghanistan. The Reagan administration, for whatever reason, was able to achieve terms much more satisfactory to conservatives in the Strategic Arms Reduction Treaty. Even in doing so, those critics of SALT could not discard entirely the political imperative of undertaking strategic arms control negotiations or ignore the basic conceptual framework set out during the Nixon and Ford administrations.

Part of the problem with SALT had to do with the Nixon administration's policy-making process and obsession with secrecy and the use of the diplomatic back channel with Dobrynin, to the exclusion of the rest of the government. Despite their best efforts to centralize matters in the White House, Nixon and Kissinger were never able to control decision-making or its outcome completely. Managing the SALT negotiations also competed for their attention with other critical foreign policy matters, such as Vietnam, which meant that details were overlooked due to the sheer press of events. Nixon's obsession with getting the credit for SALT, and Kissinger's management style, meant that the professionals—not only Gerard Smith but willing skeptics like Paul Nitze—could not weigh in fully on critical issues that later haunted strategic arms control.

Nixon sincerely believed that his defeat at the hands of a Democratic candidate in 1972, given the leftward turn of the party and demoralization of the Eastern establishment, would mean catastrophe for the republic. In his own mind, this justified a by-any-means-necessary approach to reelection. This did not mean that he made major concessions in SALT strictly for that purpose—the evidence from the White House tapes do not support such a straightforward argument. To be sure, no president is unmindful of the political value of timely diplomatic success, and Nixon did want a SALT agreement and Soviet summit for that purpose. He intended to take full advantage of being seen as a peacemaker, including SALT and, to a lesser extent, other WMD control initiatives. But his extreme obsession with control, secrecy, and credit—including the search for and punishment of leakers in SALT—went to such extremes that it contributed to his ultimate downfall.

This brings us back to the question of why a relatively conservative administration went as far as it did with WMD controls, although not nearly as far as advocates wanted. And are significant arms control agreements and unilateral initiatives most likely to occur under conservative administrations, on the general principle "Only Nixon can go to China"? The answer to the first, as we have laid out in the foregoing chapters, is that the context of the times matters greatly, as does the precise nature of a conservative administration. Opposition to the Vietnam War, economic difficulties at home and abroad, and the civil rights revolution and unrest, mandated changes in American national security policy. The solution developed by the peculiar combination of American and European realism represented by Nixon and Kissinger, together with their distinct personal qualities (to put it kindly), is unlikely to recur. The conservatism of Ronald Reagan, George H. W. Bush, George H. Bush, and Donald Trump have been distinctive in their own way, but the first three at least did seek to advance WMD controls, following the general path of Nixon. (George W. Bush did, however, step back by withdrawing from the ABM Treaty, although without challenging the logic behind mutual deterrence with Russia, and added overt, preventive action against state and nonstate WMD threats). The polarization of American politics—with fewer liberal or moderate Republicans and fewer conservative Democrats—makes WMD arms control, and support for nonnegotiated international norms, even more of a partisan issue.

And what have been the enduring consequences of Nixon's arms control and nonproliferation agenda? Current top-level policy makers and practitioners within the WMD field are grappling with the possible demise of the Nixon-era arms control framework as a means to curtail nuclear arsenals—especially, by choice or necessity, if the United States enters a period of great power competition. Should the United States continue to pursue a reduction in its nuclear arsenal? How does arms control fit within US-Russian relations? Should strategic nuclear arms control be multilateralized, a concept that Nixon rejected? Should the United States reenergize efforts to bring about the abolition of nuclear weapons, an approach that Nixon also rejected but one that has been supported, at least by some senior members of his administration, including Kissinger? And with respect to the international nonproliferation regime of which the NPT is the cornerstone, this edifice has been under sharp criticism for apparent treaty "loopholes" and hypocrisies that have long undercut the very objectives the treaty was intended to address. Although Nixon largely inherited a signed NPT, did the low significance he placed on it forestall correctives that might perhaps have been made at the time?

Another legacy of the Nixon period initiatives is a binary construct for approaching WMD. None of the very real accomplishments, whether SALT or the BWC, were treated holistically. These policy tendencies have persisted. Are they appropriate for today's policy makers? What alternative approaches to constraining biological and chemical weapons in particular were posited during this critical time period that might have bearing on deliberations today? Was the US government wise in forswearing offensive BW use, and was a multilateral treaty the best mechanism, especially given its lack of verification features? Did separating BW from CW in policy impede consideration of a multilateral treaty governing the latter, since after all, the Chemical Weapons Convention was not signed until 1993? Lastly, what modifications to the arms control and NPT regimes established during the Nixon era should be made to ensure a reliable global security structure?

Despite an impressive number of agreements and treaties, then, the Nixon administration left a host of questions and issues that have bearing today. And the refusal to view these treaties and agreements as an interconnected "whole" quite possibly created lost opportunities and future impediments for policy makers by limiting courses of action. Still, even with its shortcomings, Nixon's presidency represents a critical inflection point in US efforts to curb and control the entire spectrum of WMD.

COMMON ABBREVIATIONS

ABM	antiballistic missile
ACDA	Arms Control and Disarmament Agency
AEC	Atomic Energy Commission
BW	biological weapons
BWC	Biological Weapons Convention
CBW	chemical and biological weapons
CDU	Christian Democratic Union
CHASE	Cut Hole and Sink 'Em
CIA	Central Intelligence Agency
CTB	comprehensible test ban
CW	chemical weapons
CWC	Chemical Weapons Convention
DCI	Director of Central Intelligence
DNSA	Digital National Security Archive
DoD	Department of Defense
ENCD	Eighteen Nation Committee on Disarmament
FBS	forward-based system
FRG	Federal Republic of Germany
GOCO	government-owned, contractor-operated
IAEA	International Atomic Energy Agency
ICBM	intercontinental ballistic missile
IRBM	intermediate-range ballistic missile
LANWFZ	Latin America nuclear-weapons-free zone
LTBT	Limited Test Ban Treaty
MIRV	multiple independently targetable reentry vehicle
MRBM	medium-range ballistic missile
MRV	multiple reentry vehicles
NATO	North Atlantic Treaty Organization
NCA	National Command Authority
NIE	National Intelligence Estimate
NPT	Nonproliferation Treaty
NSC	National Security Council
NSDM	National Security Decision Memorandum
NSSM	National Security Study Memorandum
OSI	on-site inspection
OSD	Office of the Secretary of Defense

PNE	peaceful nuclear explosion
PRC	People's Republic of China
PSAC	President's Science Advisory Committee
R&D	research and development
SALT	Strategic Arms Limitation Talks
SLBM	submarine-launched ballistic missile
SSBN	ballistic missile submarine (nuclear)
TTB	threshold test ban
UK	United Kingdom
UN	United Nations
USSR	Union of Soviet Socialist Republics
VEE	Venezuelan equine encephalitis
WHT	White House tapes

NOTES

PREFACE

1. Nixon White House Tapes, Conversation between Nixon and Haldeman, Conversations 501–16, 19 May 1971, Oval Office. All Nixon White House tapes come from the collections of the Nixon Presidential Library. The authors have accessed the digitized version in the collection maintained by the Miller Center of Public Affairs, University of Virginia. Unless otherwise indicated, the transcripts from the White House tapes were prepared by the authors. Hereinafter referred to as WHT.

1. NIXON'S ARMS CONTROL INHERITANCE

1. United Nations Office for Disarmament Affairs, *The United Nations and Disarmament: 1945–1970*, 28, 349. See also W. Seth Carus, "Defining 'Weapons of Mass Destruction,'" Occasional Paper no. 8, revised and updated (Washington, DC: National Defense University Press, 2012).
2. For an overview, see Richard Dean Burns, *The Evolution of Arms Control: From Antiquity to the Nuclear Age* (Santa Barbara, CA: Praeger Security International, 2009). For critical assessments of various historical approaches to arms control and disarmament, see Lawrence Freedman, *Arms Control: Management or Reform?* (Routledge and Kegan Paul, 1986); Bruce D. Berkowitz, *Calculated Risks: A Century of Arms Control, Why It Has Failed, and How It Can Be Made to Work* (New York: Simon and Schuster, 1987); and Colin S. Gray, *House of Cards: Why Arms Control Must Fail* (Ithaca, NY: Cornell University Press, 1992).
3. W. Seth Carus, "A Short History of Biological Warfare: From Pre-History to the 21st Century," Occasional Paper no. 12 (Washington, D.C.: National Defense University Press, 2017).
4. See Rodney J. McElroy, "The Geneva Protocol of 1925," in *The Politics of Arms Control and Treaty Ratification*, ed. Michael Krepon and Dan Caldwell (New York: St. Martin's, 1991). For a review of earlier efforts at disarmament and arms control, including efforts to prohibit WMD, see Burns, *The Evolution of Arms Control*.
5. For Roosevelt's declaration about US government CW use, see "Statement Warning the Axis against Using Poison Gas," 8 June 1943, American Presidency Project, University of California at Santa Barbara, https:// abmceducation.org/sites/default/files/Statement-Warning-Axis.pdf.

6. See generally Thomas I. Feith, *Behind the Gas Mask: The U.S. Chemical Warfare Service in War and Peace* (Urbana: University of Illinois Press, 2014), 107–16; and John Ellis van Courtland Moon, "Chemical Weapons and Deterrence: The World War II Experience," *International Security* 8, no. 4 (Spring 1984): 3–35.

7. *U.S. Army Activity in the U.S. Biological Warfare Programs* (vol. 1 and 2), US Department of the Army, 24 February 1977, reprinted in *Biological Testing Involving Human Subjects by the Department of Defense, 1977,* Hearings before the Subcommittee on Health and Scientific Research of the Committee on Human Resources, 8 March and 23 May 1977, US Senate, 95th Congress, 1st session (Washington, DC: Government Printing Office, 1977), Document 26, National Security Archives, vol. 3, Biowar, National Security Archive Electronic Briefing Book no. 58, ed. Robert A Wampler, updated 7 December 2001, https://nsarchive2.gwu .edu/NSAEBB/NSAEBB58/#doc25. See also Wendy Barnaby, *The Plague Makers: The Secret World of Biological Warfare* (New York: Continuum International Publishing Group, 2000), 81–91; and Barton J. Bernstein, "The Birth of the U.S. Biological Warfare Program," *Scientific American* 255 (June 1987): 116–21.

8. For quote, see Richard M. McCarthy, *The Ultimate Folly: War by Pestilence, Asphyxiation, and Defoliation* (New York: Alfred A. Knopf, 1969), 24.

9. *U.S. Army Activity in the U.S. Biological Warfare Programs,* vol. 2, Appendix I-C-7, https://nsarchive2.gwu.edu/NSAEBB/NSAEBB58/RNCBW _USABWP.pdf.

10. Ed Regis, *The Biology of Doom: The History of America's Secret Germ Warfare Project* (New York: Henry Holt, 1999), 143–46.

11. Fifth Pugwash Conference, "On Chemical and Biological Warfare," *Bulletin of the Atomic Scientists* 15, no. 9 (October 1959): 338–39; "Biological and Chemical Weapons: A Symposium," *Bulletin of the Atomic Scientists,* 16, no. 6 (June 1960): 226–56.

12. For US use of riot agents, defoliants, and herbicides during the Vietnam War, see Caroline D. Harnly, *Agent Orange and Vietnam: An Annotated Bibliography* (London: Scarecrow, 1988); and Wil D. Verwey, *Riot Control Agents and Herbicides in War: Their Humanitarian, Toxicological, Ecological, Military, Polemological, and Legal Aspects* (Leiden: A. W. Sijthoff International, 1977). For CW and Third World conflicts, see Edward M. Spiers, *Chemical Warfare* (London: Palgrave Macmillan, 1986), 89–119.

13. Richard G. Hewlett and Oscar E. Anderson Jr., *A History of the United States Atomic Energy Commission,* vol. 1, *The New World, 1939–1946* (University Park: Pennsylvania State University Press, 1962); Hewlett and Anderson, *A History of the United States Atomic Energy Commission,*

vol. 2, *Atomic Shield, 1947–1952* (University Park: Pennsylvania State University Press, 1969); Campbell Craig and Sergey Radchenko, *The Atomic Bomb and the Origins of the Cold War* (New Haven, CT: Yale University Press, 2008).

14. Amy F. Woolf and James D. Werner, "The U.S. Nuclear Weapons Complex: Overview of Department of Energy Sites," Congressional Research Service (6 September 2018): 8–9.

15. For the size of the US force structure, see "Minimize Harm and Security Risks of Nuclear Energy," in National Resources Defense Council, *Table of U.S. Strategic Offensive Force Loadings: Archive of Nuclear Data,* http://www.nrdc.org/nuclear/nudb/datab1.asp. See Department of State Fact Sheet, 29 April 2014.

16. For a succinct account of the "new thinking" see Lawrence Freedman, *The Evolution of Nuclear Strategy,* 3rd ed. (New York: Palgrave Macmillan, 2003), 165–205, 226–43.

17. Jennifer Sims, *Icarus Restrained: An Intellectual History of Nuclear Arms Control* (Boulder, CO: Westview, 1990). Among early influential works were Thomas C. Schelling and Morton H. Halperin, *Strategy and Arms Control* (New York: Twentieth Century Fund, 1961); Donald Brennan, ed., *Arms Control, Disarmament, and National Security* (New York: George Braziller, 1961); and David Frisch, ed., *Arms Reduction: Program and Issues* (New York: Twentieth Century Fund, 1961). See also Hedley Bull, *The Control of the Arms Race: Disarmament and Arms Control in the Missile Age* (New York: Frederick A. Praeger, 1961). For a later critique of this "technical" line of argument about arms control and deterrence, see Gray, *House of Cards.* John D. Mauer describes this as the "assured destruction" school of arms control and contrasts it with an emergent "competitive strategies" approach, which was not yet fully formed in the 1960s. John D. Mauer, "Divided Counsels: Competing Approaches to SALT, 1969–1970," *Diplomatic History* 43, no. 2 (April 2019): 353–77.

18. See generally Robert A. Divine, *Blowing on the Wind: The Nuclear Test Ban Debate, 1954–1960* (New York: Oxford University Press, 1978).

19. Glenn T. Seaborg with Benjamin S. Loeb, *Kennedy, Khrushchev, and the Test Ban* (Berkeley: University of California Press, 1981); Ronald J. Terchek, *The Making of the Test Ban* (The Hague: Martinus Nijhoff, 1970).

20. This assertion is out of step with much of the scholarly literature on US grand strategy during the Cold War but in sync with a thoughtful analysis offered by Francis J. Gavin, "Strategies of Inhibition: U.S. Grand Strategy, the Nuclear Revolution, and Nonproliferation," *International Security* 40, no. 1 (Summer 2015): 9–46.

21. See generally Robert Divine, *Eisenhower and the Cold War* (New York: Oxford University Press, 1981), 105–55; and Matthew Fhurmann, *Atomic Assistance: How "Atoms for Peace" Programs Cause Nuclear Insecurity* (Ithaca, NY: Cornell University Press, 2012).

22. For an excellent overview, see Joseph M. Siracusa and Aiden Warren, "The Nuclear Non-Proliferation Regime: An Historical Perspective," *Diplomacy and Statecraft* 29, no. 1 (2018): 3–28. See also Scott D. Sagan and Kenneth N. Waltz, *The Spread of Nuclear Weapons* (New York: W. W. Norton, 2003); and John Lewis Gaddis et al., eds., *Cold War Statesmen Confront the Bomb: Nuclear Diplomacy since 1945* (New York: Oxford University Press, 1999). For a thoughtful case study of the "rollback" phenomenon, see Rebecca K. C. Hersman and Robert Peters, "Nuclear U-Turns: Learning from South Korean and Taiwanese Rollback," *Nonproliferation Review* 13, no. 3 (November 2006): 539–553.

23. On US perennial concerns about nuclear proliferation, see Francis J. Gavin, "Same as It Ever Was: Nuclear Alarmism, Proliferation, and the Cold War," *International Security* 34, no. 3 (Winter 2009/2010): 7–37; and Gavin, "Blasts from the Past: Proliferation Lessons from the 1960s," *International Security* 29, no. 3 (Winter 2004/2005): 100–35; on France, West Germany, and NATO nuclear dilemmas see Erin R. Mahan, *Kennedy, De Gaulle, and Western Europe* (London: Palgrave Macmillan, 2002); Marc Trachtenberg, *A Constructed Peace: The Making of the European Settlement, 1946–1963* (Princeton, NJ: Princeton University Press, 1998); and Thomas Alan Schwartz, *Lyndon Johnson and Europe: In the Shadow of Vietnam* (Cambridge, MA: Harvard University Press, 2003).

24. For the Gilpatric report, see "A Report to the President by the Committee on Nuclear Proliferation," The White House, 21 January 1965, in *Foreign Relations of the United States, 1964–1968*, vol. 11, *Arms Control and Disarmament*, ed. Evans Gerakas, David S. Patterson, and Carolyn B. Yee (Washington, DC: Government Printing Office, 1997), https://history.state.gov/historicaldocuments/frus1964-68v11/d64, hereinafter referred to as *FRUS, Arms Control, 1964–1968*. For analysis of the report, see Hal Brands, "Rethinking Nonproliferation: LBJ, the Gilpatric Committee, and U.S. National Security Policy," *Journal of Cold War Studies* 8, no. 2 (Spring 2006): 83–113; and Francis J. Gavin, *Nuclear Statecraft: History and Strategy in American Atomic Age* (Ithaca, NY: Cornell University Press, 2012), 80–103.

25. The most comprehensive account of the NPT remains the two volumes by Mohamed I. Shaker, *The Nuclear Non-Proliferation Treaty: Origin and Implementation, 1959–1979*, 2 vols. (New York: Oceana, 1980), but surprisingly little is offered on the machinations during the Nixon

administration. Two useful treatments of the NPT prior to the Nixon administration are offered by Hal Brands, "Progress Unseen: US Arms Control Policy and the Origins of Détente, 1963–1968," *Diplomatic History* 30, no. 2 (April 2006): 253–85; and George Quester, *The Politics of Nuclear Proliferation* (Baltimore: Johns Hopkins University Press, 1973).

26. For a review of the Kennedy-Johnson change of thinking about nuclear strategy, force posture, and strategic arms control, see Freedman, *The Evolution of Nuclear Strategy*, 215–42.

27. Freedman, *The Evolution of Nuclear Strategy*, 215–42. The declaratory policy of flexible response was meant to address a variety of political problems, especially those involving West Germany and the NATO alliance, not just military problems with the Soviet Union. See Gavin, *Nuclear Statecraft*, 30–33. For a compressive history, see David N. Schwartz, *NATO's Nuclear Dilemmas* (Washington, DC: Brookings Institution, 1983).

28. Freedman, *The Evolution of Nuclear Strategy*, 233–40.

29. Ted Greenwood, *Making the MIRV: A Study of Defense* (Cambridge, MA: Ballinger, 1975). For discussion of force planning from 1969 to 1972 and the McNamara legacy, see Walter S. Poole, *The Joint Chiefs of Staff and National Policy, 1969–1972* (Washington, DC: Office of Joint History, 2013), 35–47.

30. For McNamara's thinking, no first use, and related topics, see Henry S. Rowen, "The Evolution of Strategic Nuclear Doctrine," in *Strategic Thought in the Nuclear Age*, ed. Lawrence Martin (Baltimore: Johns Hopkins University Press, 1979), 151. Kissinger wrote in his memoirs: "When I entered office, former Defense Secretary Robert McNamara told me that he had tried for seven years to give the President more options. He had finally given up, he said, in face of bureaucratic opposition and decided to improvise." Henry Kissinger, *White House Years* (New York: Simon and Schuster, 2011), location 4627, Kindle.

31. Poole, *The Joint Chiefs of Staff*, 31–40. For a consideration of the political-military context of these discussions, see John Newhouse, *Cold Dawn: The Story of SALT* (New York: Holt, Rinehart and Winston, 1973), 66–113. For a general overview of the Johnson arms control and disarmament policy, see Brands, "Progress Unseen" 253–85.

32. Memorandum of Conversation, 23 June 1967, *Foreign Relations of the United States, 1964–1968*, vol. 14, *Soviet Union, October 1971–May 1972*, ed. David C. Humphrey and Charles S. Sampson (Washington, DC: Government Printing Office, 2001), Document 231.

33. Edward J. Drea, *History of the Office of the Secretary of Defense*, vol. 6, *McNamara, Clifford, and the Burdens of Vietnam, 1965–1969* (Washington, DC: Government Printing Office, 2011) 367–71.

34. Letter from President Johnson to Chairman Kosygin, 2 May 1968, in *Foreign Relations of the United States, 1964-1968*, vol. 11, Arms Control and Disarmament, ed. Evans Gerakas, David S. Patterson, and Carolyn B. Yee (Washington, DC: Government Printing Office, 1997), Document 237.

35. Drea, *History of the Office of the Secretary of Defense*, 6:337; Lyndon B. Johnson, Remarks at the Signing of the Nuclear Nonproliferation Treaty, 1 July 1968, at Gerhard Peters and John T. Woolley, The American Presidency Project, https://www.presidency.ucsb.edu/node/236878.

36. On the Johnson disarmament policy, see Brands, "Progress Unseen," 253-85. See also Drea, *History of the Office of the Secretary of Defense*, 6:344.

2. NATIONAL SECURITY LANDSCAPE AND ARMS CONTROL AGENDA

1. See Richard Nixon, *RN: The Memoirs of Richard Nixon* (New York: Grosset and Dunlap, 1978), 118-228; and Henry Kissinger, *American Foreign Policy: Three Essays by Henry Kissinger* (New York: W. W. Norton, 1969), 51-97.

2. Henry Kissinger, *Nuclear Weapons and Foreign Policy* (New York: Harper and Row, 1957). For insightful critiques of Kissinger's years as a Harvard professor and government consultant as well as the early development of the Nixon-Kissinger partnership, see Walter Isaacson, *Kissinger: A Biography* (New York: Simon and Schuster, 1992), 94-128; and Robert Dallek, *Partners in Power: Nixon and Kissinger* (New York: Harper, 2007), 60-86. See also, for example, Niall Ferguson, *Kissinger, 1923-1968: The Idealist* (New York: Penguin Books, 2015).

3. See Gavin, *Nuclear Statecraft*; Freedman, *The Evolution of Nuclear Strategy*; and McGeorge Bundy, *Danger and Survival: Choices about the Bomb in the First Fifty Years* (New York: Random House, 1988). Schwartz, *NATO's Nuclear Dilemmas*, discusses the specific issues of deterrence and Europe.

4. Dale Van Atta, *With Honor: Melvin Laird in War, Peace, and Politics* (Madison: University of Wisconsin Press, 2008); Richard A. Hunt, *Melvin Laird and the Foundations of the Post-Vietnam Military, 1969-1973* (Washington, DC: Government Printing Office, 2015), 395-403.

5. Richard Nixon, 20 January 1969, Inaugural Address, at Peters and Woolley, American Presidency Project.

6. See for instance William Bundy, *A Tangled Web: The Making of Foreign Policy in the Nixon Presidency* (New York: Hill and Wang, 1998); Dallek, *Partners in Power*; Jeremi Suri, *Henry Kissinger and the American Century*

(Cambridge, MA: Harvard University Press, 2009), 138–96; John Lewis Gaddis, *Strategies of Containment: A Critical Appraisal of American National Security Policy During the Cold War*, rev. and exp. ed. (New York: Oxford University Press, 2005), 272–341; and Fredrik Logevall and Andrew Preston, eds., *Nixon in the World: American Foreign Relations, 1969–1977* (New York: Oxford University Press, 2008). The president offered his remarks on what became known as the Nixon Doctrine on 27 July 1969. Richard Nixon, "Informal Remarks in Guam with Newsmen," 26 July 1969, online at Peters and Woolley, The American Presidency Project.

7. Richard Nixon, "Address at the Air Force Academy Commencement Exercises in Colorado Springs, Colorado," 4 June 1969, online at Peters and Woolley, The American Presidency Project.

8. Kissinger discussed the Nixon administration's perception of the linkage between political, strategic, and arms control issues during a background briefing for the press at the White House. See editorial note, 6 February 1969, *Foreign Relations of the United States, 1969–1976*, vol. 1, *Foundations of Foreign Policy, 1969–1972*, ed. Louis J. Smith, David H. Herschler, and David S. Patterson (Washington, DC: Government Printing Office, 2003), Document 11, hereinafter referred to as *FRUS, Foundations, 1969–1972*.

9. WHT, 10 April 1972, Conversation 705-015, Oval Office.

10. Both exchanges are recorded and cited in Avner Cohen, *The Worst Kept Secret: Israel's Bargain with the Bomb* (New York: Columbia University Press, 2010), 6.

11. Quoted in Seymour Hersh, *Chemical and Biological Warfare: America's Hidden Arsenal* (New York: Bobbs-Merrill, 1968), 303. A search by these authors of the *Washington Post, New York Times,* and *Wall Street Journal* from 1960 to 1968 yielded no reported public statements by either Nixon or Kissinger related to CBW.

12. Joel Primack and Frank von Hippel, "Matthew Meselson and the United States Policy on Chemical and Biological Warfare," in *Advice and Dissent: Scientists in the Political Arena*, ed. Joel Primack (New York: Basic Books, 1974), 150–53.

13. Gavin, *Nuclear Statecraft,* 108.

14. Henry Kissinger, *Years of Upheaval* (New York: Simon and Schuster, 2011; originally published 1982), location 5450, Kindle.

15. Conversation between Nixon and Kissinger, 26 February 1971, Conversation 460-027. For a review and assessment of Nixon's no-holds-barred political style, see Kenneth Hughes, *Chasing Shadows: The Nixon Tapes, the Chennault Affair, and the Origins of Watergate* (Charlottesville: University of Virginia Press, 2014); and Hughes, *Fatal Politics: The Nixon*

Tapes, the Vietnam War, and the Casualties of Reelection (Charlottesville: University of Virginia Press, 2015).

16. Nixon reflects on his political and strategic ambitions in WHT, Conversation 468-095, 16 March 1971, Oval Office; WHT, Conversation 494-004, 8 May 1971, Oval Office; WHT, Conversation 502-012, 20 May 1971, Oval Office. See also Raymond Garthoff, *Détente and Confrontation: American-Soviet Relations from Nixon to Reagan*, rev. ed. (Washington, DC: Brookings Institution, 1994), 30.

17. Kissinger, *White House Years*, location 2818; Kissinger, *Years of Upheaval*, location 5181–5248.

18. Dallek, *Partners in Power*, 268–69. Examples of Nixon's thoughts on his "Big Play" can be found in WHT, Conversation 456-024, 23 February 1971, Oval Office; WHT, Conversation 460-025, 26 February 1971, Oval Office; WHT, Conversation 481-007, 17 April 1971, Oval Office; WHT, Conversation 493-010, 6 May 1971, Oval Office.

19. Both authors have spent over a decade listening to and transcribing foreign policy–related Nixon presidential recordings through their association with the Miller Center of Public Affairs Presidential Recordings Project.

20. Kissinger, *White House Years*, location 4200–43; Kissinger, *Years of Upheaval*, location 20970–82.

21. Kissinger, *White House Years*, locations 1851–1960, 4594–4648.

22. Kissinger made this remark during a meeting of the National Security Council's Senior Review Group. Editorial note, 6 February 1969, *FRUS, Foundations, 1969–1972*, Document 11.

23. Kissinger would eventually use Pakistan as an intermediary to contact the Chinese on matters such as SALT before he traveled to Beijing in July 1971. See WHT, Conversation 498-002, 13 May 1971, Oval Office; WHT, Conversation 499-024, 14 May 1971, Oval Office; and WHT, Conversation 502-012, 20 May 1971, Oval Office; and Message from the Government of the United States to the Government of the Peoples Republic of China, 20 May 1971, *Foreign Relations of the United States, 1969–1976*, vol. 17, *China, 1969–1972*, ed. Steven E. Phillips and Edward C. Keefer (Washington, DC: Government Printing Office, 2006), Document 126, hereinafter referred to as *FRUS, China, 1969–1972*.

24. Kissinger, *Years of Upheaval*, location 20930–74, discusses his view of the distinction between the two defense and arms control camps. On Rogers and his relationship with Nixon and his national security advisor, see Dallek, *Partners in Power*, 82–83; Kissinger, *White House Years*, location 775–837. Nixon discusses one of the frequent contretemps between Rogers and Kissinger in WHT, Conversation 456-005, 23 February 1971, Oval Office.

25. Gerard Smith, *Disarming Diplomat: The Memoirs of Ambassador Gerard C. Smith, Arms Control Negotiator* (New York: Madison Books, 1996), 147–52, 160, 169–70.

26. Gerard Smith to Henry Kissinger, 3 February 1969, *Foreign Relations of the United States, 1969–1972*, vol. E-2, *Documents on Arms Control and Nonproliferation, 1969–1972*, ed. David I. Goldman, David C. Humphrey, and Edward C. Keefer (Washington, DC: Government Printing Office, 2007), Document 65, hereinafter referred to as *FRUS, Arms Control, 1969–1972*.

27. For examples of Nixon's fear that Smith might undermine the president's political strategy for SALT see, among others, WHT, Conversations 460–025 and 460–027, both 26 February 1971, Oval Office; and WHT, Conversation 467-011, 12 March 1971, Oval Office.

28. Among the influential scholarly works of this period were Thomas C. Schelling, *The Strategy of Conflict* (Cambridge, MA: Harvard University Press, 1960); Schelling, *Arms and Influence* (New Haven, CT: Yale University Press, 1966); and Schelling and Morton H. Halperin, *Strategy and Arms Control* (New York: Twentieth Century Fund, 1961). Schelling offered later reflections in "What Went Wrong with Arms Control?," *Foreign Affairs* 64, no. 2 (Winter 1985–86): 221–23. See also Bull, *The Control of the Arms Race*. For a later critique of the "technical" line of argument about arms control and deterrence, see Gray, *House of Cards*.

29. For a snapshot of the "theologians" or strategic traditionalists at the outset of the Nixon administration, see Poole, *The Joint Chiefs of Staff*, 15–20, 84–87. An earlier account of these views can be found in Robert Gilpin, *American Scientists and Nuclear Weapons Policy* (Princeton, NJ: Princeton University Press, 1962). The traditionalists were influenced by the thought and writings of Herman Kahn. Keith B. Payne, *The Great American Gamble: Deterrence Theory and Practice from the Cold War to the Twenty-First Century* (Fairfax, VA: National Institute for Public Policy, 2008), location 1419–1777, Kindle. John D. Mauer contends that the traditionalists/skeptics were actually advocating a positive arms control agenda based on a "competitive strategies" approach, designed to gain strategic advantages over the Soviets; see Mauer, "Divided Counsels."

30. The issue of nuclear testing is covered in depth in chapter 7.

31. Erin Mahan, "Historical Perspectives on the Secretary of Defense: Nixon and Melvin Laird," unpublished remarks, 2016 Ambassador William and Carol Stevenson Conference: What the Next Defense Secretary Should Know, 8 December 2016, Miller Center of Public Affairs, University of Virginia. See also Van Atta, *With Honor*, 3–6.

32. Hunt, *Melvin Laird*, 410. For an overview of Nitze's thinking about nuclear weapons and arms control, see Nicholas Thompson, *The Hawk and*

the Dove: Paul Nitze, George Kennan, and the History of the Cold War (New York: Henry Holt, 2009); and Strobe Talbott, *Master of the Game: Paul H. Nitze and U.S. Cold War Strategy from Truman to Reagan* (New York: Knopf, 1988).

33. Nixon offered one of his frequent criticisms of the military leadership's mindset in WHT, Conversation 603-001, 27 October 1971, Oval Office.

34. See generally Dallek, *Partners in Power;* and Suri, *Henry Kissinger.*

3. Two Paths

1. Quoted in Robert A. Strong, *Bureaucracy and Statesmanship: Henry Kissinger and the Making of American Foreign Policy* (Lanham, MD: University Press of America, 1986), 5.

2. Robert M. Neer, *Napalm: An American Biography* (Cambridge, MA: Harvard University Press, 2013), 109–25. For quote, see 111. Incidentally, accusations against the US for use of BW were leveled in the UN. The absence of compelling microbiologic or epidemiologic data, however, precluded verification of US use of BW during the Korean War. See Jean Gulliam, *Biological Weapons: From the Invention of State-Sponsored Programs to Contemporary Bioterrorism* (New York: Columbia University Press, 2005), 99–101.

3. Neer, *Napalm,* 126–133. For quote, 126.

4. See generally David Maraniss, *They Marched into Sunlight: War and Peace, Vietnam and America, October 1967* (New York: Simon and Schuster, 2004) about the demonstrations in Wisconsin.

5. See generally Verwey, *Riot Control Agents and Herbicides in War;* Harnly, *Agent Orange and Vietnam;* and R. R. Baxter and Thomas Buergenthal, "Legal Aspects of the Geneva Protocol of 1925," in *The Control of Chemical and Biological Weapons* (New York: Carnegie Endowment for International Peace, 1971), 1–23.

6. The influence of Hersch's book is rarely mentioned in the histories of US CBW programs and policy changes. For one notable exception, see Robert W. McElroy, *Morality and American Foreign Policy: The Role of Ethics in International Affairs* (Princeton, NJ: Princeton University Press, 1992), 101.

7. Jonathan Tucker, "A Farewell to Germs: The U.S. Renunciation of Biological and Toxin Warfare, 1969–1970," *International Security* 27, no. 1 (Summer 2002): 113.

8. Regis, *The Biology of Doom,* 209. See also David I. Goldman, "The General and the Germs: The Army Leadership's Response to Nixon's Review of Chemical and Biological Warfare Policies in 1969," *Journal of Military History* 73, no. 2 (April 2009): 540–41.

9. See generally McCarthy, *The Ultimate Folly*. For the phrase "transmission belt," see Forrest Frank, "U.S. Arms Control Policymaking: The 1972 Biological Weapons Convention Case," PhD diss. (Stanford University, 1975), 150.

10. "Soviet Leads in Chemical Warfare," 5 March 1969, *Washington Post*, A3.

11. McCarthy, *The Ultimate Folly*, 153–71. For McCarthy's comments on the floor of the House of Representatives, see Cong. Rec. H10910–11 (30 April 1969).

12. McCarthy, *The Ultimate Folly*, 140.

13. A composite of Laird's motivations is formed from several sources. The secretary's official biographer, Van Atta, declares that Laird entered office intent upon changing US CBW policy; see Van Atta, *With Honor*, 293. A more nuanced perspective was provided in Mahan telephone interview with Laird, 13 January 2013, and suggested by Frank, "U.S. Arms Control Policymaking," 105–7.

14. Memorandum from Laird to Kissinger, 30 April 1969, *FRUS, Arms Control, 1969–1972*, Document 139.

15. 1Cong. Rec. 9732–39 (21 April 1969),.

16. Morton Halperin remarks, in Ivo H. Daalder and I. M. Destler, moderators, "Arms Control Policy and the National Security Council," *The National Security Council Project: Oral History Roundtables*, 23 March 2000 (Washington, DC: Center for International and Security Studies at Maryland and Brookings Institution, 2000), 9–10.

17. Memorandum from Laird to Kissinger, 30 April 1969, *FRUS, Arms Control, 1969–1972*, Document 139; Memorandum from Kissinger to Nixon, 23 May 1969, *FRUS, Arms Control, 1969–1972*, Document 140; NSSM 59, 28 May 1969, National Security Council, National Security Memoranda, Richard M. Nixon Presidential Library and Museum, Yorba Linda, California, https://www.nixonlibrary.gov/sites/default/files/virtuallibrary/documents/nssm/nssm_059.pdf.

18. For an analysis of the early phases of the NSC review process, see Erin R. Mahan and Jonathan B. Tucker, "President Nixon's Decision to Renounce the U.S. Offensive Biological Weapons Program," Case Study 1, Center for the Study of WMD Case Studies Series (Washington, DC: National Defense University Press, 2009), 2–4. Because of opposition from the US Chemical Warfare Service (later the US Army Chemical Corps) and the chemical industry, the United States had signed but never ratified the 1925 Geneva Protocol. The treaty had languished for years in the US Senate and had finally been withdrawn by President Harry Truman in 1948.

19. Michael Guhin quoted in Ivo H. Daalder and I. M. Destler, "The Nixon Administration National Security Council," Oral History

Roundtables, *The National Security Project* (Washington, DC: Brookings Institution), 38.

20. Stephen S. Rosenfeld, "Russian Capability for Chemical, Biological War," *Washington Post*, A22.

21. For the now declassified NIE, see "Soviet Chemical and Biological Warfare Capabilities," National Intelligence Estimate 11-11-69, 13 February 1969, National Intelligence Council Collection, Document 0000283815, https://www.cia.gov/library/readingroom/docs/DOC_0000283815.pdf. For the Soviet BW program generally during this period, see Milton Leitenberg and Raymond A. Zilinskas with Jens H. Kuhn, *The Soviet Biological Weapons Program: A History* (Cambridge, MA: Harvard University Press, 2012), 34–50.

22. Jonathan B. Tucker, "Biological Weapons in the Former Soviet Union: An Interview with Dr. Kenneth Alibek," *Nonproliferation Review* 6, no. 3 (Spring/Summer 1999), 2–3. See also Raymond A. Zilinskas, "The Soviet Biological Weapons Program and Its Legacy in Today's Russia," Occasional Paper no. 11 (Washington, DC: Center for the Study of WMD, National Defense University Press, 2016), 5–18.

23. Primack and von Hippel, "Matthew Meselson and the United States Policy," 148.

24. Ibid., 149–51. For Meselson's testimony, see Hearing before the Committee on Foreign Relations, US Senate, 91st Congress, 1st session, 30 April 1969 (Washington, D.C.: Government Printing Office, 1969), 2–25.

25. Dr. Matthew Meselson, "Plague War," interview by PBS *Frontline*, https://www.pbs.org/wgbh/pages/frontline/shows/plague/interviews/meselson.html. In this same interview Meselson erroneously recalls the *Boston Globe* citing Soviet sites, but he was mistaken by several years. In the PBS *Frontline* interview he stated: "If you go back to 1968 or 1969, in *The Boston Globe*, an article by William B. Church named with perfect accuracy all the places where the Soviets were developing and producing biological weapons. So we did know. Up until 1969 we could hardly raise a fuss about it because we were doing the same things . . . Exactly how much we knew in detail with what degree of confidence, I don't know. Looking back, one can say from what was in the open press . . . we did know, but the question is, what you do with this kind of knowledge and how certain is it." Articles appeared in 1974–75 after the BWC was signed and concerns were raised that lack of verification requirements had permitted Soviet cheating that went unchecked. See, for example, William Beecher, "Photographic Evidence Cited: Soviets Feared Violating Germ Weapon Ban," *Boston Globe*, 28 September 1975, 1.

26. Hearings before the Subcommittee on International Organizations and Movements of the Committee on Foreign Affairs, House of Representatives, 91st Congress, 1st session, 8, 13–15 May 1969 (Washington, DC: Government Printing Office, 1969).

27. Hearings before a Subcommittee of the Committee on Government Operations, House of Representatives, 91st Congress, 1st session, 20–21 May 1969 (Washington, DC: Government Printing Office, 1969). For McCarthy's summary and comments on the House floor, see Cong. Re. 12460–63 (14 May 1969).

28. Roy Reed, "Army Admits Its Nerve Gas Killed 6,000 Sheep," *New York Times,* 22 May 1969, 14.

29. Van Atta, *With Honor,* 291–95; Hunt, *Melvin Laird,* 336; Robert Keatley, "Nerve Gas Accident: Okinawa Mishap Bares Overseas Deployment of Chemical Weapons," *Wall Street Journal,* 18 July 1969, 1.

30. Transcript of telephone conversation between Laird and Kissinger, 21 July 1969, 12:55 p.m., Digital National Security Archive, George Washington University, Washington, DC; transcript of a telephone conversation between Kissinger and Laird, 17 July 1969, ibid.

31. James M. McCullough, "Chemical and Biological Warfare Issues and Developments during 1971," *Congressional Research Service Report,* 13 December 1971 (Washington, DC: Library of Congress), 39–40.

32. Little discussion is given in the historiography of US biological weapons to the decoupling of BW and CW. There is a passing reference in Barnaby, *The Plague Makers,* 23. For a masterful survey of the US Army's position on resisting the renouncement of BW warfare, see Goldman, "The General and the Germs."

33. Minutes of the Secretary of Defense's Staff Meeting, 4 August 1969, *FRUS, Arms Control, 1969–1972,* Document 142.

34. Although somewhat self-serving, a glimpse into Laird's savviness and motivations was provided by a telephone interview with Laird, Fort Myers, Florida, 16 January 2013.

35. For quote, see "Laird Says Soviets Lead in Germ Weapons," *Boston Globe,* 29 July 1969, 15; for similar accounts, see "Laird Defends Chemical Weaponry as Deterrent," *New York Times,* 29 July 1969, 4; and "Pentagon Says Chemical War Deterrent Vital," *Los Angeles Times,* 7 September 1969, 1.

36. See generally Tucker and Mahan, "President Nixon's Decision to Renounce the U.S. Offensive Biological Weapons Program," 4–5; and Frank, "U.S. Arms Control Policymaking," 114.

37. For Laird's views and instructions, see Memorandum from Secretary of Defense Laird to the Assistant Secretary of Defense for International

Security Affairs (Nutter), Washington, DC, 6 August 1969, *FRUS, Arms Control, 1969–1972*, Document 143.

38. Ibid. For characterization of the army's role, see Goldman, "The General and the Germs," 551, 553 (for quote).

39. Cong. Re. 22197–23658, 23068 (5–12 August 1969). For DoD positions, see Memorandum, Vice Admiral Nels C. Johnson to the Chairman of the Joint Chiefs of Staff, Subject: S2546, McIntyre Amendment #131, CBW, Chairman Wheeler's Files, folder 471: Chemical and Biological Weapons, RG 218, National Archives and Records Administration (NARA), College Park, Maryland; and Memorandum, H. B. Switzer to General Wheeler, Subject: McIntyre Amendment on CBW to FY 70 DOD Authorization Bill, 11 August 1969, Chairman Wheeler's Files, folder 471: Chemical and Biological Weapons, RG 218, NARA.

40. Warren Weaver, "Laird Backs Senate Curb on Chemical War Agents," 10 August 1969, *New York Times*, 1, 26.

41. See, respectively, "Report by Secretary-General Thant on Chemical and Bacteriological (Biological) Weapons and the Effect of Their Possible Use [Extracts]," US Arms Control and Disarmament Agency, *Documents on Disarmament, 1969* (Washington DC: ACDA, 1970), 264–98; "Twelve-Nation Working Paper Submitted to the ENDC: Proposed General Assembly Declaration Regarding Prohibition of the Use of Chemical and Biological Methods of Warfare," ibid., 433–35; and "Address by Foreign Minister Gromyko [Extracts]," ibid., 457–58.

42. See, for example, "Statement by the British Representative (Mulley) to the Eighteen Nation Disarmament Committee: Chemical and Biological Warfare [Extract]," 10 July 1969, US Arms Control and Disarmament Agency, *Documents on Disarmament, 1969*, 318–23; "British Proposal Submitted to the Eighteen Nation Disarmament Committee: Draft Security Council Resolution on Biological Warfare," 10 July 1969, ibid., 324–27; "Revised British Draft Security Council Resolution on Biological Warfare," 26 August 1969, ibid., 433–34; "Statement by the British Representative (Porter) to the Conference of the Committee on Disarmament: Prohibition of Biological Warfare," ibid., 435–36. We are grateful to John Moon for providing us with the quotation from Zuckerman.

43. Report to the NSC on US Policy on Chemical and Biological Warfare and Agents, prepared by the Interdepartmental Political-Military Group in response to NSSM 59, 15 October 1969, posted at the US Department of State, FOIA website, copy in authors' files. Minutes of NSC Review Group Meeting, 30 October 1969, *FRUS, Arms Control, 1969–1972*, Document 155.

44. Minutes of NSC Meeting, 18 November 1969, *FRUS, Arms Control, 1969–1972*, Document 161.

45. Ibid.

46. Richard Nixon, "Statement on Chemical and Biological Defense Policies and Programs," 25 November 1969, *Public Papers of the Presidents, 1969* (Washington: Government Printing Office, 2004), 968–69. Nixon codified his plans with NSDM 35, issued the same day. See NSDM 35, 25 November 1969, National Security Council, National Security Memoranda, Richard M. Nixon Presidential Library and Museum, Yorba Linda, California, https://www.nixonlibrary.gov/sites/default/files/virtuallibrary/documents/nsdm/nsdm_035.pdf.

47. Harry R. Haldeman, *The Haldeman Diaries: Inside the Nixon White House* (Santa Monica, CA: Sony Imagesoft, 1994), entry for 26 November 1969, 111.

48. Office of the White House Press Secretary, Fact Sheet (Fort Detrick), 18 October 1971, White House Press Office, White House Central Files: Staff Member and Office Files, Box 23, Richard M. Nixon Presidential Library and Museum, Yorba Linda, California.

49. NSDM 85, 31 December 1969, National Security Council, National Security Memoranda, Richard M. Nixon Presidential Library and Museum, Yorba Linda, California, https://www.nixonlibrary.gov/sites/default/files/virtuallibrary/documents/nssm/nssm_085.pdf. Memorandum from Michael Guhin of the National Security Council Staff to the President's Assistant for National Security Affairs (Kissinger), Washington, DC, 30 December 1969, *FRUS, Arms Control, 1969–1972*, Document 172.

50. Minutes of the National Security Council Review Group Meeting, Washington, DC, 29 January 1970, *FRUS, Arms Control, 1969–1972*, Document 176. For the options paper, see Report Prepared by the Interdepartmental Politico-Military Group, Washington, DC, 21 January 1970, NSC Institutional Files, Meeting Files, Box H-26, NSC Meeting 2/11/70, Policy on Toxins, Richard Nixon Presidential Library, Yorba Linda, California.

51. Memorandum from Acting Secretary of State Elliott Richardson to President Nixon, Washington, DC, 10 February 1970, *FRUS, Arms Control, 1969–1972*, Document 185; Memorandum from Acting Secretary of State Richardson to President Nixon, Washington, DC, 10 February 1970, National Archives, RG 59, Central Files 1970–1973, POL 27-10, NARA II.

52. Memorandum from the Deputy Secretary of Defense (Packard) to the President's Assistant for National Security Affairs (Kissinger), 12 February 1970, *FRUS, Arms Control, 1969–1972*, Document 187.

53. Minutes of NSC Review Group Meeting, 29 January 1970, *FRUS, Arms Control, 1969–1972*, Document 176; Memorandum from the Director of

the US Information Agency (Shakespeare) to the President's Assistant for National Security Affairs (Kissinger), Washington, DC, undated, *FRUS, Arms Control, 1969–1972*, Document 182.

54. Memorandum from the President's Adviser for National Security Affairs (Kissinger) to President Nixon, Washington, DC, undated, *FRUS, Arms Control, 1969–1972*, Document 188.

55. Dr. Matthew Meselson, "What Policy for Toxins?" 22 January 1979, reprinted in Cong. Rec. E1042–43 (18 February 1970).

56. Mahan and Tucker, "President Nixon's Decision to Renounce the U.S. Offensive Biological Weapons Program," 15.

57. For quote, Office of the White House Press Secretary (Key Biscayne, FL), Statement on Toxins, 14 February 1970, *FRUS, Arms Control, 1969–1972*, Document 189; NSDM 44, 20 February 1970, National Security Council, National Security Memoranda, Richard M. Nixon Presidential Library and Museum, Yorba Linda, California.

58. Smith to Kissinger, memorandum, 10 March 1972, *FRUS, Arms Control, 1969–1972*, Document 252. Kissinger then had to give Dobrynin personal assurances that the president would be present. See transcript of a telephone conversation between Kissinger and Dobrynin, 17 March 1972, ibid., Document 253.

59. For a record of the conversation, see Memorandum of Conversation, 6 November 1969, in US Department of State, *Soviet-American Relations: The Détente Years, 1969–1972*, ed. Edward C. Keefer, David C. Geyer, and Douglas E. Selvage (Washington, DC: Government Printing Office, 2007), 101–2.

60. Leonard quote is in Leitenberg, Zilinskas, and Kuhn, *The Soviet Biological Weapons Program*, 533.

61. Richard Nixon, "First Annual Report to the Congress on United States Foreign Policy for the 1970s," 18 February 1970, *Public Papers of the Presidents, 1970*, 116–90.

62. For the Soviet proposal, see "Communist Draft Convention on the Prohibition of the Development, Production, and Stockpiling of Bacteriological (Biological) Weapons and Toxins and on Their Destruction," 30 March 1971, US Arms Control and Disarmament Agency, *Documents on Disarmament, 1971*, 190–94. Quote is in Leitenberg, Zilinskas, and Kuhn, *The Soviet Biological Weapons Program*, 539.

63. Quoted in Leitenberg, Zilinskas, and Kuhn, *The Soviet Biological Weapons Program*, 535.

64. "Convention on the Prohibition of the Development, Production, and Stockpiling of Bacteriological (Biological) and Toxin Weapons and on Their Destruction," 10 April 1972, US Arms Control and Disarmament

Agency, *Documents on Disarmament, 1972*, 133–38; US Arms Control and Disarmament Agency, *Arms Control and Disarmament Agreements: Texts and Histories of the Negotiations* (Washington, DC: ACDA, 1990), 129–38.

65. For the full text of Nixon's speech at the signing ceremony, see *Public Papers of the Presidents, 1972*, 525–26.

66. WHT, Conversation 705-013, 10 April 1972, Oval Office.

67. Transcript of background briefing, "Administration Policy Concerning Toxins," with Presidential Press Secretary Ronald Ziegler and National Security Advisor Henry Kissinger, Key Biscayne, Florida, 14 February 1970, *FRUS, Arms Control, 1969–1972*, Document 189. For an example of press accolades, see Alvin Schuster, "Capitals in Western Europe Welcome Nixon's Move," *New York Times*, 26 November 1969, 17.

68. Tucker, "A Farewell to Germs," 2.

69. The Soviet program produced the most deadly accident in biological warfare programs during the Cold War—the anthrax release at Sverdlovsk in 1979. For quote, see Meselson, "Plague War."

70. Tucker, "Biological Weapons in the Former Soviet Union," 2.

71. For Nixon's decision, see NSDM 35, 25 November 1969, National Security Council, National Security Memorandum, Richard M. Nixon Presidential Library and Museum, Yorba Linda, California, https://www.nixonlibrary.gov/sites/default/files/virtuallibrary/documents/nsdm/nsdm_035.pdf. For congressional disclosure of CIA activities, see "Hearings before the Select Committee to Study Governmental Operations with Respect to Intelligence Activities of the United States Senate [Church Committee], Ninety-fourth Congress, First Session, Volume I: Unauthorized Storage of Toxic Agents, September 16, 17 and 18, 1975" (Government Printing Office, 1976), Document 125, National Security Archives, vol. 3, Biowar, National Security Archive Electronic Briefing Book No. 58, ed. Robert A Wampler, updated 7 December 2001, https://nsarchive2.gwu.edu/NSAEBB/NSAEBB58/#doc25.

72. Gulliam, *Biological Weapons*, 129.

73. *U.S. Army Activity in the U.S. Biological Warfare Programs*, vol. 1, https://nsarchive2.gwu.edu/NSAEBB/NSAEBB58/RNCBW_USABWP.pdf, 277.

74. George W. Christopher, Theodore J. Cieslak, Julie A. Pavlin, and Edward M. Eitzen Jr., "Biological Warfare: A Historical Perspective," in *Biological Weapons: Limiting the Threat*, ed. Joshua Lederberg (Cambridge, MA: MIT Press, 1999), 27–30. See also *U.S. Army Activity in the U.S. Biological Warfare Programs*, vol. 1, https://nsarchive2.gwu.edu/NSAEBB/NSAEBB58/RNCBW_USABWP.pdf.

75. Memorandum from Melvin Laird to Henry Kissinger, 6 July 1970, *FRUS, Arms Control, 1969–1972*, Document 199.

76. Leitenberg, Zilinskas, and Kuhn, *The Soviet Biological Weapons Program*, 530.

77. Nathan E. Busch and Daniel H. Joyner, eds., *Combating Weapons of Mass Destruction: The Future of International Nonproliferation Policy* (Athens: University of Georgia Press, 2009), 78.

78. Michael Nguyen, "Senate Struggles with Riot Control Agent Policy," *Arms Control Today*, January/February 2006, available at https://www.armscontrol.org/act/2006_01-02/JANFEB-RiotControl. For text of Ford's executive order, see, "Executive Order 11850—Renunciation of Certain Uses in War of Chemical Herbicides and Riot-Control Agents," 8 April 1975, available at https://www.archives.gov/federal-register/codification/executive-order/11850.html.

79. Roger Morris, *Uncertain Greatness: Henry Kissinger and American Foreign Policy* (New York: Harper and Row, 1977) 99.

80. Ibid.

81. Guhin quoted in Daalder and Destler, "The Nixon Administration National Security Council," 37.

82. Regis, *The Biology of Doom*, 222.

83. William Safire, "Weapons of Mass Destruction: Obnubilating Aside, It's Bone Stupid to Launch Them," *New York Times Magazine*, 19 April 1998, 22–23.

84. Nixon Presidential Recordings, WHT, Conversation 706-005, 11 April 1972, Oval Office.

4. Nixon's Crown Jewel of Arms Control

1. Garthoff, *Détente and Confrontation*, 148–49; Kissinger, *Years of Upheaval*, location 2895.

2. See Patrick J. Garrity and Erin R. Mahan, *Nixon and Arms Control: Forging the Offensive/Defensive Link in the SALT Negotiations, February–May 1971* (Charlottesville: University of Virginia Press, 2014), https://prde.upress.virginia.edu/content/nixon_SALT. Other recent studies that survey SALT include Gavin, *Nuclear Statecraft*; David Tal, *U.S. Strategic Arms Control Policy in the Cold War: Negotiation and Confrontation over SALT, 1969–1979* (London: Routledge, 2017); James Cameron, *The Double Game: The Demise of America's First Missile Defense System and the Rise of Strategic Arms Limitation* (New York: Oxford University Press, 2017); Matthew J. Ambrose, *The Control Agenda: A History of the Strategic Arms Control Talks* (Ithaca, NY: Cornell University Press, 2018), Kindle edition; and Mauer, "Divided Counsels."

3. Richard Nixon: "The President's News Conference," 27 January 1969, online at Peters and Woolley, American Presidency Project. For the letters

to Rogers and Laird, see editorial note in *Foreign Relations of the United States, 1969–1976*, vol. 32, *SALT I, 1969–1972*, ed. Erin R. Mahan and Edward C. Keefer (Washington, DC: Government Printing Office, 2010), Document 1, hereinafter referred to as *FRUS, SALT I, 1969–1972*. On several occasions at the outset of the administration, Kissinger expressed the view that the United States should even consider the possibility that the talks would never open. See, for example, Review Group Meeting, 6 February 1969, *Foreign Relations of the United States, 1969–1976*, vol. 34, *National Security Policy, 1969–1972*, ed. M. Todd Bennet (Washington, DC: Government Printing Office, 2011), Document 4, hereinafter referred to as *FRUS, National Security Policy, 1969–1972*. On the approach to the Soviets, Memorandum of Conversation (US) Washington, DC, 17 February 1969, Ambassador Dobrynin's Initial Call on the President, in US Department of State, *Soviet-American Relations*, Document 5; Letter from President Nixon to the Chairman of the Council of Ministers of the Soviet Union Kosygin, 26 March 1969, in *Foreign Relations of the United States, 1969–1976*, vol. 12, *Soviet Union, January 1969–October 1970*, ed. Erin R. Mahan and Edward C. Keefer (Washington, DC: Government Printing Office, 2006), Document 28, hereinafter referred to as *FRUS, Soviet Union, January 1969–October 1970*. Dobrynin advised the Soviet leadership that it was the Americans who needed arms control because of the economic costs of the arms race. Telegram from Ambassador Dobrynin to the Soviet foreign minister, 13 March 1969, in US Department of State, *Soviet-American Relations: The Détente Years*, Document 14. Kosygin rejected Nixon's attempt at linkage. Letter from Chairman of the Council of Ministers of the Soviet Union Kosygin to President Nixon, 27 May 1969, Tab A, in Memorandum from the President's Assistant for National Security Affairs (Kissinger) to President Nixon, 28 May 1969, *FRUS, Soviet Union, January 1969–October 1970*, Document 51. David Tal discusses the various, and to his judgment, unsuccessful, attempts at linkage in SALT in "'Absolutes' and 'Stages' in the Making and Application of Nixon's SALT Policy," *Diplomatic History* 37, no. 5 (November 2013): 1090–1116. Tal concludes that Nixon distinguished between a "hard" version of linkage, in which progress in SALT (for instance) would depend on progress in other areas, and a "soft" version, in which linkage was simply a fact of diplomatic and political life. For the most part, he contends, Nixon and Kissinger followed the soft version in their dealings with Dobrynin and Soviet leaders. Tal, *U.S. Strategic Arms Control Policy in the Cold War*, 8. For a similar view, see Ambrose, *The Control Agenda*, location 607–33.

4. WHT, Conversation 501-029, 19 May 1971, Oval Office.

5. Minutes of a National Security Council Meeting, Washington, DC, 19 February 1969, *FRUS, SALT I, 1969–1972*, Document 5. Kissinger,

however, did have an idea about how to short-circuit the entire process and apply linkage practically. Nixon would appoint Cyrus Vance, a former senior national security official in the Kennedy and Johnson administrations, as a special envoy, with powers to negotiate SALT and to open discussions with a North Vietnamese representative in Moscow on a diplomatic solution to the war. There were numerous problems with this idea, even assuming the Soviets and the North Vietnamese were willing to negotiate along these lines. Among these: What if progress in one channel was slower than progress in another? Would Moscow (or Hanoi) apply linkage of their own? There were no clear answers, and the proposal did not advance beyond some discussions with Vance. Memorandum from the President's Assistant for National Security Affairs (Kissinger) to President Nixon, 3 April 1969, *Foreign Relations of the United States, 1969–1976*, vol. 6, *Vietnam, January 1969–July 1970*, ed. Edward C. Keefer and Carolyn Yee (Washington, DC: Government Printing Office, 2006), Document 52; Kissinger, *White House Years*, location 5617–32.

6. Kissinger, *White House Years*, location 3230–37; Smith, *Disarming Diplomat*, 158; Tal, *U.S. Strategic Arms Control Policy in the Cold War*, 23.

7. See, for example, WHT, 19 May 1972, Conversation 726-011, Oval Office; Ambrose, *The Control Agenda*, location 581–95.

8. See generally Garrity and Mahan, *Nixon and Arms Control*.

9. See for example, WHT, Conversation 460-025, 26 February 1971, Oval Office; and WHT, Conversation 460-027, 26 February 1971, Oval Office. For an analysis of the SALT-related White House tapes, see Erin Mahan, "The SALT Mindset: Détente through the Nixon Tapes," unpublished paper delivered at NATO, the Warsaw Pact and Détente, 1965–1973, Machiavelli Center for Cold War Studies and the Parallel History Project, 26–28 September 2002, Dobbiaco, Italy.

10. NSSM 3, 21 January 1969, *FRUS, National Security Policy, 1969–1972*, Document 2; Garthoff, *Détente and Confrontation*, 147–48. For Kissinger's argument that NSSM 3 and NSSM 28 had the same basic principles, see Minutes of a Review Group Meeting, 12 June 1969, *FRUS, SALT I, 1969–1972*, Document 17.

11. NSDM 16, Washington, DC, 24 June 1969, *FRUS, National Security Policy, 1969–1972*, Document 39. The four criteria for strategic sufficiency were to (1) maintain high confidence that our second strike capability is sufficient to deter an all-out surprise attack on our strategic forces; (2) maintain forces to ensure that the Soviet Union would have no incentive to strike the United States first in a crisis; (3) maintain the capability to deny to the Soviet Union the ability to cause significantly more

deaths and industrial damage in the United States in a nuclear war than they themselves would suffer; and (4) deploy defenses that limit damage from small attacks or accidental launches to a low level. For Kissinger's comment on the guidance for SALT provided by NSDM 16, see Minutes of a National Security Council Meeting, 18 June 1969, *FRUS, SALT I, 1969–1972*, Document 19, note 1.

12. Cited in Lawrence Freedman, *The Evolution of Nuclear Strategy*, 3rd ed. (New York: St. Martin's, 1981), 341; Poole, *The Joint Chiefs of Staff*, 107–10; Minutes of Review Group Meeting, "Review of U.S. Strategic Posture," 29 May 1969, *FRUS, National Security Policy, 1969–1972*, Document 32, 97–116; Memorandum of Conversation, "Defense Budget," 19 August 1970, *FRUS, National Security Policy, 1969–1972*, Document 153, 589; Minutes of an NSC Meeting, untitled, 25 March, 1970, *FRUS, SALT I, 1969–1972*, Document 59, 211–13.

13. In his memoirs, Nixon recalled that it was clear to him by 1969 that "absolute parity" between the two superpowers was illusory given the quantitative and qualitative asymmetries between the US and Soviet nuclear arsenals. Furthermore, the United States, if it had chosen to pursue nuclear superiority once again, would succeed only in escalating the arms race. "Consequently, at the beginning of the administration I began to talk in terms of sufficiency rather than superiority to describe my goals for our nuclear arsenal." Nixon, *RN: The Memoirs of Richard Nixon*, 415; Notes of National Security Council Meeting, Washington, DC, 14 February 1969, *FRUS, National Security Policy, 1969–1972*, Document 7; Minutes of National Security Council Meeting, 18 June 1969, *FRUS, National Security Policy, 1969–1972*, Document 36. For Nixon's insistence that the CIA had repeatedly underestimated the pace and quality of Soviet nuclear programs, missing the mark on the low side by 50 percent between 1965 and 1968, see, for example, Minutes of a National Security Council Meeting, Washington, DC, 18 June 1969, *FRUS, SALT I, 1969–1972*, Document 19. The intelligence community's judgment especially carried little weight with him when they seemed conveniently designed to support the case against ABM being promoted by Smith and by Nixon's opponents in Congress. For an account of the intergovernmental debate over Soviet strategic nuclear force sizing and intentions, see John Prados, *The Soviet Estimate: U.S. Intelligence Analysis and Soviet Strategic Forces*, updated ed. (Princeton, NJ: Princeton University Press, 1986).

14. Minutes of a National Security Council Meeting, Washington, DC, 12 February 1969, *FRUS, National Security Policy, 1969–1972*, Document 5.

15. Cameron, *The Double Game*, 107–35.

16. Hunt, *Melvin Laird*, 396–400. For the White House staff perspective, see Memorandum from the President's Assistant for Congressional Relations (Harlow) to President Nixon, Washington, DC, 10 March 1969, *FRUS, National Security Policy, 1969–1972*, Document 21.

17. Tal, *U.S. Strategic Arms Control Policy in the Cold War*, 18–19; Hunt, *Melvin Laird*, 400–401. Kissinger, *White House Years*, location 4406–14.

18. Hunt, *Melvin Laird*, 403–6; Lori Esposito Murray, "SALT and Congress: Building a Consensus for Arms Control" (PhD diss., Johns Hopkins University, 1990), 281. Congressional opponents of ABMs, such as Senators William Fulbright (D-AR) and Albert Gore (D-TN), contended that the judgment of the intelligence community about Soviet capabilities was not nearly so categorical. At the root of the debate was the question of whether the Soviets were deliberately seeking a first-strike capability. CIA director Helms and his agency argued that they were not. Many in the Department of Defense felt otherwise, based on the character and pace of its missile program. Memorandum from Director of Central Intelligence Helms to the President's Assistant for National Security, 26 May 1969, *FRUS, National Security Policy, 1969–1972*, Document 30; editorial note in Minutes of the NSC Meeting, 13 June 1969, *FRUS, National Security Policy, 1969–1972*, Document 35; Memorandum to the Holders of NIE 11-8-68, 23 June 1969, *FRUS, National Security Policy, 1969–1972*, Document 38.

19. Dallek, *Partners in Power*, 137–39. Laird, for his part, felt that Nixon personally was a poor lobbyist and that only his own contacts and credibility on Capitol Hill won the day, especially with Senator Margaret Chase Smith (R-ME). Hunt, *Melvin Laird*, 406–8; Van Atta, *With Honor*, 191.

20. In his memoirs Nixon concluded that "I am absolutely convinced that had we lost the ABM battle in the Senate, we would not have been able to negotiate the first nuclear arms control agreement in Moscow in 1972." Nixon, *RN: The Memoirs of Richard Nixon*, 415–418.

21. Memorandum from the President's Assistant for National Security Affairs (Kissinger) to President Nixon, 24 June 1969, *FRUS, SALT I, 1969–1972*, Document 21; Minutes of a National Security Council Meeting, 25 June 1969, *FRUS, SALT I, 1969–1972*, Document 22. In that NSC meeting, Laird warned that material prepared for the North Atlantic Council would get into Soviet hands. In March, during a meeting of the North Atlantic Council, Nixon acknowledged that the era of Western nuclear superiority was over and that any strategic arms agreement with the Soviets would codify the present balance of forces. For an agreement to be consistent with the security of the alliance, the various parties, despite the diversity of national policies and interests, must develop a common

worldview and strategy through a new and deeper form of political consultation—which Nixon pledged to undertake, without offering any specifics, because he then had no specifics to offer. Address by President
Nixon to the North Atlantic Council, 10 April 1969, *FRUS, Foundations,
1969–1972*, Document 18.

22. Kissinger, *White House Years*, location 3901–32; President Nixon's Notes
on a National Security Council Meeting, 14 August 1969, undated, *FRUS,
China, 1969–1972*, Document 25.

23. Memorandum from William Hyland of the National Security Council
Staff to the President's Assistant for National Security Affairs (Kissinger), 18 August 1969, *FRUS, China, 1969–1972*, Document 27; Minutes
of the Senior Review Group Meeting, 25 September 1969, *FRUS, China,
1969–1972*, Document 36.

24. Memorandum of Conversation, 20 October 1969, President Nixon,
Ambassador Dobrynin, Henry A. Kissinger, *FRUS, Soviet Union, Janu-
ary 1969–October 1970*, Document 93; Kissinger, *White House Years*, lo-
cation 3186; Memorandum from Secretary of State Rogers to President
Nixon, Washington, DC, 2 December 1969, *FRUS, China, 1969–1972*,
Document 49.

25. Ambrose, *The Control Agenda*, location 692–703.

26. William P. Bundy observed that Nixon and Kissinger never tried "to
frame a coherent statement of what the U.S. objectives and strategy
should be for the talks what the U.S. objectives and strategy should be
for the talks." To be sure, he acknowledged that such a statement would
have been difficult to formulate given the disagreements within the
government, but "surely discussion would have clarified the likely problems and trade-offs and identified the essential objectives," beyond that
of constraining the Soviet offensive forces buildup. "In the absence of
such a statement," Bundy wrote, "the preparations for negotiations ignored long-term goals in favor of details, with the result that Kissinger
ended up with a remarkably free hand." Bundy, *A Tangled Web*, location
2056–64. Which is precisely what Kissinger wanted. The White House
approach to SALT, like the rest of the Nixon-Kissinger national security policy, relied heavily on improvisation and keeping options open—
something that the bureaucracy and Congress, in their opinion, would
never allow.

27. Prepared by the Interagency SALT Steering Committee, undated, Summary of NSSM-28 report, *FRUS, SALT I, 1969–1972*, Document 14. A
more comprehensive option was circulated concurrently by ACDA,
known as "Stop Where We Are," formulated by the agency's Sidney
Graybeal, involved "a quantitative and qualitative freeze on all aspects

[of] strategic offensive and defensive forces that are subject to adequate verification by national means." This included a ban on MIRVs and a prohibition of additional construction of ABM systems and radars, presumably including the first phase of Safeguard. According to ACDA, a "Stop Where We Are" agreement would keep the strategic balance in its currently stable state, where "both sides have a confident second-strike capability, and are far from achieving a first-strike capability." See Proposal for SALT, prepared by ACDA, 11 June 1969, ACDA-3356, A "Stop Where We Are" Proposal for SALT, *FRUS, SALT I, 1969–1972*, Document 16.

28. For example, Minutes of a National Security Council Meeting, 25 March 1969, *FRUS, SALT I, 1969–1972*, Document 59. See also Gerard Smith, *Doubletalk: The Story of the First Strategic Arms Limitation Talks* (Garden City, NY: Doubleday, 1980), 159–63; Stephan Kieninger, "'Diverting the Arms Race into the Permitted Channels': The Nixon Administration, the MIRV-Mistake, and the SALT Negotiations," NPIPH Working Paper no. 9, November 2016 (Washington, DC: Woodrow Wilson Center), 18. As Mauer points out, policy disagreements over the objective of arms control were often subsumed in debates over technological issues, such as verification capabilities. See Mauer, "Divided Counsels," 372–74.

29. Hunt, *Melvin Laird*, 411–12.

30. Memorandum from the Deputy Secretary of Defense (Packard) to the President's Assistant for National Security Affairs (Kissinger), 30 May 1969, *FRUS, SALT I, 1969–1972*, Document 13; Memorandum from the Chairman of the Joint Chiefs of Staff (Wheeler) to Secretary of Defense Laird, Washington, DC, 1 August 1969, CM-4469-69, *FRUS, SALT I, 1969–1972*, Document 31.

31. Minutes of National Security Council Meeting, 14 February 1969, *FRUS, SALT I, 1969–1972*, Document 5; Minutes of National Security Council Meeting, 18 June 1969, *FRUS, SALT I, 1969–1972*, Document 19; editorial note to Verification Panel Meeting, 6 April 1970, *FRUS, SALT I, 1969–1972*, Document 62.

32. Memorandum from the President's Assistant for National Security Affairs (Kissinger) to President Nixon, 22 January 1970, *FRUS, SALT I, 1969–1972*, Document 49.

33. Kissinger, *White House Years*, location 4453–60.

34. Ibid., location 3266. In his memoirs, Smith denied that ACDA had done any lobbying for its position on Capitol Hill—a clear indication that the White House suspected otherwise and had made known its unhappiness to the ACDA director. Smith, *Doubletalk*, 163–64.

35. NSDM 33, 12 November 1969, *FRUS, SALT I, 1969–1972*, Document 40.

36. For details on the opening round of SALT, see Smith's reports to President Nixon: Letter from the Chief of the Delegation to the Preliminary Strategic Arms Limitations Talks (Smith) to President Nixon, 9 December 1969, *FRUS, SALT I, 1969–1972*, Document 44; and Memorandum for the File by the Director of the Arms Control and Disarmament Agency (Smith), 9 January 1970, *FRUS, SALT I, 1969–1972*, Document 46; Memorandum from the President's Assistant for National Security Affairs (Kissinger) to President Nixon, 22 January 1970, *FRUS, SALT I, 1969–1972*, Document 49; and Smith, *Doubletalk*, 83–99.

37. The FBSs issue is considered by Stephen M. Millett, "Forward-Based Nuclear Weapons and SALT I," *Political Science Quarterly* 98, no. 1 (Spring 1983): 79–97.

38. See Smith's correspondence with Nixon during this period, summarized in editorial note, *FRUS, SALT I, 1969–1972*, Document 41; and Letter from the Chief of the Delegation to the Preliminary Strategic Arms Limitation Talks (Smith) to President Nixon, 9 December 1969, *FRUS, SALT I, 1969–1972*, Document 44.

39. Bundy, *A Tangled Web*, location 2092–99.

40. Kissinger, *White House Years*, location 3272–80.

41. See, for example, Smith to Nixon, 30 December 1969, cited in Memorandum for the File by the Director of the Arms Control and Disarmament Agency (Smith), 9 January 1970, *FRUS, SALT I, 1969–1972*, Document 46; Letter from General Lauris Norstad of the General Advisory Committee for Arms Control and Disarmament to the President's Assistant for National Security Affairs (Kissinger), 20 January 1970, *FRUS, SALT I, 1969–1972*, Document 47. On Kissinger's reassurance to Dobrynin about the deliberate pace of Safeguard deployment, see Memorandum of Conversation, 18 February 1970, *FRUS, SALT I, 1969–1972*, Document 52.

42. Kissinger, *White House Years*, location 1160–68.

43. Minutes of National Security Council Meeting, 25 March 1970, *FRUS, SALT I, 1969–1972*, Document 59; Memorandum from Secretary of Defense Laird to President Nixon, 9 April 1970, *FRUS, SALT I, 1969–1972*, Document 67.

44. Kissinger, *White House Years*, location 11200–11217; Memorandum of Conversation, NSC Meeting, 8 April 1970, *FRUS, SALT I, 1969–1972*, Document 65; Smith, *Doubletalk*, 118.

45. NSDM 51, 10 April 1970, *FRUS, SALT I, 1969–1972*, Document 68; Memorandum of Conversation, NSC Meeting, 8 April 1970, *FRUS, SALT I, 1969–1972*, Document 65; Memorandum of Conversation, Meeting between SALT Delegation and President Nixon, 11 April 1970, *FRUS, SALT I, 1969–1972*, Document 69; Memorandum from Secretary of

State Rogers to President Nixon, 15 April 1970, *FRUS, SALT I, 1969–1972*, Document 70.

46. Smith, *Doubletalk*, 121; Garthoff, *Détente and Confrontation*, 159.

47. Memorandum from Secretary of Defense Laird to the President's Assistant for National Security, 18 April 1970, *FRUS, SALT I, 1969–1972*, Document 71; Tal, *U.S. Strategic Arms Control Policy in the Cold War*, 38–39.

48. NSDM 69, 9 July 1970, *FRUS, SALT I, 1969–1972*, Document 94. NSDM 73, 22 July 1970, *FRUS, SALT I, 1969–1972*, Document 97, modified NSDM-69 with respect to heavy missiles and silos. A detailed statement of the US negotiating position was set out in NSDM 74, 31 July 1970, *FRUS, SALT I, 1969–1972*, Document 100.

49. See the discussions between Kissinger and Dobrynin,10 June 1970, in US Department of State, *Soviet-American Relations*, Document 62; discussions between Kissinger and Dobrynin, 13 June 1970, in ibid., Document 64; discussions between Kissinger and Dobrynin, 20 June 1970, in ibid., Document 70. Kissinger informed Smith of the Soviet position in Back-channel Message from the President's Assistant for National Security Affairs (Kissinger) to the Chief of the Delegation to the Strategic Arms Limitation Talks (Smith), San Clemente, California, 4 July 1970, *FRUS, SALT I, 1969–1972*, Document 88.

50. The Semenov démarche to Smith stated, "What we need to do is jointly take a stand that the two governments intend to act together to prevent the outbreak of war by accidental, unauthorized or provocative action from any quarter. We need to let them [other countries] know that we would act together to deal with any attempted provocations." See Kissinger, *White House Years*, location 11338.

51. Kissinger, *White House Years*, location 11340–48. Kissinger's staff provided him with numerous critical assessments of the Soviet's "political" proposals. See for example Memorandum from Laurence Lynn and Helmut Sonnenfeldt of the National Security Council Staff to the President's Assistant for National Security Affairs (Kissinger), 1 July 1970, *FRUS, SALT I, 1969–1972*, Document 86.

52. Letter from Secretary of Defense Laird to the President's Assistant for National Security Affairs (Kissinger), 27 October 1970, *FRUS, SALT I, 1969–1972*, Document 111. A Joint Staff study of option D, commissioned by Admiral Moorer, indicated that illustrative US strategic forces under such an agreement could accomplish assured destruction, albeit at a lower level of confidence than the Joint Staff deemed desirable. However, lacking an effective warfighting capability, the United States probably would emerge from any "high-level" nuclear conflict in a position of relative disadvantage. Poole, *The Joint Chiefs of Staff*, 93–94.

53. Smith, *Doubletalk,* 176–77; Paul Nitze, *From Hiroshima to Glasnost: At the Center of Decision, A Memoir* (New York: Grove Weidenfeld, 1989), 311–12.

54. On 16 December a Department of Defense spokesman disclosed that the Soviets were apparently slowing the deployment of SS-9 missiles. William Beecher, "U.S. Data Indicate Moscow Is Slowing ICBM Deployment," *New York Times,* 17 December 1970, 1–2. The Soviet proposal also contained constraints on FBSs and reductions in US offensive forces that Kissinger regarded as completely unacceptable. Memorandum from the President's Assistant for National Security Affairs (Kissinger) to President Nixon, Washington, DC, 10 December 1970, *FRUS, SALT I, 1969–1972,* Document 118. As Tal notes, the Soviets were really proposing different forms of agreement—ABM limits in the form of a treaty, offense limits by less binding unilateral restraint. Tal, *U.S. Strategic Arms Control Policy in the Cold War,* 52.

55. Memorandum from Helmut Sonnenfeldt of the National Security Council Staff to the President's Assistant for National Security Affairs (Kissinger), 5 December 1970, *FRUS, SALT I, 1969–1972,* Document 116, note 4, contains excerpts of Smith's back-channel communication (3 December) on this point. Smith further wrote, "In view of large stakes here, the President may want to direct a review of our policy against ABM only arrangement and would note that US/USSR positions appear to have switched 180 degrees since McNamara/Johnson/Kosygin meeting in 1967."

56. Memorandum from the President's Assistant for National Security Affairs (Kissinger) to President Nixon, Washington, DC, 10 December 1970, *FRUS, SALT I, 1969–1972,* Document 118.

57. Letter from the Chief of the Delegation to the Strategic Arms Limitation Talks (Smith) to President Nixon, 6 May 1970, *FRUS, SALT I, 1969–1972,* Document 76. Tal, *U.S. Strategic Policy in the Cold War,* 38–39, 45–46, reviews the summit matter. He concludes that the Soviets initiated the discussion, that Kissinger argued that SALT and Vietnam and the Middle East must be included on the summit agenda, that Dobrynin and Kissinger agreed to work on limited SALT agreement for the summit, that the SALT delegations were to work on comprehensive agreement, and that President Nixon was to get full credit.

58. Kissinger, foreword to US Department of State, *Soviet-American Relations,* xvi.

59. This case is offered in Smith, *Doubletalk,* 224–44.

60. Memorandum of Conversation between Presidential Assistant Kissinger and Soviet Ambassador Dobrynin (US), 9 January 1971, in US

Department of State, *Soviet-American Relations*, Document 109; Memorandum of Conversation between Presidential Assistant Kissinger and Soviet Ambassador Dobrynin (USSR), in ibid., Document 110.

61. Memorandum from Kissinger to Nixon, 22 January 1970, *FRUS, SALT I, 1969–1972*, Document 49.

62. These January–May 1971 back-channel discussions may be followed in US Department of State, *Soviet-American Relations*.

63. Memorandum of Conversation between Presidential Advisor Kissinger and Soviet Ambassador Dobrynin (USSR), 22 February 1971, in US Department of State, *Soviet-American Relations*, Document 126, in which Dobrynin discusses and critiques the contents of the draft letter. At this time, Kissinger and his staff were devoting considerable time to the production of the president's Second Annual Report to Congress, a document in which Kissinger took great pride as a means to pull together publicly the administration's grand strategy. The draft included a section that made the case for offense-defense linkage in SALT. Someone leaked information about the interagency debate and whether to continue to insist on that linkage to nationally syndicated columnist Joseph Kraft, infuriating Kissinger, who blamed "the ACDA people." He told Nixon: "I'm afraid [this] is going to blow up my negotiation with Dobrynin because they put in there that—they put the whole debate on the arms control section, which I thought was entirely editorial. . . . I want to hold them to an option which they want to change. . . . I don't think Rogers has studied the problem with our position, but Rogers and Smith want to give them—have an ABM-only agreement. Now here, the Russians have already accepted your proposal [in the Dobrynin back channel]. And now, they get this column. I would bet they are going to back off now, to see whether they can't get more." What Smith, Kissinger warned, "wants is a completely free hand, so that he gets the credit for whatever is achieved." WHT, Conversation 451-004, 18 February 1971, Oval Office.

64. Transcript of a telephone conversation between the President's Assistant for National Security and the Soviet Ambassador, 26 March 1971, US Department of State, *Foreign Relations of the United States, 1969–1976*, vol. 13, *Soviet Union, October 1970–October 1971*, ed. David C. Geyer and Edward C. Keefer (Washington DC: Government Printing Office, 2011), Document 160, note 2, hereinafter referred to as *FRUS, Soviet Union, October 1970–October 1971*; Memorandum of telephone conversation (USSR), 26 March 1971, in US Department of State, *Soviet-American Relations*, Document 140.

65. WHT, Conversation 245-006, 6 April 1971, Executive Office Building; WHT, Conversation 479-002, 14 April 1971, Oval Office.

66. WHT, Conversation 245-006, 6 April 1971, Executive Office Building; WHT, Conversation 481-007, 17 April 1971, Oval Office.

67. Kissinger, *White House Years*, location 14734–68.

68. WHT, Conversation 489-017, 26 April 1971, Oval Office. Tal and other scholars argue that Kissinger vastly exaggerated the leverage that the United States was able to bring to bear over the Berlin issue, especially as it related to SALT. Tal, "'Absolutes' and 'Stages' in the Making and Application of Nixon's SALT Policy," 1109. See also David C. Geyer, "The Missing Link: Henry Kissinger and the Backchannel Negotiations on Berlin," in *American Detente and German Ostpolitik, 1969–1972*, ed. David C. Geyer and Bernd Schaefer (Washington, DC: German Historical Institute, 2004), 91–92.

69. WHT, Conversation 249-016, 15 April 1971, Executive Office Building; WHT, Conversation 495-026, 7 May 1971, Oval Office; WHT, Conversation 498-002, 13 May 1971, Oval Office.

70. WHT, Conversation 481-007, 17 April 1971, Oval Office; WHT, Conversation 482-010, 19 April 1971, Oval Office.

71. NSDM 102, 11 March 1971, *FRUS, SALT I, 1969–1972*, Document 138; Letter from President Nixon to Secretary of State Rogers, 18 March 1971, *FRUS, SALT I, 1969–1972*, Document 142.

72. WHT, Conversation 487-021, 23 April 1971, Oval Office; Memorandum of Conversation, 23 April 1971, in US Department of State, *Soviet-American Relations*, Document 143 (US) and Document 144 (USSR); conversation between President Nixon and the President's Assistant for National Security, 23 April 1971, *FRUS, Soviet Union, October 1970–October 1971*, Document 188.

73. WHT, Conversation 496-009, 10 May 1971, Oval Office; Kissinger, *White House Years*, location 16869–903.

74. For details, see Garrity and Mahan, *Nixon and Arms Control*.

75. WHT, Conversation 501-003, 19 May 1971, Oval Office.

76. Smith, *Doubletalk*, 224–44; Nitze, *From Hiroshima to Glasnost*, 313.

77. WHT, Conversation 501-004, 19 May 1971, Oval Office; WHT, Conversation 460-025, 26 February 1971, Oval Office; WHT, Conversation 501-007, 18 May 1971, Oval Office; WHT, Conversation 501-016, 18 May 1971, Oval Office; WHT, Conversation 003-067, 19 May 1971, White House telephone.

78. WHT, Conversation 501-018, 19 May 1971, Oval Office; WHT, Conversation 501-016, 19 May 1971, Oval Office; WHT, Conversation 501-024, 19 May 1971, Oval Office. On the morning of 20 May, Nixon and Smith met with a group of legislative leaders. Prior to that session, Kissinger warned Nixon not to use the word "freeze" in his description of the

interim agreement on offensive forces because that might seem to echo an earlier proposal made by Senator Hubert H. Humphrey (D–MN). WHT, Conversation 501-029, 19 May 1971, Oval Office. After the meeting with legislators, Nixon told Kissinger and Haldeman that Smith had done well in briefing the leaders. Nixon complained, however, that key Democratic senators, including Mansfield and Senate Foreign Relations Committee chairman J. William Fulbright (D–AR), were behaving like poor sports. Nixon acknowledged that Mansfield was doubtless disappointed that he had lost a critical Senate vote on his amendment to reduce the number of US forces in Europe the day before, and the president would later note that Mansfield had issued a gracious and favorable statement about SALT. WHT, Conversation 502-012, 20 May 1971, Oval Office. Just before he made his televised SALT announcement, Nixon spoke briefly by telephone with House Minority Leader Gerald R. Ford (R-MI) to discuss the effects of the statement on congressional opinion. WHT, Conversation 003-080, 20 May 1971, White House telephone.

79. Richard Nixon, "Remarks Announcing an Agreement on Strategic Arms Limitation Talks," 20 May 1971, online at Peters and Woolley, American Presidency Project. WHT, Conversation 502-009, 18 May 1971, Oval Office; WHT, Conversation 501-016, 19 May 1971, Oval Office; WHT, Conversation 502-006, 20 May 1971, Oval Office; WHT, Conversation 502-009, 20 May 1971, Oval Office. Kissinger held such conversations in subsequent weeks to defend the administration's position in SALT and to argue for conservative support.

80. J. D. Crouch, "Strategic Defense and the ABM Treaty: An Examination of the Effect of the ABM Treaty on U.S. Defense Programs, 1972–1986" (PhD diss., University of Southern California, August 1987), 46.

81. William Beecher, "U.S. Urges Soviet[s] to Join in a Missiles Moratorium," *New York Times*, 23 July 1971, 1; Smith, *Doubletalk*, 253; Newhouse, *Cold Dawn*, 224–25.

82. Message from the Government of the United States to the Government of the People's Republic of China, 20 May 1971, *FRUS, China, 1969–1972*, Document 126.

83. Memorandum of Conversation, Beijing, 10 July 1971, *FRUS, China, 1969–1972*, Document 140. For his part, Chou said very little about arms control, other than to insist that China would never participate in the Soviet-proposed Five-Power Nuclear Conference and that while "we don't know the content in your SALT talks, . . . the only thing we know is that your defense budget rises every year and the result is that the more you talk about disarmament, the more armaments expand and that adds to the disquiet, the turmoil of the world."

84. Telephone conversation between President Nixon and Henry Kissinger, 19 November 1971, Telcon; Conversation between President Nixon and the President's Assistant for National Security (Kissinger), 3 January 1972, *FRUS, SALT I, 1969–1972,* Document 219.

85. Memorandum from Secretary of Defense Laird to the President's Assistant for National Security Affairs (Kissinger), Washington, DC, 12 July 1971, *FRUS, SALT I, 1969–1972,* Document 117; Memorandum from the Acting Chairman of the Joint Chiefs of Staff (Zumwalt) to Secretary of Defense, 31 July 1971, *FRUS, SALT I, 1969–1972,* Document 186; Hunt, *Melvin Laird,* 420–21. In Kissinger's assessment, the Accidents Measures Agreement was successfully watered down from its original anti-Chinese formulation. See Kissinger, *White House Years,* locations 11485, 17277.

86. See, for example, Poole, *The Joint Chiefs of Staff,* 99.

87. Memorandum from the Chairman of the Joint Chiefs of Staff (Moorer) to Secretary of Defense Laird, Washington, DC, 13 July 1971, *FRUS, SALT I, 1969–1972,* Document 176; Hunt, *Melvin Laird,* 411–12; Poole, *The Joint Chiefs of Staff,* 99.

88. Smith, *Disarming Diplomat,* 301–18.

89. Ibid., 202–9, 261–65; personal letter from Smith to President Nixon, 12 August 1971, Smith, *Doubletalk,* appendix 5; Back-channel Message from the Chief of the Delegation to the Strategic Arms Limitation Talks (Smith) to the President's Assistant for National Security Affairs (Kissinger), 7 August 1971, *FRUS, SALT I, 1969–1972,* Document 189. According to the final language in the ABM Treaty: "Further, to decrease the pressures of technological change and its unsettling impact on the strategic balance, both sides agree to prohibit development, testing, or deployment of sea-based, air-based, or space-based ABM systems and their components, along with mobile land-based ABM systems. Should future technology bring forth new ABM systems 'based on other physical principles' than those employed in current systems, it was agreed that limiting such systems would be discussed, in accordance with the Treaty's provisions for consultation and amendment."

90. Memorandum from Secretary of Defense Laird to President Nixon, 18 January 1972, *FRUS, SALT I, 1969–1972,* Document 226. See the summary of the Kissinger-Dobrynin conversation on the SLBM trade-in option, 9 March 1972, and subsequent discussions, editorial note, *FRUS, SALT I, 1969–1972,* Document 237.

91. Kissinger, *White House Years,* location 22999–23060.

92. Semenov had previously introduced this idea of a 2:2 ABM deployment in the formal negotiations, and Dobrynin and Kissinger discussed it in the back channel. NSDM 158, 23 March 1972, *FRUS, SALT I, 1969–1972,*

Document 243; Memorandum of Conversation, 22 April 1972, *FRUS, SALT I, 1969–1972*, Document 262; Kissinger, *White House Years*, location 23581–608; Tal, *U.S. Strategic Arms Control Policy in the Cold War*, 79.

93. Editorial note, including Memorandum from President Nixon to Presidential Assistant Kissinger, 23 April 1972, *FRUS, SALT I, 1969–1972*, Document 264; Kissinger, *White House Years*, location 23684–875.

94. Conversation among President Nixon, Secretary of State Rogers, the President's Assistant for National Security Affairs (Kissinger), the President's Deputy Assistant for National Security Affairs (Haig), and the White House Press Secretary (Ziegler), 1 May 1972, *FRUS, SALT I, 1969–1972*, Document 270; Smith, *Disarming Diplomat*, 160. The two sides established a baseline of 44 modern SSBNs and 740 modern SLBMs, from which the Soviet Union could build up to the 62/950 limit if they fully applied the trade-in rules. The United States was capped at the 44/740 limit if it chose to build up beyond its current sea-based force.

95. Smith, *Disarming Diplomat*, 370–77; Bundy, *A Tangled Web*, location 6808–17.

96. Smith, *Disarming Diplomat*, 404–15, 432.

97. Kissinger, *White House Years*, location 25692–769.

98. Back-channel Message from the President's Deputy Assistant for National Security Affairs (Haig) to the President's Assistant for National Security Affairs (Kissinger), 25 May 1972, *FRUS, SALT I, 1969–1972*, Document 310, text and note 4, a telegram from Haig to Kissinger, which contains the "in accord" language finally endorsed by the Joint Chiefs (who at one point considered going on the record merely as "acquiescing"). This *Foreign Relations of the United States* volume contains many documents recording the back-channel negotiations between Nixon, Kissinger, Haig, and the Joint Chiefs during the Moscow summit. See also Hunt, *Melvin Laird*, 429.

99. Hunt, *Melvin Laird*, 429; Poole, *The Joint Chiefs of Staff*, 109.

100. Minutes of an NSC Meeting, 11 February 1971, *FRUS, National Security Policy, 1969–1972*, Document 174.

101. For quote, see Garthoff, *Détente and Confrontation*, 30. For an analysis of the political aspects enveloping Nixon's foreign policy, see generally Dallek, *Partners in Power*. For a recent treatment of the political aspects of arms control, the ABM Treaty, and SALT, see James Cameron, *The Double Game*, 107–12, 136–37, 157–60, 165–67.

102. Mahan, "The SALT Mindset."

103. Conversation between Nixon and Haldeman, WHT, Conversation 717-019, 2 May 1972, Oval Office.

104. For one of the better revisionist approaches, see Niccolo Petrelli and Giordana Pulcini, "Nuclear Superiority in the Age of Parity: US

Planning, Intelligence Analysis, Weapons Innovation and the Search for a Qualitative Edge 1969–1976," *International History Review* 40, no. 5 (2018): 1191–1209.

5. NUCLEAR NONPROLIFERATION AND A STRATEGY OF AMBIVALENCE

1. See, for example, "Nixon Says He Has Doubts Concerning Nuclear Treaty," *Washington Post*, 9 September 1968; and "Nixon Sharpens Attacks on Humphrey," *New York Times*, 24 September 1968.
2. Treaty on the Non-Proliferation of Nuclear Weapons (NPT), United Nations Office for Disarmament Affairs, accessed 6 January 2019, https:// www.un.org./disarmanet/wemd/nuclear/npt.
3. One prominent exception to the prevailing "lost years" thesis is offered by James Cameron and Or Rabinowitz, "Eight Lost Years? Nixon, Ford, Kissinger and the Non-Proliferation Regime, 1969–1977," *Journal of Strategic Studies* 40, no. 6 (January 2016): 1–27. Although not covering the Nixon era per se, an insightful overview of the "1970s as the crucial decade" for the crafting of an international nuclear regime is offered in Leopoldo Nuti, "The Making of the Nuclear Order and the Historiography on the 1970s," *International History Review*, 40, no. 5 (2018): 965–74.
4. There is a general paucity of scholarship covering the period after the initial signing of the NPT. A notable exception and an influence on these authors' thesis is offered by the works of Francis J. Gavin. See, for example, Gavin, "Nuclear Proliferation and Non-Proliferation during the Cold War," in *The Cambridge History of the Cold War*, vol. 2, ed. Melvyn P. Leffler and Odd Arne Westad (New York: Cambridge University Press), 410–12; and Gavin, *Nuclear Statecraft*, 104–19.
5. Rostow to Johnson, 14 November 1968, US Declassified Documents Online.
6. Rostow to Johnson, 12 December 1968, ibid.
7. Memorandum of Conversation, 2 January 1969, *FRUS, Arms Control, 1969–1972*, Document 1.
8. Minutes of National Security Council Meeting, 29 January 1969, *FRUS, Arms Control, 1969–1972*, Document 5. The centrality of West Germany has been overlooked by even the best treatments of Nixon's nonproliferation policies, most notably Cameron and Rabinowitz, "Eight Lost Years?" Gavin is a notable exception, but he does not delve deeply into the issues. See Gavin, "Nuclear Proliferation and Non-Proliferation during the Cold War," 410–11.
9. Members of the NSC staff summarized the lengthy report for Kissinger with the key remark: "The recommended courses of action are in every

case quite moderate and none involve putting pressure on the countries to sign or ratify. This is basically an operational problem which could now be assigned to the Under Secretaries Committee." See Memorandum from Keeny and Halperin to Kissinger, 5 March 1969, *FRUS, Arms Control, 1969–1972,* Document 67.

10. "Message to the Senate Requesting Advice and Consent to Ratification of the Treaty on Non-Proliferation of Nuclear Weapons," 5 February 1969, *Public Papers of the President, 1969,* 62. For text of the Senate Foreign Relations Committee report, see US Arms Control and Disarmament Agency, *Documents on Disarmament, 1969,* 78–97. For Nixon's "expressed delight," see "The President's News Conference of 14 March 1969," *Public Papers of the President, 1969,* 214.

11. NSDM 6, 5 February 1969, National Security Council, National Security Memoranda, Richard M. Nixon Presidential Library and Museum, Yorba Linda, California, https://www.nixonlibrary.gov/sites/default/files/virtuallibrary/documents/nsdm/nsdm_006.pdf.

12. For quote, see "Talking Paper on European Trip," prepared by the NSC staff, undated (circa February 1969), US Declassified Documents Online. These concerns crept into many conversations between Kissinger or Department of State diplomats and representatives of the FRG. See, for example, Memorandum of Conversation, 3 February 1969, *FRUS, Arms Control, 1969–1972,* Document 7; Memorandum of Conversation, 9 April 1969, *FRUS, Arms Control, 1969–1972,* Document 18; and Telegram 14146 from the Embassy in Germany to the Department of State, 28 October 1969, *FRUS, Arms Control, 1969–1972,* Document 28. On West Germany signing the NPT, see "Statement by the Federal Republic of Germany on Signature of the Nonproliferation Treaty," 28 November 1969, US Arms Control and Disarmament Agency, *Documents on Disarmament, 1969,* 612–13.

13. Although somewhat dated, see generally Catherin Kelleher, *Germany and the Politics of Nuclear Weapons* (New York: Columbia University Press, 1975); see also Stephen F. Szabo, ed., *The Bundeswehr and Western Security* (New York: Palgrave Macmillan, 1990), 71–86; and Wolfram Hanrieder, ed., *Arms Control, the FRG, and the Future of East-West Relations* (Boulder, CO: Westview, 1987).

14. Memorandum of Conversation, 17 February 1969, in US Department of State, *Soviet-American Relations,* 10.

15. Telegram from Dobrynin to the Soviet Foreign Ministry, 13 March 1969, in US Department of State, *Soviet-American Relations,* 43.

16. See generally *FRUS, Arms Control, 1969–1972,* Documents 6, 18, 35, 36, and 39; Oliver Bange, "NATO and the Non-Proliferation Treaty," in

Transforming NATO in the Cold War: Challenges Beyond Deterrence in the 1960s, ed. Andreas Wenger, Christian Nuenlist, and Anna Locher (New York: Routledge, 2007), 169–72; and Dallek, *Partners in Power,* 214–16.

17. See NIE 41–69, 17 February 1969, *Foreign Relations of the United States, 1969–1976,* vol. 19, *Part 2, Japan, 1969–1972,* ed. David P. Nickels, Edward C. Keefer, and Adam M. Howard (Washington, DC: Government Printing Office, 2018), Document 3, hereinafter referred to as *FRUS, Japan, 1969–1972:* "There is no indication that the Japanese are now planning for the production of nuclear weapons, though they have the capability to build them." See also special NIE 4-1-74, "Prospects for Further Proliferation of Nuclear Weapons," 23 August 1974, National Security Archive, accessed at nsarchive2.gwu.edu: "The Japanese are unlikely to make a decision to produce nuclear weapons unless there is a major adverse shift in relationships among the major powers. . . . If Japan decided to develop a nuclear weapon as rapidly as possible, in violation of safeguards, it probably could have an initial device within two or three years," 30.

18. The scholarly literature on US-Japanese foreign relations during the Nixon era is sparse. For a thoughtful article, see Liang Pan, "Whither Japan's Military Potential? The Nixon Administration's Stance on Japanese Defense Power," *Diplomatic History* 31, no. 1 (January 2007): 111–42. For two overviews, see Poole, *The Joint Chiefs of Staff,* 232–50; and Hunt, *Melvin Laird,* 329–46.

19. George H. Quester, "Japan and the Nuclear Non-Proliferation Treaty," *Asian Survey* 10, no. 9 (September 1970): 765–78.

20. Daniel I. Okimoto, "Japan's Non-Nuclear Policy: The Problem of the NPT," *Asian Survey* 15, no. 4 (April 1975): 313.

21. Robert F. Reed, *The US-Japan Alliance: Sharing the Burden of Defense* (Washington, DC: National Defense University Press, 1983), 23.

22. Gavin, *Nuclear Statecraft,* 118.

23. Letter from the Under Secretary of State for Political Affairs (Johnson) to the President's Assistant for National Security Affairs (Kissinger), 7 June 1972, *FRUS, Japan, 1969–1972,* Document 120.

24. See generally Timothy J. Botti, *The Long Wait: The Forging of the Anglo-American Nuclear Alliance, 1945–1958* (New York: Greenwood, 1987). Although somewhat dated, for this early period, a comprehensive study is offered by Margaret Gowing, *Independence and Deterrence: Britain's Atomic Energy, 1945–1952* (New York: Palgrave Macmillan, 1975).

25. For background on the British nuclear deterrent and its relationship to NATO during the 1960s, see generally Beatrice Heuser, "The Development

of NATO's Nuclear Strategy," *Contemporary European History* 4, no. 1 (Winter 1995): 37–66; Lawrence S. Kaplan, *NATO and the United States: The Enduring Alliance*, rev. ed. (New York: Twayne, 1994), 91–95; and Mahan, *Kennedy, De Gaulle, and Western Europe*, 39–40, 137–42.

26. For Nixon's visit to the UK, see, for example, "Talking Points in Preparation for President Nixon's Trip to Great Britain," undated, US Declassified Documents Online, http://tinyurl.galegroup.com/tinyurl/6Mg971; and Memorandum of Conversation (UK and US Official Delegations), 25 February 1969, US Declassified Documents Online; see also summary reported in Telegram from Secretary of State Rogers to the Department of State, 28 February 1969, 0050Z, *Foreign Relations of the United States, 1969–1976*, vol. 41, *Western Europe; NATO, 1969–1972*, ed. James E. Miller and Laurie Van Hook (Washington, DC: Government Printing Office, 2012), Document 311, hereinafter referred to as *FRUS, Western Europe, 1969–1972*.

27. A succinct summary of US-UK nuclear relations, especially pertaining to the Super Antelope program is offered in Response to NSSM 123, 2 July 1971, *FRUS, Western Europe, 1969–1972*, Document 344. For Nixon's approval of US assistance to the UK Super Antelope program, see NSDM 124, 29 July 1971, *FRUS, Western Europe, 1969–1972*, Document 345.

28. For the British perspective, see Peter Hennessy, *Cabinets and the Bomb* (Oxford: Oxford University Press, 2007), 219–322. Hennessy's work provides not only analysis of UK-US nuclear issues but also facsimiles of declassified copies of photocopies of British documents on the subject from the UK Public Records Office at Kew.

29. For de Gaulle's antipathy toward the NPT, see Shane J. Maddock, *Nuclear Apartheid: The Quest for American Atomic Supremacy From World War II to the Present* (Chapel Hill: University of North Carolina Press, 2014), 251–84. For details on French nuclear testing, see, for example, NIE 22–68, "French Nuclear Weapons and Delivery Capabilities," 31 December 1968, Woodrow Wilson Center Digital Archive, https://digitalarchive .wilsoncenter.org; and "24 August 1968—French 'Canopus' Test," Comprehensive Nuclear-Test-Ban-Organization, https://www.ctbto.org/specials /testing-times/24-august-1968-french-canopus-test.

30. See generally Drea, *History of the Office of the Secretary of Defense*, 6:375–88. On Kissinger's optimism that the Nixon administration could work in "turning" de Gaulle, see, for example, Memorandum from the President's Assistant for National Security Affairs (Kissinger) to President Nixon, 14 February 1969, *FRUS, Western Europe, 1969–1972*, Document 117. On the affinity and admiration felt by Nixon toward de Gaulle, see Thomas C. Reed and Danny B. Stillman, *The Nuclear Express: A Political History of*

the Bomb and Its Proliferation (Voyageur, 2010), 122; and C. L. Sulzberger, *The World and Richard Nixon*, 1st ed. (New York: Prentice Hall, 1987), 150–67. For senior French official quote, see Richard H. Ullman, "The Covert French Connection," *Foreign Policy* 75 (Summer 1989): 8. Ullman's provocative and insightful article draws extensively on interviews with former US and French officials who spoke under the condition of anonymity.

31. Memorandum of Conversation, 1 March 1969, *FRUS, Western Europe, 1969–1972*, Document 118.

32. See generally Ullman, "The Covert French Connection." The nuclear assistance continued under Carter and Reagan.

33. For quote, ibid., 12. For insight into Laird's resistance, see author's telephone interview with Robert Pursley (former senior military assistant to Secretary Laird), 5 February 2016.

34. For Pompidou's discussions with Nixon, see Memorandum from Assistant to the President for National Security Affairs (Kissinger) to President Nixon, 23 February 1970; and Memorandum from Helmut Sonnenfeldt of the NSC Staff to the Assistant to the President for National Security Affairs (Kissinger), 28 February 1970. On US-French parameters of cooperation, see Memorandum from Kissinger to Laird, 16 March 1970; Memorandum from Helmut Sonnenfeldt of the NSC Staff to Kissinger, 16 April 1970; Memorandum from Laird to Kissinger, 14 July 1970. All documents obtained through History and Public Policy Program Digital Archive, FOIA Release, available at https://www.wilsoncenter.org/publication/us-secret-assistance-to-the-french-nuclear-program-1969-1975-fourth-country-to-strategic.

35. NSDM 103, 29 March 1971, *FRUS, Western Europe, 1969–1972*, Document 153; and NSDM 104, 29 March 1971, *FRUS, Western Europe, 1969–1972*, Document 154.

36. For discussion of legalities surrounding nuclear safety and other forms of cooperation, see, for example, Memorandum from the Executive Secretariat of the Department of State (Eliot) to Kissinger, 13 August 1971, US Declassified Documents Online, and Letter from Laird to Kissinger, 29 July 1971, History and Public Policy Program Digital Archive, FOIA Release, by William Burr, available at https://digitalarchive.wilsoncenter.org/document/112255. On DoD's skepticism, see, for example, Memorandum from the Deputy Director of the Office of Strategic and Space Systems, Department of Defense (Walsh) to Secretary of Defense Schlesinger, 6 March 1974, *Foreign Relations of the United States, 1969–1976*, vol. E-15, Part 2, *Documents on Western Europe, 1973–1976*, ed. Kathleen B. Rasmussen and Adam M. Howard (Washington, DC:

Government Printing Office, 2014), Document 320, hereinafter referred to as *FRUS, Documents on Western Europe, 1973–1976*. For quotes, see Ullman, "The Covert French Connection," 10, 31.

37. Leopoldo Nuti, "A Turning Point in Postwar Foreign Policy: Italy and the NPT Negotiations, 1967–1969," in *Negotiating the Nuclear Non-Proliferation Treaty: Origins of the Nuclear Order,* ed. Roland Popp, Liviu Horovitz, and Andreas Wenger (New York: Routledge, 2016),78–79 (the authors thank Nuti for providing a prepublication draft of a forthcoming manuscript chapter). See also "Italy's Nuclear Choices," UNISCI Discussion Papers, 25 (January 2011): 171–74.

38. Leopoldo Nuti, "Italy as a Hedging State? The Problematic Ratification of the Non-Proliferation Treaty," EUT Edizioni Università di Trieste, 2017, https://www.openstarts.units.it/handle/10077/15331, 122. For an insightful look at the role of nuclear safeguards and the early history of the IAEA, see Elisabeth Roehrlich, "Negotiating Verification: International Diplomacy and the Evolution of Nuclear Safeguards, 1945–1972, *Diplomacy and Statecraft* 29, no. 1 (March 2018): 29–50. For Italian sensitivities to their place in NATO, see for example, Talking Paper For European Trip, undated (February 1969), US Declassified Documents Online.

39. For a persuasive account of Italy as a "nuclear hedging" state, see Nuti, "Italy as a Hedging State?," 139.

40. Depending on whether Algeria is considered a Middle Eastern country, it had also not signed the NPT by 1969. As far as these authors know, Okimoto coined the term "nuclear metastasis." See Okimoto, "Japan's Non-Nuclear Policy," 323.

41. One of the most comprehensive and thoroughly researched seminal accounts remains George Perkovich, *India's Nuclear Bomb: The Impact on Global Proliferation,* updated ed. (Berkeley: University of California Press, 1999), 125–89.

42. Meeting between Kissinger and Dobrynin, in US Department of State, *Soviet-American Relations,* 24.

43. The Intelligence and Research Bureau (INR) at the State Department was revealing the most telling information on India's nuclear capabilities, but it was rarely looked at by Nixon or Kissinger. For Nixon's skepticism toward the State Department, see Sulzberger, *The World and Richard Nixon,* 168–90. For INR assessments, see William Burr, "The Nixon Administration and the Indian Nuclear Program, 1972–1974," National Security Archive Briefing Book no. 367, 5 December 2011, https://nsarchive2.gwu.edu/nukevault/ebb367/index.htm.

44. Richard Betts, "Nuclear Incentives: India, Pakistan, Iran," *Asian Survey* 19, no. 11 (November 1979): 1055–57; and Perkovich, 161–66.

45. Perkovich, "Could Anything Be Done to Stop Them? Lessons from Pakistan's Proliferating Past," in *Pakistan's Nuclear Future: Worries beyond War*, ed. Henry D. Sokolski (Carlisle Barracks, PA: Strategic Studies Institute, 2008); Reed and Stillman, *The Nuclear Express*, 157–161.

46. "Kissinger Regrets 1971 Remarks on India," *New York Times*, 2 July 2005.

47. Zafar Kahn, "Pakistan and the NPT: Commitments and Concerns," *Margalla Papers*, 2012, 14; and Perkovich, "A Nuclear Third Way in South Asia," *Foreign Policy* 91 (Summer 1993): 89–91.

48. For Nixon's memoir reflections, see Francine Klagsbrun, *Lioness: Golda Meir and The Nation of Israel* (Knopf Doubleday, 2017), 519.

49. Conversation among Nixon, MacArthur, and Haig, 8 April 1971, *FRUS, Arms Control, 1969–1972*, Document 122.

50. On Nixon's tilt toward Iran, see Roham Alvandi, *Nixon, Kissinger, and the Shah: The United States and Iran in the Cold War* (New York: Oxford University Press, 2014), 54–55. For text of the NSDM, see NSDM 92, 7 November 1970, National Security Council, National Security Memoranda, Richard M. Nixon Presidential Library and Museum, Yorba Linda, California https://www.nixonlibrary.gov/sites/default/files/virtuallibrary/documents/nsdm/nsdm_092.pdf.

51. Mustafa Kibaroğlu, "Iran's Nuclear Ambitions from a Historical Perspective and the Attitude of the West," *Middle Eastern Studies* 43, no. 2 (March 2007): 225–29; see also Alvandi, *Nixon, Kissinger, and the Shah*, 130–31.

52. On Iran's quest for nuclear energy and concern about regional nuclear ambitions, see George Quester, "The Shah and the Bomb," *Policy Sciences* 8 (1977): 21–32. See also Gawdat Bahgat, "Nuclear Proliferation: The Islamic Republic of Iran," *Iranian Studies* 39, no. 3 (September 2006): 307–27.

53. Alvandi, *Nixon, Kissinger, and the Shah*, 139–43.

54. Nixon's stance on Israel and the NPT and nonproliferation is one subject that has been explored in depth by many scholars. An overview will suffice here, as no new documentation has been released to modify existing accounts.

55. "Memorandum from Secretary of Defense (Laird) to Secretary of State (Rogers) and Assistant to the President for National Security Affairs (Kissinger)," 17 March 1969, https://www.jewishvirtuallibrary.org/jsource/US-Israel/Nixon/Nixon031769.pdf; "Minutes, Meeting of the Special NSC Review Group on Israeli Assistance Requests," 26 January 1970, https://www.jewishvirtuallibrary.org/jsource/US-Israel/Nixon/Nixon012670.pdf.

56. "Memorandum from Executive Secretariat (John Walsh) to Assistant to the President for National Security Affairs (Kissinger), Deputy Secretary of Defense (Packard), Director of CIA (Helms), and Chairman of JCS

(Wheeler)," 30 May 1969, https://www.archives.gov/files/declassification /iscap/pdf/2009-076-doc1.pdf; "Memorandum from Deputy Secretary of State (Richardson) to President Nixon," 17 October 1969, https://www .archives.gov/files/declassification/iscap/pdf/2009-076-doc1.pdf. The reactions of Kissinger and the various departments are set out in Rodger Davies to Distribution, "Review Group Consideration of Response to NSSM 40," 30 June 1969, https://www.jewishvirtuallibrary.org/jsource /US-Israel/Nixon/Nixon063069.pdf. The memorandum of the 29 July conversation with Rabin is attached to "Elliot Richardson to President Nixon," 1 August 1969, https://www.jewishvirtuallibrary.org/jsource/US -Israel/Nixon/Nixon080169.pdf.

57. The most comprehensive analyses remain Cohen, *The Worst Kept Secret*, and Avner Cohen, *Israel and the Bomb* (New York: Columbia University Press, 1998). Nixon met privately with Meir and recorded his own memorandum of their conversation. For months afterward, senior officials complained that they still had not been given a copy. "Harold Saunders to Henry Kissinger, Record of the President's Talk with Henry Kissinger," 8 December 1969, https://www.jewishvirtuallibrary.org /jsource/US-Israel/Nixon/Nixon120869.pdf. For a discussion of the differing terminologies, see for instance, "Joseph Sisco to Acting Secretary of State, Talking Points for Initial Meeting with Israelis on Nuclear and NSSM Issues," 29 July 1969, briefing memorandum, 28 July 1969, https:// www.jewishvirtuallibrary.org/jsource/US-Israel/Nixon/Nixon072869 .pdf; and "Theodore Eliot to Henry Kissinger, Briefing Book—Visit of Mrs. Golda Meir," 19 September 1969, https://www.jewishvirtuallibrary .org/jsource/US-Israel/Nixon/Nixon091969.pdf.

58. For background on and provisions of the Treaty of Tlatelolco, see Davis R. Robinson, "The Treaty of Tlatelolco and the United States: A Latin American Nuclear Free Zone," *American Journal of International Law* 64, no. 2 (April 1970): 282–309.

59. On the verification and enforcement mechanisms of the LANWFZ as well as the implications on regional nuclear ambitions, see John R. Redick, "Regional Nuclear Arms Control in Latin America," *International Organization* 29, no. 2 (Spring 1975): 415–45. For examples of the State Department's lead at key inflection points, see for example, Letter from the Under Secretary of State (Richardson) to the Deputy Secretary of Defense (Packard), 10 June 1970; Memorandum from Secretary of State Rogers to President Nixon, 24 June 1970; and Memorandum from the Executive Secretary of the Department of State (Eliot) to the President's Assistant for National Security Affairs (Kissinger), 16 July 1970, all in *FRUS, Arms Control, 1969–1972*, Documents 355–57.

60. See generally Reddick, "Regional Nuclear Arms Control in Latin America."
61. The body of works related to the Seabed Treaty is sparse. For a succinct description and background, see Bennett Ramberg, "The Seabed Treaty, 1971 to the Present," in *Encyclopedia of Arms Control and Disarmament*, ed. Richard Dean Burns, vol. 2 (New York: Charles Scribner's Sons, 1993), 887–94. See also James A. Barry Jr., "The Seabed Arms Control Issue: 1967–1971, A Superpower Symbiosis?" *Naval War College Review* 24, no. 2 (November–December 1972): 87–101. For a political scientist approach to the seabed treaty negotiations, see Terrence Hopmann, "Bargaining in Arms Control Negotiations: The Seabed Denuclearization Treaty," *International Organization* 28, no. 3 (Summer 1974): 313–43.
62. *FRUS, Arms Control, 1969–1972,* Document 63.
63. Journal Entry by Seaborg, 15 March 1969, *FRUS, Arms Control, 1969–1972,* Document 74.
64. The Joint Chiefs most forcibly argued their position in an NSC Review Group meeting prior to the NSC meeting. See memorandum for the record, 7 March 1969, *FRUS, Arms Control, 1969–1972,* Document 68. See also Talking Paper Prepared for Secretary of Defense Laird and the Chairman of JCS (Wheeler), undated (March 1969), *FRUS, Arms Control, 1969–1972,* Document 72. For the evolution of Laird's position, see Journal Entry by Seaborg, 15 March 1969, *FRUS, Arms Control, 1969–1972,* Document 74; and Seaborg Diary, NSC Meeting, 30 April 1969, *FRUS, Arms Control, 1969–1972,* US Declassified Documents Online.
65. For Kissinger's quotes, *FRUS, Arms Control, 1969–1972.*
66. Journal entry by Seaborg, 15 March 1969, *FRUS, Arms Control, 1969–1972,* Document 74.
67. Notes of Telephone Conversation between the President's Assistant for National Security Affairs (Kissinger) and the Director of the Arms Control and Disarmament Agency (Smith), 28 March 1969, *FRUS, Arms Control, 1969–1972,* Document 82; NSSM 41, 11 April 1969, *FRUS, Arms Control, 1969–1972,* Document 84; Study Prepared by Ad Hoc National Security Council Steering Committee, 18 April 1969, *FRUS, Arms Control, 1969–1972,* Document 86; and Draft minutes of NSC Meeting, 30 April 1969, *FRUS, Arms Control, 1969–1972,* Document 89.
68. See, for example, telegram 2978 from the mission in Geneva to the Department of State, 19 August 1969, 2120Z, National Archives, RG 59, Central Files 1967–1969, POL 33–36; and Letter from Director of the ACDA (Smith) to Secretary of State Rogers, 21 August 1969, *FRUS, Arms Control, 1969–1972,* Document 109. For a pithy description of various

proposals and evolution of the negotiations, see US Arms Control and Disarmament Agency, *International Negotiations on the Seabed Arms Control Treaty* (Washington, DC: ACDA, 1973).

69. For Nixon's statement, see "Message from President Nixon to the ENDC," 3 July 1969, US Arms Control and Disarmament Agency, *Documents on Disarmament, 1969,* 300. See generally Bennett Ramberg, "Tactical Advantages of Opening Positioning Strategies: Lessons from the Seabed Arms Control Talks, 1967–1970," *Journal of Conflict Resolution* 21, no. 4 (December 1977): 691–94.

70. Richard Nixon, "First Annual Report to the Congress on United States Foreign Policy for the 1970s," 18 February 1970, online at Peters and Woolley, American Presidency Project.

71. Laura Iandola, "Foreign Relations of the United States, Vol. E-2, Documents on Arms Control and Nonproliferation, 1969–1972," *H-Diplo FRUS Review,* 12 July 2013.

72. Ramberg is tepid but more generous than these authors in his assessment. Ramberg, "The Seabed Treaty, 1971 to the Present." A more scathing critique is provided in Barry, "The Seabed Arms Control Issue," 98–99.

73. WHT, Conversation 732-011, 13 June 1972, Oval Office.

74. This perspective is shared by many proponents of the NPT. See, for example, Joseph Cirincione, "Lessons Lost," *Bulletin of the Atomic Scientists* 61, no. 6 (December 2005): 43–53.

75. During the Ford administration, Secretary of Defense Donald Rumsfeld informed the president, for example, that cooperation with France should be contingent upon its cooperation with the US and NATO and that "it may be time to review our policies with respect to some sensitive programs of assistance with national directives: 1) Missile Engineering, 2) Vulnerability Assessment, 3) Testing of Reentry Vehicle Material, 4) Basic Knowledge of Material Behavior, 5) Nuclear Safety, 6) Underground testing." Memorandum from Secretary of Defense Rumsfeld to President Ford, 13 May 1976, *FRUS, Documents on Western Europe, 1973–1976,* Document 336.

76. Gavin, "Strategies of Inhibition." Gavin provides a thoughtful, even provocative account of the range of tools employed to slow, halt, and reverse the spread of nuclear weapons.

77. John Simpson, "The Future of the NPT," in *Combating Weapons of Mass Destruction: The Future of International Nonproliferation Policy,* ed Nathan E. Busch and Daniel Joyner (Athens: University of Georgia Press, 2009), 46–47. See also Paul Lettow, *Strengthening the Nuclear Nonproliferation Regime* (Council on Foreign Relations, 2010), 6.

6. Unfinished Business of SALT II

1. Richard Nixon, "Address to a Joint Session of the Congress on Return from Austria, the Soviet Union, Iran, and Poland," 1 June 1972, online at Peters and Woolley, American Presidency Project.
2. Lori Esposito Murray, "The Selling of SALT," *Foreign Service Journal* 59 (February 1982): 20–24.
3. Murray, "SALT and Congress," 377–79, 381–84, 393–95.
4. Memorandum from President Nixon to the President's Deputy Assistant for National Security (Haig), 20 May 1972, *Foreign Relations of the United States, 1969–1976*, vol. 14, *Soviet Union, October 1971–May 1972*, ed. David C. Geyer, Nina D. Howland, and Kent Sieg (Washington, DC: Government Printing Office, 2006), Document 250, hereinafter referred to as *FRUS, Soviet Union, 1971–1972*; Telephone conversation between President Nixon and Henry Kissinger, 2 June 1972, Digital National Security Archive.
5. Richard Nixon, "Address to a Joint Session of the Congress on Return from Austria, the Soviet Union, Iran, and Poland," https://www.presidency.ucsb.edu/documents/address-joint-session-the-congress-return-from-austria-the-soviet-union-iran-and-poland; Murray, "SALT and Congress," 381–84, 395–96. For a recent discussion of the interaction of SALT, strategy, and technology that prizes weapon-system capabilities, see Steven Pomeroy, *An Untaken Road: Strategy, Technology, and the Hidden History of America's Mobile ICBMs* (Annapolis, MD: Naval Institute Press, 2016), 129–74.
6. Briefing by the President's Assistant for National Security Affairs (Kissinger) for the Senate Foreign Relations Committee, 15 June 1972, *FRUS, Foundations, 1969–1972*, Document 118.
7. Murray, "SALT and Congress," 396–97, 404–10.
8. Robert Kauffman, *Henry M. Jackson: A Life in Politics* (Seattle: University of Washington Press, 2000), 254–57.
9. Senator Henry Jackson, Amendment to Senate Joint Resolution 241 on the Interim Strategic Offensive Arms Agreement, Cong. Rec. S30623e.
10. Telephone conversation between Henry Kissinger and Senator Henry Jackson, 27 July 1972, Digital National Security Archive (DNSA), Telcon; telephone conversation between President Nixon and Henry Kissinger, 10 August 1972, DNSA, Telcon; Murray, "SALT and Congress," 396–97, 421–27.
11. Back-Channel Message from the Chief of the Delegation to the Strategic Arms Limitation Talks (Smith) to President Nixon, 20 December 1972, *Foreign Relations of the United States, 1969–1976*, vol. 33, *SALT II, 1972–1980*,

ed. Erin R. Mahan (Washington, DC: Government Printing Office, 2013), Document 10, hereinafter referred to as *FRUS, SALT II, 1972–1980*.

12. NSDM 197, 18 November 1972, *FRUS, SALT II, 1972–1980*, Document 7; Kissinger, *Years of Upheaval*, Kindle edition, location 5671–79. For an unclassified but well-informed account of the SALT negotiations during this period, see Thomas Wolfe, *The SALT Experience: Its Impact on U.S. and Soviet Policy and Decisionmaking* (Santa Monica, CA: RAND Corporation, 1975).

13. Minutes of a Meeting of the National Security Council, 8 March 1973, *FRUS, SALT II, 1972–1980*, Document 14; Kissinger, *Years of Upheaval*, location 5684; Poole, *The Joint Chiefs of Staff*, 48–49, 60–65.

14. For a description of the opening position of the Joint Chiefs, which remained fairly consistent in terms of the acceptable range of equal aggregates (though some were willing to go as low as two thousand), see Poole, *The Joint Chiefs of Staff*, 57.

15. Nitze, *From Hiroshima to Glasnost*, 335–36.

16. Henry Kissinger, *Years of Renewal* (New York: Simon and Schuster, 1999), 125–28.

17. Kissinger, *Years of Upheaval*, location 21078–96; Minutes of a Meeting of the National Security Council, 8 March 1973, *FRUS, SALT II, 1972–1980*, Document 14.

18. Minutes of a Meeting of the National Security Council, 8 March 1973, *FRUS, SALT II, 1972–1980*, Document 14.

19. Kissinger, *Years of Upheaval*, location 5604–12.

20. Defense conservatives frequently cited the views of the former chief of Naval Operations, Admiral Elmo Zumwalt, who alleged that Kissinger made such pessimistic statements in private. Zumwalt, *On Watch: A Memoir* (New York: Quadrangle, 1976), x, xiv. William Shawcross wrote a highly influential critique from the left shortly after Kissinger left office, which served as a template for subsequent indictments. Shawcross, *Sideshow: Kissinger, Nixon and the Destruction of Cambodia* (New York: Simon and Schuster, 1979). Journalist Seymour Hersh later published an account that excoriated Kissinger, including his alleged errors and transgression in SALT; see Hersh, *The Price of Power: Kissinger in the Nixon White House* (New York: Summit Books, 1983).

21. Tal, *U.S. Strategic Policy in the Cold War*, 118–19; Ambrose, *The Control Agenda*, location 1293–1316; U. Alexis Johnson, *The Right Hand of Power: The Memoirs of an American Diplomat* (Englewood Cliffs, NJ: Prentice-Hall, 1984), 576.

22. Tal, *U.S. Strategic Policy in the Cold War*, 119. This did not mean that Iklé himself had any significant influence over policy. According to Odeen,

"Fred, really, was reduced to non-proliferation because it didn't really carry much weight at that time. . . . Henry would never see Fred Iklé. Fred would ask to see Henry and Henry wouldn't see him at the last minute, and I ended up getting stuck listening to Fred go on for two hours about some esoteric subject." National Security Council Project, Oral History Roundtables, The Nixon Administration National Security Council, 8 December 1998, 23–24. Iklé later served as undersecretary of defense for policy in the Reagan administration.

23. Kissinger regarded Laird's immediate successor, Eliot Richardson, as a strong secretary and bureaucratic ally of the White House. Richardson, however, was soon shifted over to the Department of Justice as attorney general, to be succeeded in DoD by Schlesinger.

24. NSDM 213, 3 May 1973, *FRUS, SALT II, 1972–1980*, Document 23; NSDM 216, 7 May 1973, *FRUS, SALT II, 1972–1980*, Document 25.

25. Editorial note, *FRUS, SALT II, 1972–1980*, Document 24, which summarizes Kissinger's reporting on his May 1973 meetings in Moscow pertaining to SALT. Kissinger reviews the tortured history of these Soviet "political" approaches to arms control in *Years of Upheaval*, location 5825–6054.

26. Kissinger, *Years of Upheaval*, location 3629–39, 5901, 5968–73, 19257–77.

27. Memorandum of Conversation (Ford and Kissinger), 25 October 1975, *Foreign Relations of the United States, 1969–1976*, vol.18, *China, 1973–1976*, ed. David P. Nickels and Edward C. Keefer (Washington, DC: Government Printing Office, 2007), Document 129, hereinafter referred to as *FRUS, China, 1973–1976*. As to Mao's health, Kissinger told President Ford: "When you see him you think he is finished; he can hardly articulate. He speaks a few words of English but it is impossible to understand. The interpreter has to guess at the words until he nods—or he writes out the words." On Soviet perception of American weakness see also Memorandum from Secretary of State Kissinger to President Ford, 20 November 1975, *FRUS, China, 1973–1976*, Document 132.

28. See, for example, Memorandum from Winston Lord of the National Security Council Staff to the President's Military Assistant (Scowcroft), 16 April 1973, *FRUS, China, 1973–1976*, Document 27, summarizing Kissinger's meeting with Huang Zhen, head of the PRC Liaison Office in Washington.

29. The SALT basic principles agreement is reprinted in *Department of State Bulletin*, 23 July 1973, 158. The Agreement on the Prevention of Nuclear War is reprinted in Kissinger, *Years of Upheaval*, location 25865–913. Raymond Garthoff reviews the background of the agreement in *Détente and Confrontation*, 376–86.

30. Minutes of a Meeting of the Verification Panel, 15 August 1973, *FRUS, SALT II, 1972–1980*, Document 34; Poole, *The Joint Chiefs of Staff*, 64; Ambrose, *The Control Agenda*, location 1384–1418.

31. Minutes of a Meeting of the National Security Council, 24 January 1974, *FRUS, SALT II, 1972–1980*, Document 47; Kissinger, *Years of Upheaval*, location 21105–13.

32. Memorandum for the Record, 30 August 1973, *FRUS, SALT II, 1972–1980*, Document 36; Minutes of a Meeting of the Verification Panel, 28 December 1973, *FRUS, SALT II, 1972–1980*, Document 45; Minutes of a Meeting of the National Security Council, 24 January 1974, *FRUS, SALT II, 1972–1980*, Document 47. On Schlesinger's conceptual agreement but practical differences with Kissinger, see Tal, *U.S. Strategic Policy in the Cold War*, 150–52.

33. NSDM 242, 17 January 1974, Foreign Relations of the United States, 1969–1976, vol. 35, *National Security Policy, 1973–1976*, ed. M. Todd Bennett and Adam M. Howard (Washington DC: Government Printing Office, 2014), Document 31, hereinafter referred to as *FRUS, National Security Policy, 1973–1976*; James R. Schlesinger, "Secretary of Defense Report to Congress, FY 1975," 4 March 1974, ibid., 4, 38. For a comprehensive overview of the Nixon administration's approach, see Terry Terriff, *The Nixon Administration and the Making of U.S. Nuclear Strategy* (Ithaca, NY: Cornell University Press, 1995); and Gavin, *Nuclear Statecraft*, 104–19.

34. Memorandum from the President's Assistant for National Security Affairs (Kissinger) to President Nixon, undated, *FRUS, National Security Policy, 1973–1976*, Document 30, lays out the rationale for NSDM 242. On military secrecy surrounding the SIOP, see Terriff, *The Nixon Administration and the Making of Nuclear Strategy*, 61–62; Janne Nolan, *Guardians of the Arsenal: the Politics of Nuclear Strategy* (New York: Basic Books, 1989), 125, 249. On the Soviet response, see Garthoff, *Détente and Confrontation*, 466–68.

35. For contrasting views of the Jackson-Vanik amendment, see Kissinger, *Years of Upheaval*, location 5351–5461; and Kauffman, *Henry M. Jackson*, 266–73. For an analysis of what was considered acceptable and unacceptable behavior under the umbrella of détente, see Garthoff, *Détente and Confrontation*, 1125–80.

36. Minutes of a Meeting of the National Security Council, 21 March 1974, *FRUS, SALT II, 1972–1980*, Document 58; Kissinger, *Years of Upheaval*, location 21149–75.

37. Kissinger, *Years of Upheaval*, location 21307–16; Memorandum of Conversation, Moscow, 25 March 1974, *FRUS, SALT II, 1972–1980*, Document 60.

38. Minutes of a Meeting of the Verification Panel, 23 April 1974, *FRUS, SALT II, 1972–1980*, Document 64; Memorandum of Conversation (Nixon and Schlesinger), 6 June 1974, Gerald R. Ford Presidential Library and Museum, Ann Arbor, Michigan, https://www.fordlibrarymuseum .gov/library/document/0314/1552719.pdf (accessed 7 June 2018); Poole, *The Joint Chiefs of Staff*, 68–69; Kissinger, *Years of Upheaval*, location 23956, 23968–30264.

39. Kissinger, *Years of Upheaval*, location 21327–36, 23979–95; Memorandum of Conversation (Kissinger and Gromyko), 29 April 1974, *FRUS, SALT II, 1972–1980*, Document 66; Minutes of a Meeting of the National Security Council, 20 June 1974, *FRUS, SALT II, 1972–1980*, Document 68.

40. Letter from Senator Henry Jackson to President Nixon, 29 January 1974, *FRUS, SALT II, 1972–1980*, Document 50. Nixon responded in a letter to Jackson on 8 March 1974, which did not address the senator's arguments directly but insisted that the president was committed to maintaining US quantitative superiority. In a memo to Nixon on 5 March, Kissinger had made the following observations about Jackson's letter: (1) the proposed reductions to 1,760 strategic launchers would be one-sided and unacceptable to the Soviets, requiring them to reduce more than twice as many of their existing launchers as the United States; (2) a reductions-only program "places no real restraint" on new Soviet programs, especially their MIRV capacity; (3) Jackson's threat of a new series of US strategic programs if the Soviets did not respond to his proposed reductions would probably cause SALT to collapse. Letter from President Nixon to Senator Henry Jackson, 8 March 1974, *FRUS, SALT II, 1972–1980*, Document 56.

41. Poole, *The Joint Chiefs of Staff*, 69.

42. Quoted in Kissinger, *Years of Upheaval*, location 21339–48.

43. Memorandum of Conversation, 6 June 1974, Gerald R. Ford Presidential Library and Museum, Ann Arbor, Michigan, https://www .fordlibrarymuseum.gov/library/document/0314/1552719.pdf (accessed 7 June 2018).

44. Minutes of a Meeting of the National Security Council, 20 June 1974, *FRUS, SALT II, 1972–1980*, Document 68; Poole, *The Joint Chiefs of Staff*, 69.

45. Minutes of a Meeting of the National Security Council, 20 June 1974, *FRUS, SALT II, 1972–1980*, Document 68; Kissinger, *Years of Upheaval*, location 24011–22; Nixon, *RN: The Memoirs of Richard Nixon*, 1023–24.

46. Kissinger, *Years of Upheaval*, location 24294–303.

47. Kissinger, *Years of Upheaval*, location 24361–70.

48. Letter from President Ford to Soviet General Secretary Brezhnev, 9 August 1974, *Foreign Relations of the United States, 1969–1976*, vol. 16,

Soviet Union, August 1974–December 1976, ed. David C. Geyer and Edward C. Keefer (Washington, DC: Government Printing Office, 2012), Document 4, hereinafter referred to as *FRUS, Soviet Union, August 1974–December 1976.* Memorandum of Conversation (Ford and Gromyko), 20 September 1974, *FRUS, Soviet Union, August 1974–December 1976,* Document 37; Tal, *U.S. Strategic Policy in the Cold War,* 166–67.

49. Minutes of a Meeting of the National Security Council, 14 September 1974, *FRUS, SALT II, 1972–1980,* Document 74; Minutes of a Meeting of the National Security Council, 7 October 1974, *FRUS, SALT II, 1972–1980,* Document 76; Memorandum of Conversation (Ford-Kissinger-Scowcroft), 8 October 1974, *FRUS, SALT II, 1972–1980,* Document 77; Note from the United States to the Soviet Union, undated, *FRUS, SALT II, 1972–1980,* Document 78; Kissinger, *Years of Upheaval,* 277–78.

50. Ford did offer assurances that the United States would stop basing missile-carrying submarines at Rota, Spain, after 1983; this merely formalized existing US plans, since longer-range missiles on new Poseidon and Trident submarines would make forward bases unnecessary. The best account of the details of the Vladivostok Accord is in Anatoly Dobrynin, *In Confidence: Moscow's Ambassador to Six Cold War Presidents* (New York: Crown, 1995), 322–23, 327–33. See also memorandum, Jan Lodal of the National Security Staff to Kissinger, 30 November 1974, *FRUS, SALT II, 1972–1980,* Document 89; Soviet Aide-Mémoire, 10 December 1974, *FRUS, SALT II, 1972–1980,* Document 9; and David Horrocks and Helmi Raaska, eds., *The Vladivostok Summit on Arms Control, 23–24 November 1974,* Gerald R. Ford Presidential Library and Museum, Ann Arbor, Michigan, https://www.fordlibrarymuseum.gov/library/exhibits/vladivostok/vladivostok.asp.

51. Poole, *The Joint Chiefs of Staff,* 74.

52. Kissinger, *Years of Renewal,* 301–2.

53. Kissinger, *Years of Renewal,* 849–50.

54. Johnson, *The Right Hand of Power,* 605–21, provides a good synopsis of the post-Vladivostok issues. See also Kissinger, *Years of Renewal,* 847–48.

55. Poole, *The Joint Chiefs of Staff,* 74–83.

56. Johnson, *The Right Hand of Power,* 605–21.

57. See Paul Nitze, "The Strategic Balance between Hope and Skepticism," *Foreign Policy* 17 (Winter 1974–75): 136–56; Nitze, "The Vladivostok Accord and SALT II," *Review of Politics* 37 (April 1975): 146–60; Nitze, "Assuring Strategic Stability in an Era of Detente," *Foreign Affairs* 54 (January 1976): 207–32. See also Nitze, *From Hiroshima to Glasnost.*

58. Robert G. Kaufman, *Henry M. Jackson,* 288.

59. For an account of Nitze's strategic thought, see Strobe Talbott, *The Master of the Game.* For the role of the defense right and the Committee

on the Present Danger in fostering public perceptions of SALT and the treaty's demise, see David Dunn, *The Politics of Threat: Minuteman Vulnerability in American National Security Policy* (New York: St. Martin's, 1997), 95–101; Nolan, *Guardians of the Arsenal*, 136–37; Garthoff, *Détente and Confrontation*, 680, 800, 874–75; and Anne Hessing-Cahn, *Killing Détente: The Right Attacks the CIA* (University Park: Pennsylvania State University Press, 1998), 28–30, 188–91. For a view that discounts domestic factors in the demise of SALT II and the formulation of defense policy in the Carter administration, see Brian Auten, *Carter's Conversion: The Hardening of American Defense Policy* (Columbia: University of Missouri Press, 2008), especially 280–81, 304, 308; see also Ambrose, *The Control Agenda*, locations 3022, 3339–51. Garthoff takes a dim view of the Carter administration's efforts in SALT; see *Détente and Confrontation*, 883–912. For an analysis of the argument over arms control and nuclear policy, see Gavin, *Nuclear Statecraft*, 120–33.

7. Reconciling Nuclear Testing with Arms Control

1. WHT, Conversation 468-005, Oval Office, quoted in editorial note, *FRUS, SALT I, 1969–1972*, Document 141.
2. On the history of efforts to limit nuclear testing, see among others Divine, *Blowing on the Wind*; Glenn T. Seaborg with Benjamin S. Loeb, *Kennedy, Khrushchev, and the Test Ban* (Berkeley: University of California Press, 1981); and Rebecca Johnson, *Unfinished Business: The Negotiation of the CTBT and the End of Nuclear Testing* (New York: United Nations, 2009). For Nixon's disparagement of Kennedy and the limited test ban, see for example WHT, Conversation 494-004, 8 May 1971, Oval Office; WHT, Conversation 502-012, 20 May 1971, Oval Office. All the conversations cited below have been transcribed by the authors.
3. See, for example, "Swedish Working Paper on Possible Provisions of an Underground Test-Ban Treaty," 1 April 1969, 140; "Canadian Working Paper on a Comprehensive Test Ban," 23 May 1969, 231; and "Statement by the Japanese Representative (Asakai) on Underground Test Ban," 31 July 1969, 380—all in US Arms Control and Disarmament Agency, *Documents on Disarmament, 1969*.
4. Memorandum from Spurgeon Keeny and Morton Halperin of the National Security Council Staff to the President's Assistant for National Security Affairs (Kissinger),Washington, DC, 5 March 1969, *FRUS, Arms Control, 1969–1972*, Document 57; Memorandum for the Record, Washington, 7 March 1969, NSC Review Group Meeting, 6 March 1969, *FRUS, Arms Control, 1969–1972*, Document 68; Talking Paper Prepared for Secretary of Defense Laird and the Chairman of the Joint Chiefs of Staff

(Wheeler), Washington, DC, undated, *FRUS, Arms Control, 1969–1972,* Document 72.

5. Journal entry by the Chairman of the Atomic Energy Commission (Seaborg), Washington, DC, 15 March 1969, *FRUS, Arms Control, 1969–1972,* Document 74. The NSC also decided to maintain current US policy on a fissile material production ban and on the Seabed Treaty, which were also to be discussed in the ENCD.

6. Journal Entry by the Chairman of the Atomic Energy Commission (Seaborg), Washington, DC, 28 January 1969, *FRUS, Arms Control, 1969–1972,* Document 279. See also "Executive Summary: Plowshare Program," Report, US Department of Energy, Office of Science and Technical Information, undated, https://www.osti.gov/opennet/reports/plowshar.pdf.

7. At the same time, however, the US government was also restricted by the Atomic Energy Act from sharing nuclear device design or manufacturing information with most other countries. For an overview of Plowshares, see Scott Kaufman, *Project Plowshare: The Peaceful Use of Nuclear Explosives in Cold War America* (Ithaca, NY: Cornell University Press, 2012).

8. See for example Letter from the Chairman of the Atomic Energy Commission (Seaborg) to President Nixon, 5 February 1969, *FRUS, Arms Control, 1969–1972,* Document 280.

9. Nixon ordered a review of the LTBT-PNE relationship in the context of the proposed Australian PNE shortly after the administration took office. NSSM 25, 20 February 1969, *FRUS, Arms Control, 1969–1972,* Document 283. For a review of the issues, see Memorandum from the Director of the Office of International Scientific and Technological Affairs (Pollack) to the President's Assistant for National Security Affairs (Kissinger), 22 March 1969, Subject: NSSM 25: Cape Keraudren Nuclear Excavation Project and the Treaty Banning Nuclear Weapon Tests in the Atmosphere, in Outer Space and Under Water, *FRUS, Arms Control, 1969–1972,* Document 286. See also Memorandum for the Record, 4 October 1969, Eighteenth Meeting of the NSC Under Secretaries Committee on Tuesday, 14 October 1969, *FRUS, Arms Control, 1969–1972,* Document 292.

10. NSDM 18, 27 June 1969, *FRUS, Arms Control, 1969–1972,* Document 289; National Security Council Under Secretaries Committee Decision Memorandum 22, Washington, DC, 5 November 1969, *FRUS, Arms Control, 1969–1972,* Document 293.

11. See, for example, Telegram 2322 from the Department of State to Embassy in the Soviet Union, 7 January 1971, *FRUS, Arms Control, 1969–1972,* Document 296, which reported Soviet ambassador Dobrynin's

complaints about US venting of radioactive material. On Seaborg's position, see Journal Entry by the Chairman of the Atomic Energy Commission (Seaborg), 14 October 1969, *FRUS, Arms Control, 1969–1972*, Document 292.

12. NSSM 128, 4 June 1971, *FRUS, Arms Control, 1969–1972*, Document 303; Memorandum from the Director of the Arms Control and Disarmament Agency (Smith) to the President's Assistant for National Security Affairs (Kissinger), Washington, DC, 15 May 1971, *FRUS, Arms Control, 1969–1972*, Document 301.

13. Executive Summary Prepared by Interagency, Washington, DC, undated; NSSM 128, Nuclear Test Ban Policy Review, undated, *FRUS, Arms Control, 1969–1972*, Document 313; Analytical Summary Prepared by the National Security Council Staff, undated, Results of NSSM 128, *FRUS, Arms Control, 1969–1972*, Document 314; Memorandum from the Director of the Program Analysis Staff, National Security Council (Odeen) to the President's Assistant for National Security Affairs (Kissinger), 9 June 1972, *FRUS, Arms Control, 1969–1972*, Document 315.

14. Memorandum from the Chairman of the Joint Chiefs of Staff (Moorer) to Secretary of Defense Laird, 14 March 1972, JCSM-109-72, *FRUS, Arms Control, 1969–1972*, Document 311. The president's science advisor, Edward E. David Jr. also recommended against making any further moves toward a CTBT at the time. Memorandum from the President's Science Adviser (David) to the President's Assistant for National Security Affairs (Kissinger), 5 April 1972, *FRUS, Arms Control, 1969–1972*, Document 312.

15. Memorandum from the Director of the Program Analysis Staff, National Security Council (Odeen) to the President's Assistant for National Security Affairs (Kissinger), 29 March 1972, *FRUS, Arms Control, 1969–1972*, Document 311; Memorandum from the Director of the Program Analysis Staff, National Security Council (Odeen) to the President's Assistant for National Security Affairs (Kissinger), 9 June 1972, *FRUS, Arms Control, 1969–1972*.

16. The Committee for Nuclear Responsibility had been founded in January 1971 for the express purpose of blocking the Cannikin test. It was joined in this effort by the Sierra Club, Friends of the Earth, the Wilderness Society, the National Parks and Conservation Association, the Association on American Indian Affairs, Amchitka Two, and Sane, Inc. The motion to stop the Cannikin test was filed in the United States District Court for the District of Columbia on 9 July 1971. Dean W. Kohlhoff, *Amchitka and the Bomb: Nuclear Testing in Alaska* (Seattle: University of Washington Press, 2002), 101–7.

17. Ibid., 103.

18. WHT, Conversation 269-025, 3 August 1971, Executive Office Building; WHT, Conversation 277-018, 5 September 1971, Executive Office Building.

19. WHT, Conversation 603-001, 27 October 1971, Oval Office.

20. WHT, Conversation 620-012, 17 November 1971, Oval Office.

21. WHT, Conversation 14-017, 10 November 1971, White House telephone.

22. WHT, Conversation 620-008, 17 November 1971, Oval Office. During this conversation Nixon and Kissinger compared their impressions of Reagan. President Nixon: "What's your evaluation of Reagan after meeting him several times now?" Kissinger: "Well, I think he's a—actually I think he's a pretty decent guy." Nixon: "Oh, decent, no question, but his brains—" Kissinger: "Well, his brains are negligible." President Nixon: "He's really pretty shallow, Henry." Kissinger: "He's shallow. He's got no . . . he's an actor. When he gets a line he does it very well. He said, 'Hell, people are remembered not for what they do, but for what they say. Can't you find a few good lines?' [Chuckles.] That's really an actor's approach to foreign policy—to substantive—" President Nixon: "I've said a lot of good things, too, you know damn well." Kissinger: "Well, that too."

23. WHT, Conversation 619-028, 16 November 1971, Oval Office.

24. WHT, Conversation 620-012, 17 November 1971, Oval Office.

25. WHT, Conversation 621-043, 22 November 1971, Oval Office.

26. Kohlhoff, *Amchitka and the Bomb*, 109–16; Pam Miller, *Nuclear Flashback: The Return to Amchitka* (Washington, DC: Greenpeace, 1996).

27. Kissinger, *Years of Upheaval*, location 24186–93.

28. Ibid., location 24193–204; Memorandum from Jan Lodal of the National Security Council Staff to Secretary of State Kissinger, Washington, DC, 12 March 1974, *Foreign Relations of the United States, 1969–1976*, vol. E-14, Part 2, *Documents on Arms Control and Nonproliferation, 1973–1976*, ed. Kristin L. Ahlberg, Bonnie Sue Kim, Chris Tudda, and Adam M. Howard (Washington, DC: Government Printing Office, 2015), Document 32, hereinafter referred to as *FRUS, Arms Control, 1973–1976*; Minutes of NSC Meeting, 20 June 1974, *FRUS, Arms Control, 1973–1976*, Document 56.

29. NSSM 195, 20 February 1974, *FRUS, Arms Control, 1973–1976*, Document 30; Memorandum of Conversation, Department of State, Meeting of the Secretary's Visit to Moscow, 20 March 1974, *FRUS, Arms Control, 1973–1976*, Document 34.

30. Poole, *The Joint Chiefs of Staff*, 70–71; Minutes of NSC Meeting, 20 January 1974, *FRUS, Arms Control, 1973–1976*, Document 56.

31. Zumwalt, *On Watch*, 195–97.

32. Poole, *The Joint Chiefs of Staff*, 70–71.

33. Ibid., 71–72; NSDM 256, 10 June 1974, *FRUS, Arms Control, 1973–1976*, Document 54.

34. Poole, *The Joint Chiefs of Staff*, 71; Minutes of NSC Meeting, 20 June 1974, *FRUS, Arms Control, 1973–1976*, Document 56.

35. Minutes of NSC Meeting, 20 June 1974, *FRUS, Arms Control, 1973–1976*, Document 56.

36. Kissinger, *Years of Upheaval*, location 24197–215; Nixon, *RN: The Memoirs of Richard Nixon*, location 2028; Garthoff, *Détente and Confrontation*, 476; Memorandum of Conversation, 28 June 1974, *FRUS, Arms Control, 1973–1976*, Document 58; Memorandum of Conversation, 29 June 1974, *FRUS, Arms Control, 1973–1976*, Document 60. In the 20 June NSC meeting, Kissinger had stated that the American position was 150 kilotons.

37. Kissinger, *Years of Upheaval*, location 24207; Memorandum of Conversation, 1 July 1974, *FRUS, Arms Control, 1973–1976*, Documents 61 and 62.

38. Richard Nixon, Address to the Nation on Returning From the Soviet Union, at Peters and Woolley, American Presidency Project; Garthoff, *Détente and Confrontation*, 476.

39. Telegram 6591 from the Embassy in India to the Department of State, the Interests Section in Syria, and the Embassy in the United Kingdom, 18 May 1974, *FRUS, Arms Control, 1973–1976*, Document 47; Paper Prepared by an Interagency Working Group, 30 May 1974, Implications of the Indian Test, *FRUS, Arms Control, 1973–1976*, Document 52.

40. Memorandum, Lodal and Sonnenfeldt to Kissinger, 28 September 1974, *FRUS, Arms Control, 1973–1976*, Document 85; Poole, *The Joint Chiefs of Staff*, 72.

41. Poole, *The Joint Chiefs of Staff*, 72.

8. Legacies and Implications

1. WHT, Conversation 706-005, 11 April 1972, Oval Office.

BIBLIOGRAPHY

GOVERNMENT ARCHIVES AND
PRIVATE MANUSCRIPT COLLECTIONS

Digital National Security Archive. George Washington University, Washington, DC.

Federal Register. Codification of Presidential Proclamations and Executive Orders. https://www.archives.gov/federal-register/codification.

Gerald Ford Presidential Library. Ann Arbor, Michigan.
    Memoranda of Conversations

Gerhard Peters and John T. Woolley. The American Presidency Project. University of California at Santa Barbara. https://www.presidency.ucsb.edu.

The Jewish Virtual Library. American-Israeli Cooperative Enterprise. https://www.jewishvirtuallibrary.org/.

National Archives and Records Administration II. College Park, Maryland.
    Central Files, Record Group 59
    Nixon Presidential Materials (before transfer to Nixon Presidential Library)
        Henry Kissinger Office Files
            HAK Trip Files
        NSC Files
        NSC Institutional Files (H-Files)

National Resources Defense Council. *Table of U.S. Strategic Offensive Force Loadings: Archive of Nuclear Data.* http://www.nrdc.org/nuclear/nudb/datab1.asp.

The National Security Council Project. Washington, DC: Center for International and Security Studies at Maryland and Brookings Institution, 2000.

Nixon White House Tapes (WHT). Miller Center of Public Affairs Presidential Recordings Project. University of Virginia. Charlottesville, Virginia.

Richard M. Nixon Presidential Library. Yorba Linda, California.
    Meeting Files
    National Security Decision Memoranda (NSDM)
    National Security Study Memoranda (NSSM)
    NSC Institutional Files
    White House Central Files
        Staff Member and Office Files

Treaty on the Non-Proliferation of Nuclear Weapons (NPT). United Nations
    Office for Disarmament Affairs. https://www.un.org./disarmanet/wmd
    /nuclear/npt.

U.S. Army Activity in the U.S. Biological Warfare Programs (vols. 1 and 2),
    US Department of the Army, 24 February 1977, reprinted in *Biological
    Testing Involving Human Subjects by the Department of Defense, 1977*,
    Hearings before the Subcommittee on Health and Scientific Research
    of the Committee on Human Resources, 8 March and 23 May 1977,
    US Senate, 95th Congress, 1st session (Government Printing Office,
    1977), Document 26, National Security Archives, vol. 3, Biowar, Na-
    tional Security Archive Electronic Briefing Book no. 58, edited by Rob-
    ert A Wampler, updated 7 December 2001. https://nsarchive2.gwu.edu
    /NSAEBB/NSAEBB58/#doc25.

US Declassified Documents Online. https://www.gale.com/c/us-declassified
    -documents-online.

Published Government Documents

Director of Central Intelligence. "Soviet Chemical and Biological Warfare
    Capabilities." National Intelligence Estimate, 11-11-69. 13 February 1969.
    http://www.foia.cia.gov.

McCullough, James M. "Chemical and Biological Warfare Issues and Devel-
    opments during 1971." Congressional Research Service, 13 December 1971.
    Washington, DC: Library of Congress, 1971.

Public Papers of the Presidents of the United States: Richard Nixon, 1969. Wash-
    ington, DC: Government Printing Office, 1971.

Public Papers of the Presidents of the United States: Richard Nixon, 1970. Wash-
    ington, DC: Government Printing Office, 1971.

Public Papers of the Presidents of the United States: Richard Nixon, 1972. Wash-
    ington, DC: Government Printing Office, 1974.

*Report of the Secretary of Defense James R. Schlesinger to the Congress on the
    FY 1975 Defense Budget.* 4 March 1974.

US Arms Control and Disarmament Agency. *Arms Control and Disarmament
    Agreements: Texts and Histories of the Negotiations.* Washington, D.C.:
    ACDA, 1990.

US Arms Control and Disarmament Agency. *Documents on Disarmament,
    1969.*

US Arms Control and Disarmament Agency. *Documents on Disarmament,
    1971.*

US Arms Control and Disarmament Agency. *Documents on Disarmament,
    1972.*

US Arms Control and Disarmament Agency. *International Negotiations on the Seabed Arms Control Treaty.* Washington, DC: ACDA, 1973.

US Congress. House of Representatives. *Hearings before a Subcommittee of the Committee on Government Operations.* 91st Congress, 1st session, 20–21 May 1969.

US Congress. House of Representatives. *Hearings before the Subcommittee on International Organizations and Movements of the Committee on Foreign Affairs.* 91st Congress, 1st session, 8, 13–15 May 1969.

US Congress. Senate. *Hearings before the Committee on Foreign Relations.* 91st Congress, 1st session, 30 April 1969.

US Congress. Senate. *Hearings before the Select Committee to Study Governmental Operations with Respect to Intelligence Activities of the United States Senate.* Vol. 1, *Unauthorized Storage of Toxic Agents.* 94th Congress, 1st session, 16, 17, and 18 September, 1975.

US Congress. Senate. *Hearings before the Subcommittee on Health and Scientific Research of the Committee on Human Resources.* 95th Congress, 1st session, 8 March and 23 May 1977.

US Department of Energy. Office of Science and Technical Information. "Executive Summary: Plowshare Program." Undated. https://www.osti.gov /opennet/reports/plowshar.pdf.

US Department of State. *Department of State Bulletin.* 69, no. 1778 (23 July 1973): 113–176.

US Department of State. "Fact Sheet: Transparency in the U.S. Nuclear Stockpile." 29 April 2014.

US Department of State. *Foreign Relations of the United States, 1964–1968.* Vol. 11, *Arms Control and Disarmament,* edited by Evans Gerakas, David S. Patterson, and Carolyn B. Yee. Washington, DC: Government Printing Office, 1997.

US Department of State. *Foreign Relations of the United States, 1964–1968.* Vol. 14, *Soviet Union,* edited by David C. Humphrey, Charles S. Sampson, and David S. Patterson. Washington, DC: Government Printing Office, 2001.

US Department of State. *Foreign Relations of the United States, 1969–1976.* Vol. E-2, *Documents on Arms Control and Nonproliferation, 1969–1972,* edited by David I. Goldman, David C. Humphrey, and Edward C. Keefer. Washington, DC: Government Printing Office, 2007.

US Department of State. *Foreign Relations of the United States, 1969–1976.* Vol. E-14, part 2, *Documents on Arms Control and Nonproliferation, 1973–1976,* edited by Kristin L. Ahlberg, Bonnie Sue Kim, Chris Tudda, and Adam M. Howard. Washington, DC: Government Printing Office, 2015.

US Department of State. *Foreign Relations of the United States, 1969–1976.* Vol. E-15, part 2, *Documents on Western Europe, 1973–1976,* edited by

Kathleen B. Rasmussen and Adam M. Howard. Washington, DC: Government Printing Office, 2014.

US Department of State. *Foreign Relations of the United States, 1969–1976.* Vol. 1, *Foundations of Foreign Policy, 1969–1972,* edited by Louis J. Smith, David H. Herschler, and David S. Patterson. Washington, DC: Government Printing Office, 2003.

US Department of State. *Foreign Relations of the United States, 1969–1976.* Vol. 6, *Vietnam, January 1969–July 1970,* edited by Edward C. Keefer and Carolyn Yee. Washington, D.C.: Government Printing Office, 2006.

US Department of State. *Foreign Relations of the United States, 1969–1976.* Vol. 12, *Soviet Union, January 1969–October 1970,* edited by Erin R. Mahan and Edward C. Keefer. Washington, DC: Government Printing Office, 2006.

US Department of State. *Foreign Relations of the United States, 1969–1976.* Vol. 13, *Soviet Union, October 1970–October 1971,* edited by David C. Geyer and Edward C. Keefer. Washington, DC: Government Printing Office, 2011.

US Department of State. *Foreign Relations of the United States, 1969–1976.* Vol. 14, *Soviet Union, October 1971–May 1972,* edited by David C. Geyer, Nina D. Howland and Kent Sieg. Washington, DC: Government Printing Office, 2006.

US Department of State. *Foreign Relations of the United States, 1969–1976.* Vol. 16, *Soviet Union, August 1974–December 1976,* edited by David C. Geyer and Edward C. Keefer. Washington, DC: Government Printing Office, 2012.

US Department of State. *Foreign Relations of the United States, 1969–1976.* Vol. 17, *China, 1969–1972,* edited by Steven E. Phillips and Edward C. Keefer. Washington, DC: Government Printing Office, 2006.

US Department of State. *Foreign Relations of the United States, 1969–1976.* Vol. 18, *China, 1973–1976,* edited by David P. Nickles and Edward C. Keefer. Washington, DC: Government Printing Office, 2007.

US Department of State. *Foreign Relations of the United States, 1969–1976.* Vol. 19, part 2, *Japan, 1969–1972,* edited by David P. Nickels, Edward C. Keefer and Adam M. Howard. Washington, DC: Government Printing Office, 2018.

US Department of State. *Foreign Relations of the United States, 1969–1976.* Vol. 32, *SALT I, 1969–1972,* edited by Erin R. Mahan and Edward C. Keefer. Washington, DC: Government Printing Office, 2010.

US Department of State. *Foreign Relations of the United States, 1969–1976.* Vol. 33, *SALT II, 1972–1980,* edited by Erin R. Mahan and Adam M. Howard. Washington, DC: Government Printing Office, 2013.

US Department of State. *Foreign Relations of the United States, 1969–1976.* Vol. 34, *National Security Policy, 1969–1972,* edited by M. Todd Bennett and Edward C. Keefer. Washington, DC: Government Printing Office, 2011.

US Department of State. *Foreign Relations of the United States, 1969–1976.* Vol. 35, *National Security Policy, 1973–1976,* edited by M. Todd Bennett and Adam M. Howard. Washington, DC: Government Printing Office, 2014.

US Department of State. *Foreign Relations of the United States, 1969–1976.* Vol. 41, *Western Europe; NATO, 1969–1972,* edited by James E. Miller and Laurie Van Hook. Washington, DC: Government Printing Office, 2012.

US Department of State. *Report to the NSC on U.S. Policy on Chemical and Biological Warfare and Agents.* 15 October 1969. http://www.foia.cia.gov.

US Department of State. *Soviet-American Relations: The Détente Years, 1969– 1972.* Edited by Edward C. Keefer, David C. Geyer, and Douglas E. Selvage. Washington, DC: Government Printing Office, 2007.

Woolf, Amy F., and James D. S. Werner. "The U.S. Nuclear Weapons Complex: Overview of Department of Energy Sites." Washington, DC: Congressional Research Service, September 6, 2018.

OTHER SOURCES

"24 August 1968—French 'Canopus' Test: CTBTO Preparatory Commission." Comprehensive Nuclear-Test-Ban Treaty Organization. Accessed 21 May 2020. https://www.ctbto.org/specials/testing-times/24-august-1968-french -canopus-test.

Alvandi, Roham. *Nixon, Kissinger, and the Shah: The United States and Iran in the Cold War.* New York: Oxford University Press, 2014.

Ambrose, Matthew J. *The Control Agenda: A History of the Strategic Arms Control Talks.* Kindle edition. Ithaca: Cornell University Press, 2018.

Auten, Brian. *Carter's Conversion: The Hardening of American Defense Policy.* Columbia: University of Missouri Press, 2008.

Bahgat, Gawdat. "Nuclear Proliferation: The Islamic Republic of Iran." *Iranian Studies* 39, no. 3 (September 2006): 307–27.

Bange, Oliver. "NATO and the Non-Proliferation Treaty." In *Transforming NATO in the Cold War: Challenges beyond Deterrence in the 1960s,* edited by Andreas Wenger, Christian Nuenlist, and Anna Locher, 169–72. New York: Routledge, 2007.

Barnaby, Wendy. *The Plague Makers: The Secret World of Biological Warfare.* New York: Continuum International Publishing Group, 2000.

Barry, James A., Jr. "The Seabed Arms Control Issue: 1967–1971, A Superpower Symbiosis?" *Naval War College Review* 24, no. 2 (December 1972): 87–101.

Baxter, R. R., and Thomas Buergenthal. "Legal Aspects of the Geneva Protocol of 1925." In *The Control of Chemical and Biological Weapons,* 1–23. New York: Carnegie Endowment for International Peace, 1971.

Berkowitz, Bruce D. *Calculated Risks: A Century of Arms Control, Why It Has Failed, and How It Can Be Made to Work.* New York: Simon and Schuster, 1987.

Bernstein, Barton J. "The Birth of the U.S. Biological Warfare Program." *Scientific American* 255 (June 1987): 116–21.

Betts, Richard. "Nuclear Incentives: India, Pakistan, Iran." *Asian Survey* 19, no. 11 (November 1979): 1055–57.

"Biological and Chemical Weapons: A Symposium." *Bulletin of the Atomic Scientists* 16, no. 6 (June 1960): 226–56.

Botti, Timothy J. *The Long Wait: The Forging of the Anglo-American Nuclear Alliance, 1945–1958.* New York: Greenwood, 1987.

Brands, Hal. "Progress Unseen: US Arms Control Policy and the Origins of Détente, 1963–1968." *Diplomatic History* 30, no. 2 (April 2006): 253–85.

———. "Rethinking Nonproliferation: LBJ, the Gilpatric Committee, and U.S. National Security Policy." *Journal of Cold War Studies* 8, no. 2 (Spring 2006): 83–113.

Brennan, Donald, ed. *Arms Control, Disarmament, and National Security.* New York: George Braziller, 1961.

Bull, Hedley. *The Control of the Arms Race: Disarmament and Arms Control in the Missile Age.* New York: Frederick A. Praeger, 1961.

Bundy, McGeorge. *Danger and Survival: Choices about the Bomb in the First Fifty Years.* New York: Random House, 1988.

Bundy, William. *A Tangled Web: The Making of Foreign Policy in the Nixon Presidency.* New York: Hill and Wang, 1998.

Burns, Richard Dean. *The Evolution of Arms Control: From Antiquity to the Nuclear Age.* Santa Barbara, CA: Praeger Security International, 2009.

Burr, William. "The Nixon Administration and the Indian Nuclear Program, 1972–1974." National Security Archive Briefing Book no. 367, 5 December 2011, https://nsarchive2.gwu.edu/nukevault/ebb367/index.htm.

Busch, Nathan E., and Daniel H. Joyner, eds. *Combating Weapons of Mass Destruction: The Future of International Nonproliferation Policy.* Athens: University of Georgia Press, 2009.

Cahn Hessing, Anne. *Killing Détente: The Right Attacks the CIA.* University Park: Pennsylvania State University Press, 1998.

———. "Team B: The Trillion Dollar Experiment." *Bulletin of the Atomic Scientists* 49, no. 3 (1993): 22–27.

Cameron, James. *The Double Game: The Demise of America's First Missile Defense System and the Rise of Strategic Arms Limitation.* New York: Oxford University Press, 2017.

Cameron, James, and Or Rabinowitz. "Eight Lost Years? Nixon, Ford, Kissinger and the Non-Proliferation Regime, 1969–1977." *Journal of Strategic Studies* 40, no. 6 (January 2016): 1–27.

Carus, W. Seth. "A Short History of Biological Warfare: From Pre-History to the 21st Century." Occasional Paper no. 12. Washington, DC: National Defense University Press, August 2017.

———. "Defining 'Weapons of Mass Destruction.'" Occasional Paper no. 8, revised and updated. Washington, DC: National Defense University Press, January 2012.

Christopher, George W., Theodore J. Cieslak, Julie A. Pavlin, and Edward M. Eitzen Jr. "Biological Warfare: A Historical Perspective." In *Biological Weapons: Limiting the Threat,* edited by Joshua Lederberg, 17–36. Cambridge, MA: MIT Press, 1999.

Cirincione, Joseph. "Lessons Lost." *Bulletin of the Atomic Scientists* 61, no. 6 (December 2005): 42–53.

Cohen, Avner. *Israel and the Bomb.* New York: Columbia University Press, 1998.

———. *The Worst Kept Secret: Israel's Bargain with the Bomb.* New York: Columbia University Press, 2010.

Craig, Campbell, and Sergey Radchenko. *The Atomic Bomb and the Origins of the Cold War.* New Haven, CT: Yale University Press, 2008.

Crouch, J. D. "Strategic Defense and the ABM Treaty: An Examination of the Effect of the ABM Treaty On U.S. Defense Programs, 1972–1986." PhD diss., University of Southern California, 1987.

Daalder, Ivo H., I. M. Destler, and Michael Guhin. "The Nixon Administration National Security Council." Oral History Roundtables, *The National Security Project.* Washington, DC: Brookings Institution, 1999.

Dallek, Robert. *Partners in Power: Nixon and Kissinger.* New York: Harper, 2007.

Divine, Robert A. *Blowing on the Wind: The Nuclear Test Ban Debate, 1954–1960.* New York: Oxford University Press, 1978.

———. *Eisenhower and the Cold War.* New York: Oxford University Press, 1981.

Dobrynin, Anatoly. *In Confidence: Moscow's Ambassador to Six Cold War Presidents.* New York: Crown, 1995.

Drea, Edward J. *History of the Office of the Secretary of Defense.* Vol. 6, *McNamara, Clifford, and the Burdens of Vietnam, 1965–1969.* Secretaries of Defense Historical Series, vol. 6. Washington, DC: Government Printing Office, 2011.

Dunn, David. *The Politics of Threat: Minuteman Vulnerability in American National Security Policy.* New York: St. Martin's, 1997.

Feith, Thomas I. *Behind the Gas Mask: The U.S. Chemical Warfare Service in War and Peace.* Urbana: University of Illinois Press, 2014.

Ferguson, Niall. *Kissinger, 1923–1968: The Idealist.* New York: Penguin Books, 2015.

Fhurmann, Matthew. *Atomic Assistance: How "Atoms for Peace" Programs Cause Nuclear Insecurity.* Ithaca, NY: Cornell University Press, 2012.

Fifth Pugwash Conference. "On Chemical and Biological Warfare." *Bulletin of the Atomic Scientists* 15, no. 9 (October 1959): 337–39.

Frank, Forrest. "U.S. Arms Control Policymaking: The 1972 Biological Weapons Convention Case." PhD diss., Stanford University, 1975.

Freedman, Lawrence. *Arms Control: Management or Reform?* London: Routledge and Kegan Paul, 1986.

———. *The Evolution of Nuclear Strategy.* 3rd ed. New York: Palgrave Macmillan, 2003.

Frisch, David, ed. *Arms Reduction: Program and Issues.* New York: Twentieth Century Fund, 1961.

Gaddis, John Lewis. *Strategies of Containment: A Critical Appraisal of American National Security Policy during the Cold War.* Rev. and exp. edition. New York: Oxford University Press, 2005.

Gaddis, John Lewis, et al., eds. *Cold War Statesmen Confront the Bomb: Nuclear Diplomacy since 1945.* New York: Oxford University Press, 1999.

Garrity, Patrick J., and Erin R. Mahan. *Nixon and Arms Control: Forging the Offensive/Defensive Link in the SALT Negotiations, February–May 1971.* Presidential Recordings digital edition. Charlottesville: University of Virginia Press, 2014. https://prde.upress.virginia.edu/content/nixon_SALT.

Garthoff, Raymond. *Détente and Confrontation: American-Soviet Relations from Nixon to Reagan.* Rev. ed. Washington, DC: Brookings Institution, 1994.

Gavin, Francis J. "Blasts from the Past: Proliferation Lessons from the 1960s." *International Security* 29, no. 3 (Winter 2004/2005): 100–135.

———. "Nuclear Proliferation and Non-Proliferation during the Cold War." In *The Cambridge History of the Cold War,* vol. 2, edited by Melvyn P. Leffler and Odd Arne Westad, 395–416. New York: Cambridge University Press, 2010.

———. *Nuclear Statecraft: History and Strategy in America's Atomic Age.* Ithaca, NY: Cornell University Press, 2012.

———. "Same as It Ever Was: Nuclear Alarmism, Proliferation, and the Cold War." *International Security* 34, no. 3 (Winter 2009/2010): 7–37.

———. "Strategies of Inhibition: U.S. Grand Strategy, the Nuclear Revolution, and Nonproliferation." *International Security* 40, no. 1 (Summer 2015): 9–46.

Geyer, David C. "The Missing Link: Henry Kissinger and the Backchannel Negotiations on Berlin." In *American Detente and German Ostpolitik, 1969–1972,* edited by David C. Geyer and Bernd Schaefer, 80–97. Washington, DC: German Historical Institute, 2004.

Gilpin, Robert. *American Scientists and Nuclear Weapons Policy*. Princeton, NJ: Princeton University Press, 1962.

Goldman, David I. "The General and the Germs: The Army Leadership's Response to Nixon's Review of Chemical and Biological Warfare Policies in 1969." *Journal of Military History* 73, no. 2 (April 2009): 531–69.

Gowing, Margaret. *Independence and Deterrence: Britain's Atomic Energy, 1945–1952*. New York: Palgrave Macmillan, 1975.

Gray, Colin S. *House of Cards: Why Arms Control Must Fail*. Ithaca, NY: Cornell University Press, 1992.

Greenwood, Ted. *Making the MIRV: A Study of Defense*. Cambridge, MA: Ballinger, 1975.

Gulliam, Jeanne. *Biological Weapons: From the Invention of State-Sponsored Programs to Contemporary Bioterrorism*. New York: Columbia University Press, 2005.

Haldeman, Harry R. *The Haldeman Diaries: Inside the Nixon White House*. Santa Monica, CA: Sony Imagesoft, 1994.

Hanrieder, Wolfram, ed. *Arms Control, the FRG, and the Future of East-West Relations*. Boulder, CO: Westview, 1987.

Harnly, Caroline D. *Agent Orange and Vietnam: An Annotated Bibliography*. London: Scarecrow, 1988.

Hennessy, Peter. *Cabinets and the Bomb*. Oxford: Oxford University Press, 2007.

Hersh, Seymour. *Chemical and Biological Warfare: America's Hidden Arsenal*. New York: Bobbs-Merrill, 1968.

———. *The Price of Power: Kissinger in the Nixon White House*. New York: Summit Books, 1983.

Hersman, Rebecca K. C., and Robert Peters. "Nuclear U-Turns: Learning from South Korean and Taiwanese Rollback." *Nonproliferation Review* 13, no. 3 (November 2006): 539–53.

Heuser, Beatrice. "The Development of NATO's Nuclear Strategy." *Contemporary European History* 4, no. 1 (Winter 1995): 37–66.

Hewlett, Richard G., and Oscar E. Anderson Jr. *A History of the United States Atomic Energy Commission*. vol. 1, *The New World, 1939–1946*. University Park: Pennsylvania State University Press, 1962.

———. *A History of the United States Atomic Energy Commission*. Vol. 2, *Atomic Shield, 1947–1952*. University Park: Pennsylvania State University Press, 1969.

Hopmann, Terrence. "Bargaining in Arms Control Negotiations: The Seabed Denuclearization Treaty." *International Organization* 28, no. 3 (Summer 1974): 313–43.

Horrocks, David, and Helmi Raaska, eds. *The Vladivostok Summit on Arms Control, 23–24 November 1974*. Gerald R. Ford Presidential Library and

Museum, Ann Arbor, Michigan, https://www.fordlibrarymuseum.gov /library/exhibits/vladivostok/vladivostok.asp.

Hughes, Kenneth. *Chasing Shadows: The Nixon Tapes, the Chennault Affair, and the Origins of Watergate.* Charlottesville: University of Virginia Press, 2014.

———. *Fatal Politics: The Nixon Tapes, the Vietnam War, and the Casualties of Reelection.* Charlottesville: University of Virginia Press, 2015.

Hunt, Richard A. *Melvin Laird and the Foundations of the Post-Vietnam Military, 1969–1973.* Washington, DC: Government Printing Office, 2015.

Iandola, Laura. "Foreign Relations of the United States, Vol. E-2, Documents on Arms Control and Nonproliferation, 1969–1972." *H-Diplo FRUS Review,* 12 July 2013.

Isaacson, Walter. *Kissinger: A Biography.* New York: Simon and Schuster, 1992.

Johnson, U. Alexis. *The Right Hand of Power: The Memoirs of an American Diplomat.* Englewood Cliffs, NJ: Prentice-Hall, 1984.

Johnson, Rebecca. *Unfinished Business: The Negotiation of the CTBT and the End of Nuclear Testing.* New York: United Nations, 2009.

Kaplan, Lawrence S. *NATO and the United States: The Enduring Alliance.* Rev. ed. New York: Twayne, 1994.

Kauffman, Robert. *Henry M. Jackson: A Life in Politics.* Seattle: University of Washington Press, 2000.

Kaufman, Scott. *Project Plowshare: The Peaceful Use of Nuclear Explosives in Cold War America.* Ithaca, NY: Cornell University Press, 2012.

Kelleher, Catherin. *Germany and the Politics of Nuclear Weapons.* New York: Columbia University Press, 1975.

Khan, Zafar. "Pakistan and the NPT: Commitments and Concerns." *Margalla Papers,* 2012.

Kịbaroğlu, Mustafa. "Iran's Nuclear Ambitions from a Historical Perspective and the Attitude of the West." *Middle Eastern Studies* 43, no. 2 (2007): 225–29.

Kieninger, Stephan. "'Diverting the Arms Race into the Permitted Channels': The Nixon Administration, the MIRV-Mistake, and the SALT Negotiations." NPIPH Working Paper no. 9. Washington, DC: Woodrow Wilson Center, 2016.

Kissinger, Henry. *American Foreign Policy: Three Essays by Henry Kissinger.* New York: W. W. Norton, 1969.

———. *Nuclear Weapons and Foreign Policy.* New York: Harper and Row, 1957.

———. *White House Years.* 1982. Kindle edition. Reprint, New York: Simon and Schuster, 2011.

———. *Years of Renewal.* New York: Simon and Schuster, 1999.

———. *Years of Upheaval.* 1982. Kindle edition. Reprint, New York: Simon and Schuster, 2011.

Klagsbrun, Francine. *Lioness: Golda Meir and the Nation of Israel.* New York: Knopf Doubleday, 2017.

Kohlhoff, Dean W. *Amchitka and the Bomb: Nuclear Testing in Alaska.* Seattle: University of Washington Press, 2002.

Leitenberg, Milton, and Raymond A Zilinskas with Jens H. Kuhn. *The Soviet Biological Weapons Program: A History.* Cambridge, MA: Harvard University Press, 2012.

Lettow, Paul Vorbeck. *Strengthening the Nuclear Nonproliferation Regime.* New York: Council on Foreign Relations, 2010.

Logevall, Fredrik, and Andrew Preston, eds. *Nixon in the World: American Foreign Relations, 1969–1977.* New York: Oxford University Press, 2008.

Maddock, Shane J. *Nuclear Apartheid: The Quest for American Atomic Supremacy from World War II to the Present.* Chapel Hill: University of North Carolina Press, 2014.

Mahan, Erin R., and Jonathan B. Tucker. "President Nixon's Decision to Renounce the U.S. Offensive Biological Weapons Program." Case Study 1. Center for the Study of WMD Case Studies Series. Washington, DC: National Defense University Press, 2009.

———. *Kennedy, De Gaulle, and Western Europe.* London: Palgrave Macmillan, 2002.

Maraniss, David. *They Marched into Sunlight: War and Peace, Vietnam and America, October 1967.* New York: Simon and Schuster, 2004.

Mauer, John. "Divided Counsels: Competing Approaches to SALT, 1969–1970." *Diplomatic History* 43, no. 2 (April 2019): 353–77.

McCarthy, Richard M. *The Ultimate Folly: War by Pestilence, Asphyxiation, and Defoliation.* New York: Alfred A. Knopf, 1969.

McElroy, Robert W. *Morality and American Foreign Policy: The Role of Ethics in International Affairs.* Princeton, NJ: Princeton University Press, 1992.

McElroy, Rodney J. "The Geneva Protocol of 1925." In *The Politics of Arms Control and Treaty Ratification,* edited by Michael Krepon and Dan Caldwell, 125–66. New York: St. Martin's, 1991.

Miller, Pam. *Nuclear Flashback: The Return to Amchitka.* Washington, DC: Greenpeace, 1996.

Millett, Stephen M. "Forward-Based Nuclear Weapons and SALT I." *Political Science Quarterly* 98, no. 1 (Spring 1983): 79–97.

Moon, John Ellis van Courtland. "Chemical Weapons and Deterrence: The World War II Experience." *International Security* 8, no. 4 (Spring 1984): 3–35.

Morris, Roger. *Uncertain Greatness: Henry Kissinger and American Foreign Policy.* New York: Harper and Row, 1977.

Murray, Lori Esposito. "SALT and Congress: Building a Consensus for Arms Control." PhD diss., Johns Hopkins University, 1990.

———. "The Selling of SALT." *Foreign Service Journal* 59 (February 1982): 20–24.

Neer, Robert M. *Napalm: An American Biography*. Cambridge, MA: Harvard University Press, 2013.

Newhouse, John. *Cold Dawn: The Story of SALT*. New York: Holt, Rinehart and Winston, 1973.

Nguyen, Michael. "Senate Struggles with Riot Control Agent Policy." *Arms Control Today*, January/February 2006. https://www.armscontrol.org/act /2006_01-02/JANFEB-RiotControl.

Nitze, Paul. "Assuring Strategic Stability in an Era of Détente." *Foreign Affairs* 54 (January 1976): 207–32.

———. *From Hiroshima to Glasnost: At the Center of Decision, a Memoir*. New York: Grove Weidenfeld, 1989.

———. "The Strategic Balance between Hope and Skepticism." *Foreign Policy* 17 (Winter 1974–75): 136–56.

———. "The Vladivostok Accord and SALT II." *Review of Politics* 37, no. 2 (April 1975): 146–60.

Nixon, Richard. "First Annual Report to the Congress on United States Foreign Policy for the 1970s." The American Presidency Project, 18 February 1970. https://www.presidency.ucsb.edu/documents/first-annual-report -the-congress-united-states-foreign-policy-for-the-1970s.

———. *RN: The Memoirs of Richard Nixon*. New York: Grosset and Dunlap, 1978.

Nolan, Janne. *Guardians of the Arsenal: the Politics of Nuclear Strategy*. New York: Basic Books, 1989.

Nuti, Leopoldo. "'A Turning Point in the Postwar Foreign Policy': Italy and the NPT Negotiations 1967–1969." In *Negotiating the Nuclear Non-Proliferation Treaty: Origins of the Nuclear Order*, edited by Roland Popp, Liviu Horovitz, and Andreas Wenger, 77–96. New York: Routledge, 2016.

———. "Italy as a Hedging State? The Problematic Ratification of the Non-Proliferation Treaty." EUT Edizioni Università di Trieste, 2017. https://www .openstarts.units.it/handle/10077/15331.

———. "Italy's Nuclear Choices." *UNISCI Discussion Papers* no. 25 (January 2011): 171–74.

———. "The Making of the Nuclear Order and the Historiography on the 1970s." *International History Review* 40, no. 5 (October 2018): 965–74.

Okimoto, Daniel I. "Japan's Non-Nuclear Policy: The Problem of the NPT." *Asian Survey* 15, no. 4 (April 1975): 313.

Pan, Liang. "Whither Japan's Military Potential? The Nixon Administration's Stance on Japanese Defense Power." *Diplomatic History* 31, no. 1 (January 2007): 111–42.

Payne, Keith B. *The Great American Gamble: Deterrence Theory and Practice from the Cold War to the Twenty-First Century.* Kindle edition. Fairfax, VA: National Institute for Public Policy, 2008.

Perkovich, George, and Henry D. Sokolski. "Could Anything Be Done to Stop Them? Lessons from Pakistan's Proliferating Past." In *Pakistan's Nuclear Future: Worries beyond War,* edited by Henry D. Sokolski, 59–84. Carlisle Barracks, PA: Strategic Studies Institute, US Army War College, 2008.

———. *India's Nuclear Bomb: The Impact on Global Proliferation.* Updated ed. Berkeley: University of California Press, 1999.

———. "A Nuclear Third Way in South Asia." *Foreign Policy* 91 (Summer 1993): 89–91.

Petrelli, Niccolo, and Giordana Pulcini. "Nuclear Superiority in the Age of Parity: US Planning, Intelligence Analysis, Weapons Innovation and the Search for a Qualitative Edge, 1969–1976." *International History Review* 40, no. 5 (2018): 1191–1209.

Pomeroy, Steven. *An Untaken Road: Strategy, Technology, and the Hidden History of America's Mobile ICBMs.* Annapolis, MD: Naval Institute Press, 2016.

Poole, Walter S. *The Joint Chiefs of Staff and National Policy, 1969–1972.* Washington, DC: Office of Joint History, 2013.

Prados, John. *The Soviet Estimate: U.S. Intelligence Analysis and Soviet Strategic Forces.* Updated ed. Princeton, NJ: Princeton University Press, 1986.

Primack, Joel, and Frank von Hippel. "Matthew Meselson and the United States Policy on Chemical and Biological Warfare." In *Advice and Dissent: Scientists in the Political Arena,* edited by Joel Primack, 143–64. New York: Basic Books, 1974.

Quester, George H. "Japan and the Nuclear Non-Proliferation Treaty." *Asian Survey* 10, no. 9 (September 1970): 765–78.

———. "The Shah and the Bomb." *Policy Sciences* 8 (1977): 21–32.

———. *The Politics of Nuclear Proliferation.* Baltimore: Johns Hopkins University Press, 1973.

Ramberg, Bennett. "The Seabed Treaty, 1971 to the Present." In *Encyclopedia of Arms Control and Disarmament,* edited by Richard Dean Burns, 2:887–94. New York: Charles Scribner's Sons, 1993.

———. "Tactical Advantages of Opening Positioning Strategies: Lessons from the Seabed Arms Control Talks." *Journal of Conflict Resolution* 21, no. 4 (December 1977): 691–94.

Rearden, Steven L. *Council of War: A History of the Joint Chiefs of Staff, 1942–1991.* Washington, DC: National Defense University Press, 2012.

Redick, John R. "Regional Nuclear Arms Control in Latin America." *International Organization* 29, no. 2 (Spring 1975): 415–45.

Reed, Robert F. *The US-Japan Alliance: Sharing the Burden of Defense.* Washington, DC: National Defense University Press, 1983.

Reed, Thomas C., and Danny B. Stillman. *The Nuclear Express: A Political History of the Bomb and Its Proliferation.* Voyageur, 2010.

Regis, Ed. *The Biology of Doom: The History of America's Secret Germ Warfare Project.* New York: Henry Holt, 1999.

Robinson, Davis R. "The Treaty of Tlatelolco and the United States: A Latin American Nuclear Free Zone." *American Journal of International Law* 64, no. 2 (April 1970): 282–309.

Roehrlich, Elisabeth. "Negotiating Verification: International Diplomacy and the Evolution of Nuclear Safeguards, 1945–1972." *Diplomacy and Statecraft* 29, no. 1 (March 2018): 29–50.

Rowen, Henry S. "The Evolution of Strategic Nuclear Doctrine." In *Strategic Thought in the Nuclear Age,* edited by Lawrence Martin, 131–56. Baltimore: Johns Hopkins University Press, 1979.

Safire, William. "Weapons of Mass Destruction: Obnubilating Aside, It's Bone Stupid to Launch Them." *New York Times Magazine,* 19 April 1998, 22–23.

Sagan, Scott D., and Kenneth N. Waltz. *The Spread of Nuclear Weapons.* New York: W. W. Norton, 2003.

Schelling, Thomas C. *Arms and Influence.* New Haven, CT: Yale University Press, 1966.

———. *The Strategy of Conflict.* Cambridge, MA: Harvard University Press, 1960.

———. "What Went Wrong with Arms Control?" *Foreign Affairs* 64, no. 2 (Winter 1985–86): 221–23.

Schelling, Thomas C., and Morton H. Halperin. *Strategy and Arms Control.* New York: Twentieth Century Fund, 1961.

Schwartz, David N. *NATO's Nuclear Dilemmas.* Washington, DC: Brookings Institution, 1983.

Schwartz, Thomas Alan. *Lyndon Johnson and Europe: In the Shadow of Vietnam.* Cambridge, MA: Harvard University Press, 2003.

Seaborg, Glenn T., with Benjamin S. Loeb. *Kennedy, Khrushchev, and the Test Ban.* Berkeley: University of California Press, 1981.

Shaker, Mohamed I. *The Nuclear Non-Proliferation Treaty: Origin and Implementation, 1959–1979.* 2 vols. New York: Oceana, 1980.

Shawcross, William. *Sideshow: Kissinger, Nixon and the Destruction of Cambodia.* New York: Simon and Schuster, 1979.

Simpson, John. "The Future of the NPT." In *Combating Weapons of Mass Destruction: The Future of International Nonproliferation Policy,* edited by Nathan E. Busch and Daniel Joyner, 45–73. Athens: University of Georgia Press, 2009.

Sims, Jennifer. *Icarus Restrained: An Intellectual History of Nuclear Arms Control*. Boulder, CO: Westview, 1990.

Siracusa, Joseph M., and Aiden Warren. "The Nuclear Non-Proliferation Regime: An Historical Perspective." *Diplomacy and Statecraft* 29, no. 1 (2018): 3–28.

Smith, Gerard. *Disarming Diplomat: The Memoirs of Ambassador Gerard C. Smith, Arms Control Negotiator*. New York: Madison Books, 1996.

———. *Doubletalk: The Story of the First Strategic Arms Limitation Talks*. Garden City, NY: Doubleday, 1980.

Spiers, Edward M. *Chemical Warfare*. London: Palgrave Macmillan, 1986.

Strong, Robert A. *Bureaucracy and Statesmanship: Henry Kissinger and the Making of American Foreign Policy*. Lanham, MD: University Press of America, 1986.

Sulzberger, C. L. *The World and Richard Nixon*. 1st ed. New York: Prentice Hall, 1987.

Suri, Jeremi. *Henry Kissinger and the American Century*. Cambridge, MA: Harvard University Press, 2009.

Szabo, Stephen F., ed. *The Bundeswehr and Western Security*. New York: Palgrave Macmillan, 1990.

Tal, David. "'Absolutes' and 'Stages' in the Making and Application of Nixon's SALT Policy." *Diplomatic History* 37, no. 5 (November 2013): 1090–1116.

———. *U.S. Strategic Arms Control Policy in the Cold War: Negotiation and Confrontation over SALT, 1969–1979*. London: Routledge, 2017.

Talbott, Strobe. *The Master of the Game: Paul H. Nitze and U.S. Cold War Strategy from Truman to Reagan*. New York: Knopf, 1988.

———. *The Master of the Game: Paul Nitze and the Nuclear Peace*. New York: Vintage Books, 1989.

Terchek, Ronald J. *The Making of the Test Ban*. The Hague: Martinus Nijhoff, 1970.

Terriff, Terry. *The Nixon Administration and the Making of U.S. Nuclear Strategy*. Ithaca, NY: Cornell University Press, 1995.

Thompson, Nicholas. *The Hawk and the Dove: Paul Nitze, George Kennan, and the History of the Cold War*. New York: Henry Holt, 2009.

Trachtenberg, Marc. *A Constructed Peace: The Making of the European Settlement, 1946–1963*. Princeton, NJ: Princeton University Press, 1998.

"Treaty on the Non-Proliferation of Nuclear Weapons (NPT)—UNODA." Accessed 6 January 2019. https://www.un.org/disarmament/wmd/nuclear/npt/.

Tucker, Jonathan B. "Biological Weapons in the Former Soviet Union: An Interview with Dr. Kenneth Alibek." *Nonproliferation Review* 6, no. 3 (Spring/Summer 1999): 1–10.

———. "A Farewell to Germs: The U.S. Renunciation of Biological and Toxin Warfare, 1969–1970." *International Security* 27, no. 1 (Summer 2002): 107–48.

Ullman, Richard H. "The Covert French Connection." *Foreign Policy* 75 (Summer 1989): 8, 12.

United Nations Office for Disarmament Affairs. *The United Nations and Disarmament, 1945–1970.* New York: United Nations, 1970.

"U.S. Secret Assistance to the French Nuclear Program, 1969–1975: From 'Fourth Country' to Strategic Partner." Wilson Center. Accessed 21 May 2020. https://www.wilsoncenter.org/publication/us-secret-assistance-to -the-french-nuclear-program-1969-1975-fourth-country-to-strategic.

Van Atta, Dale. *With Honor: Melvin Laird in War, Peace, and Politics.* Madison: University of Wisconsin Press, 2008.

Verwey, Wil D. *Riot Control Agents and Herbicides in War: Their Humanitarian, Toxicological, Ecological, Military, Polemological, and Legal Aspects.* Leiden: A. W. Sijthoff International, 1977.

Wolfe, Thomas. *The SALT Experience: Its Impact on U.S. and Soviet Policy and Decisionmaking.* Santa Monica, CA: RAND Corporation, 1975.

Zilinskas, Raymond A. "The Soviet Biological Weapons Program and Its Legacy in Today's Russia." Occasional Paper no. 11. Washington, DC: Center for the Study of WMD, National Defense University Press, 2016.

Zumwalt, Elmo. *On Watch: A Memoir.* New York: Quadrangle, 1976.

INDEX

Agreement on the Prevention of Nuclear War, 153–54
Alaska, Cannikin nuclear test, 171, 173–79, 191
Allende, Salvador, 151
Allison, Royal B., 87, 102, 151
Antarctic Treaty of 1959, 135
anthrax, 4, 45, 55–56, 62–63
Antiballistic Missile Program (ABM): Antiballistic Missile Treaty, ix, xiii–xiv, 33–34, 37, 68, 98–108, 119, 138, 142–47, 161–65, 194; ban on ABM proposed as part of SALT, 83–89; Sentinel ABM system, 17, 71–72. *See also* Safeguard
Arms Control and Disarmament Agency (ACDA): nuclear testing and arms control, xiii, 171–73; SALT and ABM, 70, 83; SALT II, 142, 151; Vietnam and, 38–40
Army, US: biological weapons research laboratories, 63; US Army Chemical Medical Research Institute for Infectious Diseases, 63
Atomic Energy Act, 120–24
Atomic Energy Commission (AEC), 7–8, 10–11, 32, 124, 167–85
Australia, Keraudren Bay, 169, 171

B-1 bomber, 148, 159
B-52 bomber, 149
ballistic missile submarines, 92, 138
Bhutto, Ali, 129
biological weapons (BW): Biological Weapons Convention of 1972, 37, 58–66, 189–95; dismantling of offensive program, 62–63
Brezhnev, Leonid, 152, 154, 157, 161–63, 183–85

Cambodia, 89, 178
Caribbean, 133–34
chemical and biological weapons (CBW): combatting use of, 37–43; congressional hearings, 41–42, 47–48; current issues of, ix–xiv; decoupling, 49–50; early CBW arms control policy, 1–7, 23–29; Nixon statement on, 54–55; NSC review, xi, 43–44; Operation CHASE, 40–41, 47–48; testing, 25–29; use of in Vietnam, 38–40
Chemical Warfare Service, US Army (also known as Chemical Corps), 3–4, 51
chemical weapons (CW): Chemical Weapons Convention, 61, 64, 190, 195; US weapons program, 41–57; World War I, 2–3; World War II, 1–12, 19, 32, 38–39, 116–20
China: arms control, 27–28; CBW and, 6–7; Kissinger relationship with, 99–100, 154, 167; nuclear ambitions, 12–13; nuclear nonproliferation, 130; SALT and ABM, 17, 74–75; SALT negotiation and agreement, 99–100
Cienfuegos, Cuba, 89, 178
comprehensive test ban (CBT) treaty, 10, 168–90
Conference of the Committee on Disarmament, 136–37, 212
Congress: ABM Treaty, 97–104; chemical and biological weapons programs, 41–42, 47–57; Interim Offensive Agreement, 142; SALT agreements, 37–40, 80–92, 108, 142–66
Connally, John, 66

269

MILLER CENTER STUDIES ON THE PRESIDENCY